ALABAMA AFTERNOONS

Alabama Afternoons

PROFILES AND CONVERSATIONS

ROY HOFFMAN

The University of Alabama Press • Tuscaloosa

The University of Alabama Press
Tuscaloosa, Alabama 35487-0380
uapress.ua.edu

Copyright © 2011 by Roy Hoffman
All rights reserved.

Hardcover edition published 2011.
Paperback edition published 2017.
eBook edition published 2011.

Inquiries about reproducing material from this work should be addressed to the
University of Alabama Press.

Typeface: Minion Pro

Cover image: photograph by Chip Cooper
Cover design: Michele Myatt Quinn

Paperback ISBN: 978-0-8173-5903-4

A previous edition of this book has been catalogued by the Library of Congress as follows:
Library of Congress Cataloging-in-Publication Data
Hoffman, Roy, 1953–
Alabama afternoons : profiles and conversations / Roy Hoffman.
p. cm.
Includes bibliographical references.
ISBN 978-0-8173-1739-3 (cloth : alk. paper) — ISBN 978-0-8173-8560-6
(electronic) 1. Alabama—History—Anecdotes. 2. Alabama—Biography—Anecdotes. 3.
Alabama—Social life and customs—Anecdotes. I. Title.
F326.6.H64 2011
976.1—dc22
2010036119

To Nancy
For all our Alabama afternoons

Contents

Windows: A Son Remembers

The nameplate was still on the door: Charles Hoffman, Lawyer

ALABAMA AFTERNOONS

Introduction

Alabama Afternoons is a book of character portraits—from passing visits to full-scale profiles—of some of our state's remarkable people, famous or obscure. Culled from more than a decade of my roaming the state, present and past, to find people worthy of Sunday feature spreads, *Alabama Afternoons* is a collective portrait, too. From a day spent with Selma storyteller Katherine Tucker Windham and her friend artist Charlie "Tin Man" Lucas, to an afternoon with Montgomery Improvement Association president Johnnie Carr, to reminiscences about Birmingham area native Mel Allen, a broadcast legend who became "the voice of the New York Yankees," *Alabama Afternoons* displays the wealth of compelling lives—and great storytelling—in the spirited, sometimes-melancholy, and always-involving Heart of Dixie.

This collection is not meant to be comprehensive—there are numerous source books, including the *Encyclopedia of Alabama,* for that—but reflective of my own curiosities and passions as a writer. Photographers and painters, novelists and journalists, civil rights figures, old people remembering way back when, ordinary folks with colorful stories to tell—these are some of my favorite subjects. While I am aware, of course, of the colorful traditions of Alabama in areas like sports and politics, I have bent my talents to venues not as much explored by contemporary nonfiction writers (though sports and politics do show as aspects of other pieces). Whether the profile be of New Jersey native Gay Talese, whose sojourn at The University of Alabama was the catalyst that propelled him into being one of America's most influential New Journalists, or Sara Hamm, the last Jew in Eufaula, determined to preserve the town's historic Jewish cemetery, my stories hope to turn up fresh angles on familiar folks or introduce little-known ones for the first time. Most of the people featured here have visibility within their community—or wider—but there are some famous just on their street corner, like the old domino players under the oak tree in Mobile, or the coon dog historians on a bench in Russellville.

Whatever the subject, I pay a lot of attention to how people speak, and do my best to retain idiosyncratic rhythms and colloquialisms. How we talk is sometimes as important as what we say. I'm interested in setting, too, so where these conversations take place is not just about geography, but often also about interior landscapes. My visit with E. B. Sledge, for example, author of the spectacular—and increasingly famous—World War II memoir *With the Old Breed,* occurs at his home in Montevallo, where he was battling cancer during what turned out to be his final days. That struggle, along with his joy in bird-watching through his bedroom window, became part of the story of this brave and sensitive veteran.

Most of the portraits are contemporary—people I can call up, travel to, sit with, or take a walk with—but I love history, too, especially in terms of how it shapes us today, so I have included here some stories about lesser-known figures who connect us to our state's past. While I have written sketches of world-known celebrities such as Olympian Jesse Owens, heavyweight champion Joe Louis, and the extraordinary Helen Keller, I have chosen here, instead, to include a few portraits of people who might otherwise be relegated to a footnote in the march of time: Abby Fisher of Mobile, believed to be the author of the first African American cookbook; Artelia Bendolph, who became an icon of the Depression-era South as a child from a photograph taken of her in a shack window in Gee's Bend. If I've been lucky enough to catch someone in their later years, like Bendolph—who has since passed away—I have spent time with them in person. If they are of an earlier era, like Walter Bellingrath, I try to capture a sense of them from those who knew them, in this case Edward Carl, at first Bellingrath's driver, but ultimately, it seems, his most trusted friend. My history is intended to have a personal feeling, enabling the reader to touch someone on the page who knew the person at the heart of the story.

Most of these pieces were originally written for the *Press-Register,* and my editors in Mobile have often given me ideas of where to look for interesting characters. The photographs that accompany each piece were, for the most part, taken by our newspaper's staff photographers, and show the talent of one of the best photography staffs anywhere.

The pieces were not written with categories in mind, but, in assembling them, I have put them into sections based on overt similarities, or undercurrents of connection: "The Makers," "The Tellers," "The Journeyers," "Witnesses to the Movement," "Down Back Roads," "Different Windows on Dixie," and "Personal Sojourns."

The categories, in many ways, are fluid. I put novelist and journalist Howell Raines into "Journeyers," because of the path his career has taken, though he is a teller, too. Stan Chassin and Tommy Tarrants, in the dramatic "Deliver Us from Evil," are journeyers because of their transit over time—from two teens meeting in a violent confrontation, to their meeting up again more than forty years later in an emotionally heightened moment of connection.

The artist-photographer William Christenberry is in "The Makers," but he could also be in "Down Back Roads," since I traipsed behind him as he went exploring the Alabama countryside with his camera. Bessie Papas, the last survivor of the original Greek Orthodox settlers at Malbis plantation near Spanish Fort, is in "Down Back Roads" but could also fit into "Different Windows on Dixie." That latter section highlights folks whose stories enable us to see an ages-old landscape and culture in unusual ways: through the eyes of Miss America 1951, Bebe Betbeze, or those of Alex Alvarez, a young man from the Poarch Creek reservation in Atmore, teaching Muscogee to Alabamians of Native American heritage.

Ultimately, the reader will create his or her own linkages among the pieces. An observation by novelist Sena Jeter Naslund, a reflection by journalist Diane McWhorter, an image captured by photographer Charles Moore, a story told by hairdresser Theresa Burroughs, lunch chat between Kathryn Tucker Windham and the "Tin Man," a play of language and dominoes among old men beneath a weathered oak—certain moments, surely, will stand out for the reader and create new connections. Folks I've written about may not have met one another, or even lived in the same time period, but assembled here together their voices play off one another's in varying ways.

So what do all these profiles and conversations add up to? I would like to say that, at the end of it all, I have defined what it means to be an Alabamian. But I would rather that you, the reader from here or afar, fill in the blank. What I do know is that most of the people you will meet here have been shaped, in some way, by being from Alabama, or by having spent a pivotal time in their lives here. That defining experience may be because they love the state or hate it, can never leave or can only thrive far away—no matter. The sense of identity may not be as profound as one's religion or race, family lineage or professional calling, but it's an identity that has to be reckoned with, taken into account with all the others. Whether they embrace or wrestle with it, Alabama is part of who they are.

I have traveled all over the country and lived for twenty years in New York. In the vast world beyond the Deep South I rarely heard anyone ask a native of Topeka, "What's it like to be from Kansas," or an Ann Arbor resident, "What's it mean to be a Michigander?" But I have been asked constantly—no, probed is the word—what's it like to be from Alabama? No doubt that the Civil War, the civil rights movement, movies, and famous (or infamous) politicians, athletes, musicians, and authors have generated a mythology about the state that, nationwide, cuts both ways. Alabama constantly lurks toward the bottom of the pack in literacy and high in rural poverty, but its accomplishments—the heart-piercing beauty of Harper Lee's *To Kill a Mockingbird*, the phenomenal expressiveness of Helen Keller, the simple yet history-shaking defiance of Rosa Parks on a Montgomery bus, the triumph amid bloodshed of marchers on Selma's Edmund Pettus Bridge—are woven into the sensibility of the nation. Thus *Alabama Afternoons*, I like to think, is a small part of the even bigger question of what it means to be an American.

Answers and speculations aside, these visits are above all meant to be engaging, enjoyable, memorable, so don't stand there on the porch, but open the door—and come on in.

PART I THE MAKERS

A camera, a canvas, a sculpture, tales fashioned from ghost stories whispered at night—whatever the means, the tools of the artist are used, in this section, to render up a personal vision. That vision also reflects the time and place, and stays with us long after the artist has moved on.

My process of writing about artists involves my getting as close as possible to their act of creativity.

It is 100 degrees on a summer day, and I am tromping through a field in Newbern with artist William Christenberry, standing next to him as he sets up his box camera to take an exposure of a black barn. But that's not quite close enough for me. He steps aside and lets me duck under the hood so I can see the image of the barn on the camera's viewfinder.

I am in the living room of folk artist Bernice Sims in Brewton, talking about her paintings, but I want to see her in action, too. At my request, she moves by motorized wheelchair into her kitchen, mixes some acrylics, and touches brush to canvas.

Wandering through Tuscumbia and Florence with photojournalist Charles Moore, I see how he detects interesting images and quickly snaps them, continuing to converse with me the whole time.

What's made by storyteller Katherine Tucker Windham and sculptor Charlie "Tin Man" Lucas is a special friendship, too—artists of different generations and backgrounds whose sensibility is shared. Their sense of fun is shared, too, and one of my treasured moments in Alabama Afternoons *came when heading out for lunch with the two of them. Imagine that: sitting down at a booth in a Selma bar-b-cue restaurant, listening to Windham and Lucas talk and laugh and inspire each other in their special and idiosyncratic visions.*

William Christenberry

PILGRIMAGE OF THE HEART

Stewart

The pavement hot, the air close, the thermometer groaning past 100 degrees, the afternoon unfolds along a Hale County highway a half-hour south of Tuscaloosa where William Christenberry Jr., 63—one of America's most distinguished visual artists—is driving to his grandparents' home. By kudzu-filled ditches and dilapidated garages, by forgotten gas stations and repaired fences, the native son who's lived afar for forty years is making, yet again, a pilgrimage of the heart.

From the early 1960s, Christenberry has resided up north, having taught at the Corcoran College of Art in Washington, D.C., since 1968, but it is these landscapes—general stores with bright Coca-Cola signs, wooden houses with old Pontiacs out front, churches at the end of dirt roads—that beckon.

Growing up in Tuscaloosa, he'd visit his father's parents outside Stewart on weekends and for a week in summer, picking a little cotton, listening to his grandfather's stories, relishing his grandmother's biscuits served after the morning devotional. It was during these years, also visiting with his mother's parents in nearby Akron, when he grew to love the colorful tales of the Black Belt region; when he found, in the melancholy beauty of fading farmhouses, sheds, and barns, the source of his art.

He turns into a drive and parks deep in the shade to keep his camera equipment cool. He takes a swig of water for the crushing heat and snugs on a University of Alabama cap for the pounding sun.

"I've been a Tide fan since I was a baby," he remarks of his alma mater.

William Christenberry, Hale County, Alabama. Photo courtesy of Roy Hoffman.

He gained his bachelor's degree in fine arts there in 1958, then a master's in painting in 1959. He received an honorary doctorate in 1998, when he returned as commencement speaker. In his fantasy life, he jokes, he would have been a star quarterback on the football team.

Slowly, deliberately, he steps toward the battered walls of the farmhouse, cocking his eye toward the shower of light, noting the shadows, the vine-tangled eaves. "It's a dying place," he reflects, "and you can't help but be attracted to the fact it's dying. Memory and ghost forms become very important to me."

He comes to a buckled porch with cedar tree columns. "I remember my grandfather, D. K. Christenberry, in his bed in the front room. He had one of his canes, carved in 1942. When he was well, I'd walk beside him."

His voice takes on wonderment, a boy again imagining his grandfather's strength with the cane: "He'd knock a scorpion out of the way, or a rock. One day, he slayed a dragon right before me.

"At night, we'd have cornbread and sweet milk and a lot of iced tea. There'd be Bible readings, and he'd call on different family members to pray. I always prayed he wouldn't call on me."

He reaches a sun-leached, blue-green wall at the back of the house, a one-time interior wall facing a wing of the house with a kitchen, dining room, and bathroom. The wing is gone, sawed away by a family down the road and reattached to their own place. The wall now turns to the silent yard.

Christenberry touches it with his hand. It is an image—the wall, the paint, the haunting sense of lives gone by—he has captured many times.

He walks back to his van, takes out a large tripod, and sets it up near his grandmother's tattered bedroom window. Then he lugs out a big, brown box—an old-time portrait camera—and attaches it to the tripod.

Wiping the sweat from his forehead, taking his hat off, and neatly combing his straight black hair, he readies for the shoot. He takes out a photographer's dark cloth, drapes it over the camera except for the lens, and ducks beneath it. He stays there a long moment, letting his eyes adjust to the dark.

On the grid of the viewfinder, in an upside-down image, is the window to be photographed, its pale wood, its forgotten view, its pane no resident has peered through for forty years.

He sets the controls, hurries back to the van, brings back a negative in a light-sensitive sheath, drops it into the holder and . . . *click.* "Lord," he exclaims, going back to the van with his prize, the negative carrying memory's imprint deep in its grain, "I don't know how many pictures I've made of this place."

In the old days, the house, like the fields around it, was anything but silent.

D. K. and Eula Christenberry had thirteen children, some livestock, a patch of cotton, a few pecan trees, and lived near the train tracks that thundered with freight every afternoon. Their eldest was William, who had a knack for whittling toy scissors and jackknives from the balsa wood of cigar boxes. The young man married Ruby Willard Smith, who'd grown up only a few miles from the Christenberry home. They named their first of three children William Jr.

William worked for a bakery, driving a bread route from Tuscaloosa to nearby Greensboro, then took a job with an insurance company in Clanton, in peach country. When William Jr. was in high school, William Sr. took a job with Dairy Fresh, stationed first in Tuscaloosa then in Chickasaw outside Mobile. William Jr. stayed in Tuscaloosa, living with his maternal grandmother, Caroline Smith, while finishing high school and continuing on to The University of Alabama.

For the years his parents were in Chickasaw, he'd take the Greyhound bus from Tuscaloosa to Mobile to visit. One summer, he stayed and worked at a bookstore and bindery on Government Street.

"One of the things I'm proudest of," Christenberry says of his parents, "is that they never discouraged me from becoming an artist."

In 1944, when he was 8, his parents unwittingly gave him his first artistic tool, a Brownie Holiday camera—the "Santa Claus Brownie," art critics would later dub it—to be shared with his younger sister.

While Brownie cameras were common gifts for kids in those days, in his hands, as he matured, Brownie snaps became a cornerstone of Christenberry's work. When he started taking color shots of rural Alabama as a way of recording impressions and as a basis for his paintings, he was encouraged by critics and colleagues to make more of them.

Christenberry's "visionary Brownie images," as the critic Allan Tullos called them in *Christenberry Reconstruction,* made up a solo exhibition at the Corcoran Gallery of Art in Washington in 1973. He currently uses a Brownie Bull's-Eye camera he bought at a Goodwill store in Memphis, getting film from a man who spools it for the out-of-date device. He believes that the Brownie lens has afforded him some of the "most honest" work he's ever done, "simple, direct."

For a similar reason he favors the portrait camera that requires a black cloak and a tripod to keep it absolutely still. (Usually, his exposures are a quarter-second at F/22, he says.) "I want my pictures to be a direct response to that which I see. There are no frills to it."

Richard Gruber, author of *William Christenberry: The Early Years, 1954–1968* and director of the Ogden Museum of Southern art in New Orleans, says that several generations of Christenberrys have influenced the creativity of William Jr. Christenberry's grandfather was a cane-maker, his father a carver, and his mother a seamstress and quilt maker, setting the tradition of art making in the family.

William III—the eldest of William Jr. and Sandra Christenberry's three children—graduated from the Rhode Island School of Design and is a furniture maker and sculptor.

The Christenberrys were storytellers, too. D. K. Christenberry's terse tales unfolded on a 1947 calendar the man kept beside his bed when he was ill. On it, he chronicled events as in a family Bible.

"He used the 1947 calendar to record dates in family history going back to the 1800s," Christenberry says. "He kept everyday notes too—the first pickup truck bought, the day a tree fell."

The calendar would tell of tragedy—"1949 Robert kills himself with gun in boy's room"—and expected loss. When Grandfather Christenberry died on September 5, the chronicle was picked up by William's father: "1951 D. K. Christenberry passed away at 11 minutes to 7 at Gladys's house."

Given this calendar by an aunt, Christenberry says he realized its value on many levels. Fragile and taped together in places, the calendar was not used only as an artifact but also as an art object. As an homage to his grandfather, he took the twelve months of the calendar and displayed each one in a frame. The composite work, "Calendar Wall for D. K. Christenberry," is highlighted by one of D. K. Christenberry's canes leaning amidst them.

"If I outlive my father," Christenberry explains, "I'll pencil in his passing."
One day, he says, the pencil will be taken up by his own son.

Making pictures. This simple act for William Christenberry is about taking photographs, making paintings, and creating sculpture—and in doing so, capturing the essence of a place as it inevitably changes.

From the time-battered walls of his grandparents' house in Stewart to a green shed and black barn in Newbern to a store window in Greensboro, he lingers long enough to uncover the images of his native Alabama, photographs, paints, and sculpts them and makes them his own.

In a way, it's ironic that Christenberry turns his attention to buildings rather than people. To spend a day with him in Hale County is to be in the presence of a talkative if low-key gentleman, slyly funny, who engages acquaintances and strangers alike in pleasing banter. When he lingers with an old friend from the area—such as Robert Walthall, an 85-year-old former mayor and cotton-gin owner in Newbern, who owns several sheds and barns that Christenberry photographs—the two men swap jokes and tales.

When Christenberry visits with Walthall this trip, the old-timer kids that he is going to tear down one of the sheds that the artist has made his subject. When Christenberry shows alarm, Walthall gets his laugh.

Parting company with Walthall, the two men say farewell more than once, each time pausing to tell one more tale. "It's an Alabama good-bye," Christenberry says.

Walthall has a wise, lined face with humorous eyes and does his business at a former agricultural supply office with ancient buzz fans and stacks of crinkling papers. When he tells of Newbern's busy streets and hectic commerce from his boyhood in the 1930s, he is the embodiment of Black Belt history.

Why doesn't Christenberry photograph Walthall instead of Walthall's buildings?

"He's animate," the artist answers. "These buildings are inanimate, and I feel more comfortable with them. I really like how mankind has affected things, positively mostly. I find a certain beauty, and even poignancy, in some of these places. It's not nostalgia. Strong sentiment maybe but not nostalgia."

As Robert Wilson, author and former editor of *Preservation: Magazine of the National Trust for Historic Preservation*, has explained: "What draws us to Christenberry's work is his wonderful faithfulness to a particular place and to particular buildings—often just shacks—that are meaningful to him because they exist in this place, in Hale County. The way they change over the years as he photographs them again and again defines them as surely as the original plans they were built from."

Mankind's effect has been great, hauntingly so, in the Black Belt, Alabama's struggling old cotton kingdom. Warehouses of yesteryear lean emptily into the crushing sun. Barns wait for livestock, fields for crops.

Catfish farming has helped revitalize the economy, but there is high unemployment and high poverty.

Hale County is a famous place in Alabama—indeed, in American culture—owing to journalist James Agee and photographer Walker Evans. They made their trek there in 1936, chronicling the hard lives of tenant farmers and publishing *Let Us Now Praise Famous Men,* an American classic.

"It was the same year I was born," Christenberry says.

There are far more connections between Christenberry and Evans.

In 1973 Christenberry returned from Washington as a professor at the Corcoran College of Art, accompanying a gray-bearded photographer to Hale County. It was Walker Evans himself.

Together, they visited the sites that Evans had immortalized, the tenant shacks, the fields, the corners of the Black Belt towns.

Thomas Southall, curator of photography at the High Museum of Art in Atlanta, assembled a show and wrote a book about Christenberry and Evans. The similarities were many between the two artists, he believes.

Christenberry's work, he says, "underscores some of the things Evans and Agee were talking about. It's not about a temporary situation, it's about people and family and life and the patterns of life."

But he points out a difference, too: "Christenberry had an emotional attachment growing up in this area." Evans and Agee, relatively speaking, were outsiders.

Greensboro is an antebellum town where the county courthouse has a memorial out front to the soldiers of Hale County. Christenberry's family ties are deep to this sleepy but picturesque place. One of the names on the monument is his uncle's, John Eliot Smith, who gave his life in World War II.

Ambling down its main street, Christenberry pauses to take a Brownie snapshot of an empty storefront where a flier taped in the doorway announces, "Miracles of Prayer." He points to an ornate eave, saying it's where a hotel used to be. In a local cafe, a couple calls out, "Bill? How've you been? We were just talking the other day with your mother."

Christenberry knows this town's secrets. Once he was shown upstairs to a building at the end of the block by a man who told him about the Ku Klux Klan having met there many years ago. He recalls the large hole in the masonry wall—for holding a torch.

The Klan's presence in Alabama, which he'd first seen in Tuscaloosa, was an early obsession for him, one focus of his art quite different from his elegiac vision of fading barns and old farmhouses. Exploring what he calls "that aspect of evil that manifests itself in the Klan," he began to make sculptures, drawings, and dolls driven by his vision of the hate group. He assembled 565 images into "The Klan Room."

To view photographs of this collection is to feel anxious and angered.

Viewers, he admits, often have a powerful response. In 1979 the majority of pieces from the collection, which he kept in his Washington studio, were stolen. He has had to re-create and make new images.

That there are such divergent aspects to William Christenberry's work may seem unlikely—black barns and green sheds, rural churches, Klan sheets—but like the Alabama Black Belt itself, his creative mind is one of unexpected turns and surprises.

According to the Ogden Museum's Gruber, Christenberry is "showing us the South, America, our culture and our history. He looks at it in an unflinching way, revealing, exploring, peeling off another layer."

Living outside the South, Christenberry explains, gives him that "perspective" on what he calls "the source" of his memory and his art.

"Spiritually, we're at a place I hold close to my heart," Christenberry says at his grandparents' house.

The light flickers through a pecan tree he's captured many times on film. He gazes at how the trunk enters the ground like a claw. He walks closer, examining the shadings of color on the bark. There's a scratching in the bushes and an armadillo pokes out its nose. An owl hoots.

"As I get older, this place is even more significant," he says, crossing the yard by the blue-green wall and the tattered window, lifting up his camera and, like a man cradling a treasure chest, bearing it toward the tree. "When it's gone, I don't know how I'll feel."

Charles Moore

WITNESS TO CHANGE

I profiled Charles Moore in 2001. When I saw him again in 2005 he was too busy to talk. On Selma's Edmund Pettus Bridge, for the fortieth anniversary of the civil rights march, he was hurriedly, passionately, snapping photos of the Reverend Joseph Lowery, the Reverend Fred Shuttlesworth, the Reverend Jesse Jackson, Congressman John Lewis, and Coretta Scott King. Moore passed away in 2010.

Florence

Pictures can and do make a difference. Strong images of historical events do have an impact on our society.

—CHARLES MOORE, from the preface of *Powerful Days: The Civil Rights Photography of Charles Moore*

Nearly forty years have passed since Charles Moore slung his Nikon camera over his shoulder and headed to Oxford, Mississippi, to chronicle for the nation what would be, by today's standards, a mundane event—the enrollment, in the University of Mississippi, of a young black man named James Meredith. A storm was brewing at Ole Miss—Mississippi governor Ross Barnett had sworn defiance of desegregation—and Charles Moore was heading into that storm.

Moore, an Alabama photojournalist on assignment for *Life* magazine, had already experienced the turbulence of the early civil rights movement as chief photographer for the *Montgomery Advertiser*. He had snapped dramatic im-

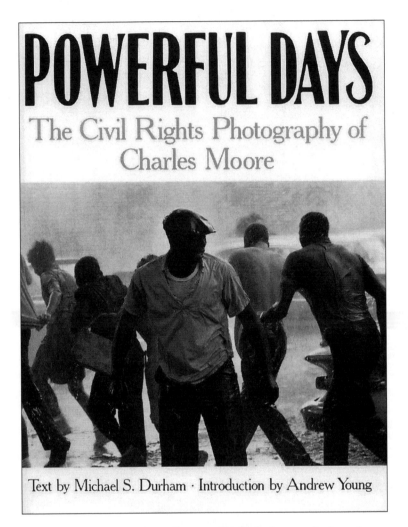

POWERFUL DAYS

The Civil Rights Photography of Charles Moore

Text by Michael S. Durham · Introduction by Andrew Young

The cover of *Powerful Days*, a collection of Moore's photographs from the civil rights movement.

ages of Martin Luther King Jr. and memorable, sometimes harrowing street scenes.

One of the most unnerving, taken in 1960 in Montgomery the day after black students tried to desegregate the capitol cafeteria, showed a white man about to crack a baseball bat over the head of a black woman—a split-second of rage captured forever by Moore's shutter. Moore says he made the picture in the midst of running down the street, which tilted the angle of the shot. The image created a sense of a moral universe turned on its side, dislocated from normal time and space.

Moore had also put himself, physically, on the line. He had been pushed, yanked, cursed at, and threatened with his life for the simple reason that his camera would not tell a lie.

The weekend of confrontations over James Meredith began not in Oxford, but in Jackson, Mississippi, during a rally downtown for the Ole Miss Rebels football team. An Ole Miss game was scheduled for that afternoon at Jackson's big stadium. As Moore remembers it, there were young men on the street waving Rebel flags and cheering on Ole Miss. But those chants soon changed to "Roll With Ross," an expression of support for the Mississippi governor.

When Moore had started taking photographs of the fans, one man with a flag had told him to stop. He then, according to Moore, began to jab Moore with the pole of the flag. Moore knocked the pole out of the young man's hand. The man swore revenge. That afternoon, while Moore was gathered with colleagues in a Jackson hotel room, the door burst open and the same young man, followed by his friends, came storming in.

The man who earlier had stuck Moore with the flagpole now grabbed him by the throat. "I ain't got nothin' against the niggers," he spat. "Every white man should own ten of them!"

Moore, now 69, trembles with anger as he recounts the story.

"He gripped me with his left hand so I could reach up like this"—he demonstrates for a visitor—"and grab hold of his left thumb. You can hurt a guy pretty bad if you turn back his thumb."

But Moore, who had learned self-defense as a combat photographer with the U.S. Marines, wanted to stay calm. "I knew if I took a swing at him we'd have chaos in that room . . . My right arm was free. It was like a coiled spring. Oh, I wanted so badly to let loose with that spring!" He shakes his head.

Moore had faced down bullies before while growing up in small-town Alabama, and he sensed the right strategy. "I told him, 'It's me you want! Forget about the rest of them. Send everybody out of the room—and it'll be just you and me.'"

The bully did not budge. Then he let go and backed away. "He'd lost face," Moore says.

Moore's photographs from Oxford tell the rest of the story: How the 28-year-old U.S. Air Force veteran, James Meredith, walked into the university with federal guards to each side; how a local law enforcement officer stood with grinning men, slapping a billy stick against his palm to show power; how the Mississippi National Guard was federalized and used tear gas to quell rioters opposed to the entrance of Meredith. In searing, now-classic photographs of the university's administration building, the Lyceum, under siege with tear gas, Moore put his viewfinder up to the goggle-eye of his own gas mask and snapped haunting images of the National Guardsmen looking like storm troopers, their otherworldly gas masks like haunting apparitions.

As Moore's first big assignment for *Life,* it was a journalistic triumph. But he was a native son of the South who says he recoiled from the very violence he captured.

Like it or not, Moore had become the young man who helped show, to the rest of the world, the anguish of his native region, and, as the civil rights movement unfolded, its sense of promise, too.

A gentle artist with an aggressive camera, Moore today is an energetic, compact man with silver hair and penetrating blue eyes. As a teenager, he boxed as a lightweight. He still betrays the instincts of a man who knew combat in the ring—quick on his feet, a little edgy, with a habit of pinning you with his gaze.

He moved back to Alabama only last spring after spending twenty-three years in California. He settled in Florence, a picturesque town on the banks of the Tennessee River in northwest Alabama, where the University of North Alabama lies close to downtown and his old hometown of Tuscumbia is a short drive away. His cozy house on a quiet block near the university—filled with art books and photographs—is one he inhabits alone. He is divorced, and his three children and their families live in southeast Alabama's Dothan and in Florida.

The heart of the house is the study where copies of his book of photographs about the civil rights movement, *Powerful Days,* lie among his landscape images of Sonora, California, where he once lived, an idyllic town just west of Yosemite National Park.

There are new images he's making, too—digital photographs of blues musicians, many from the Muscle Shoals area close by to Florence. As he talks with a visitor about his love of photography, he returns to certain words or phrases—the "excitement" of the picture, its sense of "feeling the action."

The feel of the action is dramatically evidenced in Moore's photographs of events in the civil rights movement:

- Martin Luther King Jr., on September 3, 1958, being arrested after trying to enter the Montgomery courthouse accompanying his friend, Ralph Abernathy, who was responding to a subpoena. King is being pushed against the police station counter, his arm twisted behind his back.
- Birmingham firemen turning the force of their hoses on black citizens in an effort to break up voting rights demonstrations. People huddle in doorways, cover their faces, sustain the rocket-impact of the water.
- White and black marchers, waving American flags, heading from Selma to the state capitol in Montgomery. They are tired, resolute—exultant.

Many of these images in the day when *Life* magazine came out every week, brought the movement into American homes. The pictures, as the years wore on and the images deepened, pressed on the moral nerve of the nation.

As the journalist Michael S. Durham wrote in the text of *Powerful Days* about the passage of the Civil Rights Act of 1964: "By then Charles's Birmingham photographs had become so much a part of the public memory of those events that they even received some measure of credit for the passage of the legislation. As the historian Arthur Schlesinger, Jr., later said, 'The photographs of Bull Connor's police dogs lunging at the marchers in Birmingham did as much as anything to transform the national mood and make legislation not just necessary, which it had long been, but possible.'"

If there is a sense of destiny about Moore's photographs of the movement, though, he arrived at that destiny quite by chance.

After joining up at age 17 for a stint with the Marines, he studied fashion photography at the Brooks Institute in California. Family responsibilities called him home, and he returned to Tuscumbia to work for Olan Mills, the studio portrait chain.

Restless with studio work, he turned to photojournalism and applied for a job at the *Montgomery Advertiser*. He showed up only to be directed to the local country club, where the chief photographer was doing a shoot of models dressed in evening clothes.

"You take the rest of the roll," the photographer told Moore.

By the time Moore had rearranged the models, changed the lighting, and snapped the remaining pictures, the chief photographer said, "You're hired."

It was 1957, and within the year Moore was chief photographer. By then, the world had taken note of a young minister, Martin Luther King Jr., who'd arrived at the Dexter Avenue Baptist Church in Montgomery two years earlier and had led the Montgomery Improvement Association during the Montgomery bus boycott.

"I was spellbound by his oratory," says Moore, remembering how he'd photographed King up on the altar of Dexter Avenue Baptist.

Moore found himself agreeing with King's positions, but had to be careful about what he said. "I was not on any pulpit preaching," Moore says of himself during those years. He was only serving as a witness to the drama breaking around him.

While crouching on the floor before King, taking photographs, he was exercising one of his principal philosophies of photography: Watch your subject, get to know him, be ready for the right moment to capture a sense of who he is.

"I project myself into a person," he says of his photographic technique. "I look at everything, the arms, the hands, the expression. I wait for the moment . . . I shoot."

One of Moore's famous pictures of King, in Dexter church with a cross behind him, served as the model for the Postal Service's August 1999 stamp honoring King on the thirty-sixth anniversary of the march on Washington, D.C., when King delivered his epic speech, "I Have a Dream."

On the outskirts of Tuscumbia is a community named Valdosta—railroad tracks, barns, modest one-story homes, and roads weaving off through the north Alabama hills. It is here, after being born in nearby Hackleburg, that Charles Moore spent his childhood.

Showing a visitor his boyhood home, he drives past familiar landscapes, remembering walking down the hill to home after school, crossing an old iron bridge that spans the creek, enjoying a carefree boyhood of baseball and bicycles.

The era of segregation is long over, but there are the vestiges of racial divide. "They said there was no Klan here," Moore says, pointing to a shed-like structure near the railroad tracks. "But everybody knew that's where they held their meetings."

Moore's trip to his boyhood locale evokes memories, as well, of his early rambles with his Brownie camera, a free sense of walking down lanes and through woods, which he still enjoys.

It also brings back his father, the Reverend Charles Walker Moore, a Baptist minister, and, says his son, a teacher of important moral lessons. "Dad was invited by black ministers to visit their churches," he says. "He'd be the only white there, other than me."

One of his strongest images of his father was on Sunday afternoons. "On Sundays, after church, we'd go in to the jail and he'd give a pack of cigarettes to prisoners and pray."

The white and black prisoners were kept separated in those days. Moore says his father distributed smokes to both races, a tiny gesture, but profound in its way in the segregated South. "Dad just accepted people, but he didn't go out and try to change the world."

Of his life as a photographer—and as a man—Moore says: "I wanted to look back and honor my dad about being good to people."

To this day, Moore can hardly read aloud the dedication to his book, *Powerful Days*, without having to stop to fight back tears: "To Dad, the Reverend Charles Walker Moore, in loving memory, for his gentleness and strength of faith."

Moore drives up to a lane where he grew up as a boy. A white house sits back on a rise, with a bright maple tree nearby. Across the yard is a stone house where his best friend lived. He tells how he introduced that friend to the girl who'd become his wife. The couple went on to be married fifty years, and the man became Tuscumbia's mayor. Although Moore has been home in Alabama since last spring, he has not worked up the nerve to go knock on that door, to introduce himself to the people who now live where he grew up, to ask to walk across the floorboards.

He parks the car near the house. "You stay here," he tells his visitor. He gets out, goes to the front porch, up the steps. Knocks.

He knocks again.

The shades are drawn. The house is silent. He returns to the car.

"Maybe they recognize me and don't want to answer," he says, perhaps only half joking, referring to his long-ago reputation, as a photographer, of being someone others might think wanted to paint them in an unflattering way.

Before he pulls away he tells the story of his mother, how she died from cancer when he was 13, and how it shattered his father. The Reverend Moore, still a young man, had grieved long after her passing and never remarried.

"I can see him sitting there, crying, night after night," says Moore, a grandfather now remembering like a son.

He takes a long, silent look back at the porch, then drives on.

Behind Helen Keller's home in Tuscumbia there is a water pump where Helen, as recounted in the play, *The Miracle Worker*, first uttered the word "water," after her teacher, Annie Sullivan, wrote "W-A-T-E-R" in the palm of her hand.

On a bright afternoon when the trees are turned to flame, Charles Moore shows his visitor the Helen Keller home, Ivy Green, a picturesque white house surrounded by green and a sense of hush. In the back of the house he deftly lifts his camera and takes a picture of that pump. Inside he trains his lens on antique portraits of Helen made by photographers of yesteryear. Two of those photographs show Helen as a raven-haired, sensuous young woman with captivating dark eyes. Moore says he knows of the artist who captured those images.

To travel the Tuscumbia area with Moore is to see northwest Alabama through the eyes of a native son come home, still trying, in his own, restless way, to find the place he left. He carries his camera with him, but it is his camera that seems, ultimately, to lead the direction.

At the Alabama Music Hall of Fame in Tuscumbia, he takes photographs of one of the museum directors standing in the lobby talking with his visitor.

He wanders through the galleries, praising the exploits of Alabama musicians, among them Percy Sledge, who grew up close to where Moore did.

Like a man discovering his home area anew, he reads aloud, to his visitor, information on the recording studios on Muscle Shoals, summoning great musicians who've recorded there—among them, Aretha Franklin, Greg Allman, the Oak Ridge Boys. The photographer once accused, by some southerners, of portraying his homeland in a bad light, now wants to promote it and "to help make it better," he says.

In downtown Tuscumbia he lunches in a cafe. Meeting up with a friend from high school, he ambles the familiar streets. The two men reminisce about how the town, in decades gone by, thrived with commerce on Saturday mornings; how the Tennessee Valley Authority had a research station in town and Ford had a motor plant. The town, they say, is now quiet on weekend mornings, and the research station and Ford factory are gone.

In front of a store window they pause as Moore gazes with bemusement at a pair of thong panties on a mannequin torso. He shakes his head, lifts his camera. It is a changed South.

A lady who runs the store comes out, giggling, and invites Moore and the others in. She tells a story about a man who comes in sometimes asking for ladies underclothes—for himself. "He said, 'Why, I just want a change of lifestyle!'"

It is like a scene from a comic story by Eudora Welty.

As the woman talks, Moore is snapping her picture.

If the heart of Moore's house in Florence is his study, its soul is downstairs, in his darkroom. He leads his visitor down to a series of rooms where developing trays sit near a sink, and photographs are stacked up on counters. Stunning portraits of glamorous actresses, gritty photographs of boxers in reeking gyms, bucolic landscapes from California—the images captured by Charles Moore are everywhere.

What characterizes them all is an intimacy, an artist's eye engaged by beauty and drama.

After spending seven years of his career photographing the conflict of the civil rights movement, Moore explains, he turned his attention to the world of natural beauty around him. The youngster who'd loved to ramble the back roads of Alabama became the grownup who relished the rolling hills of California. He took pictures of celebrities—Kim Novak and Raquel Welch, among them. He then turned his attention to Southeast Asia, going on photographic journeys for travel magazines.

"An artist," he says, "does not have to spend his entire life doing one kind of work."

During a later telephone conversation, Moore relates that he has not been to Oxford, Mississippi, since that tumultuous weekend in the fall of 1962. He sounds curious, perhaps a little surprised, at hearing how, today, Oxford's 19th-century courthouse rises serenely in the square. There are cozy restaurants, sporty clothing shops, and a vast, yet homey, bookstore—all looking out to a town where students, black and white, mingle casually.

Moore, who describes himself as a modest man who does not like to trumpet his talents, said there is one accomplishment he is proud to claim.

"Had it not been for the photographs I made over there, that made so many people angry, it's possible that little town would not be that way now."

Bernice Sims

A FOLK ARTIST'S STAMP ON HISTORY

Brewton

On a quiet street lined with gray mailboxes, there's one mailbox painted with bright colors of a family at a cabin. The signature of the artist, who is also the mail recipient, is printed along the side: "B. Sims."

These days, some of the letters that are put in the box bear a postage stamp with another image painted by Bernice Sims—civil rights marchers on Selma's Edmund Pettus Bridge in March 1965.

Sims, 78, has been selling her folk-art canvases for over twenty years. But the selection of her "*Selma Bridge Crossing*" as part of a ten-stamp commemorative series, called "To Form a More Perfect Union" and issued on August 30, 2005, has given the great-grandmother a national presence.

Journalists arriving at her door, art collectors traveling hundreds of miles, curious neighbors looking to see what all the fuss is about—fame has its demands.

"What is fame?" Sims asks. "How you supposed to feel?" She shrugs. "It don't feel any different. Maybe it's the age. All the fight's gone out of me. I don't get excited anymore."

She tilts her head back and laughs, a large woman in a red-pattern muumuu who, despite diabetes and arthritis, still seems full of fight and excitement about what she loves best besides church and family—making art.

Flecks of white and red paint on the backs of her strong, dark hands hint at her passion. "Sometimes it be all on my face, messy on the floor. I get so in it, I forget what I'm doing."

Folk artist Bernice Sims at work at her home in Brewton, Alabama. Her painting of the Edmund Pettus Bridge was used as the image on a U.S. postal stamp. Photo by Victor Calhoun, courtesy of the *Mobile Press-Register.*

Painted by folk artist Bernice Sims, *Selma Bridge Crossing* depicts the Selma-to-Montgomery march across the Edmund Pettus Bridge, and appears on a U.S. postage stamp. Photo by Victor Calhoun, courtesy of the *Mobile Press-Register.*

She gazes at recent canvases propped against the corner, rustic depictions of tent revivals, fieldworkers, schoolchildren, Biblical stories, civil rights scenes.

"I paint pictures of everyday," she says, "but in the past, like it used to be. I have to wait. Everything I paint I form it in my mind. It comes back to me."

On Christmas Day 1926, little Bernice was born in Butler County, Alabama, just outside of Georgiana, the first of eight children of Robert Johnson and Essie Bell Johnson. Robert worked in the sawmill and laid crossties on the railroad. Essie, Bernice says, "worked in private homes."

"Most black people were poor," she recalls.

Life in the country still had its joys, and her paintings often depict smiling children in the yard with chickens and dogs. Sometimes Bernice puts in a woman at the cabin door who represents her mother. Sometimes she also depicts herself as a child. "I'm the fat one," she says.

"We were happy kids. We didn't know anything. We made our toys. But our family was together."

Although young Bernice experienced racial prejudice in Georgiana—she remembers once being spit on—she knew kindness across racial lines, too.

"I was fortunate enough to live next door to a white family. That's how I really got started on the painting. There were five sisters, one brother. One of the sisters was an artist. She was in oil. She'd give me a little bit left in the tube and an old brush, and I'd draw and paint with that."

Bernice kept in touch with that woman, Hattie Warren, over the years.

At 16, married and starting to have children—she has four sons and two daughters, both daughters now deceased—Bernice's education and her interest in art got put on hold. Her family moved to Brewton in Escambia County, where she worked in the homes of white families as a maid, cooking, cleaning, and taking care of their little ones.

After she raised her children and was on her own, alone, she resolved to resume her education. She passed the GED for her high school degree, then got a grant to attend Jefferson Davis Community College in Brewton, where she graduated with an associate of arts degree.

She continued at Jefferson Davis, taking studio art classes. It was her art teacher, Larry Manning, who made all the difference with his encouragement, she says.

When Manning directed his class to make likenesses on the canvas of real objects—a skull, a duck, a paper bag—Sims became frustrated. "He put things on the board to copy. I can't copy. 'Well,' I thought, 'I'll just go home.'

"Larry said, 'No, Granny, don't do that. Go over there and do your thing.'"

When Manning took the art class on a field trip to Montgomery, Sims saw the work of Mose Tolliver—the famous folk artist known as Mose T—and she had an inspiration.

"It looked like children's art," Sims says of Tolliver's work. "I said, 'I know I can do better than that,' and I came home and started painting."

Sims is now part of the group of heralded "outsider" artists from Alabama that includes Mose T, Jimmy Lee Sudduth, Charlie Lucas, Lonnie Holley, and Myrtice West.

Sims' work usually falls into a subgroup of so-called self-taught art referred to as "memory" art or works depicting scenes from the painter's distant past. On a website named Voices of Civil Rights, an article says Sims has a reputation in the art world as the "Grandma Moses of the civil rights struggle."

Art galleries on the Internet typically charge $400 to $600 for her works. By her own admission, Sims has little knack for what she calls making "fine art," the realistic depictions of people and places.

"I paint what pops up in my head," she says.

Sims' postage stamp, taken from a painting she sold many years ago—she now gets paid by the Postal Service for the use of the image, she says—is part of a series on civil rights milestones that includes work by famous artists, including Jacob Lawrence.

Sims' civil rights scenes come from what she has seen in person or on television and what she has been told.

Although she did not march over Edmund Pettus Bridge, she was there watching, she says.

Her sister in Birmingham gave her a first-person account of firefighters in that city spraying activists with hoses and police setting out their dogs.

"Once I get that on the page," she says of those tumultuous times, "I can deal with it."

Whatever her subject, the childlike quality of her work and her bright colors give it a radiant simplicity.

Early on, she used a lot of green and yellow.

"I did it so much it started to drive me crazy."

Although she started with oils, the use of turpentine bothered her, and she switched to acrylics. Whatever the medium, her art has taken her on at least one welcome path.

"Before I got into this art I stayed sick all the time. I was having chest pains and such. But it was just like physical therapy. My mind got into the painting, and I didn't go to the doctor much," she says.

"It was a healing thing."

Slowly, patiently, Sims gets up from her living room chair, climbs onto a motorized scooter, and rolls into the kitchen, which doubles as her studio. She takes her place before a half-finished canvas.

With her right hand, she picks up a brush from an empty coffee can, touches it to the acrylic paint she has squeezed out into a plastic egg carton and holds the brush up to the canvas. Plagued by her arthritis, she places her left hand under her right wrist to keep her painting hand steady.

She resumes work on the canvas—a playground. Yellow, red, blue. The children's arms and legs, their faces, become vivid.

There are black faces and white faces.

Sims says that the many hours she spent on playgrounds was while working as maid, a black woman minding white children. She stopped doing that kind of work in the late 1960s, she says.

"Friday was always bridge day," she recalls. "Those ladies would play bridge. We had to get those kids out of there.

"I can visualize how we'd sit there, all the maids, with the kids playing, climbing the ladders and on the swings.

"We'd stay there until five o'clock, when the bridge game was over.

"I wasn't painting then"—she dips her brush into the acrylic, then moves it back to the canvas—"I was just memorizing."

Kathryn Tucker Windham and Charlie Lucas

KATHRYN AND THE "TIN MAN"

Selma

Kathryn Tucker Windham, 85, is short and snow-complexioned with lively blue eyes and a storyteller's voice as rich and involving as molasses. Charlie Lucas, 52, is tall and black with alert dark eyes and a way of speaking, with references to his folk art, as rhythmic as an afternoon breeze.

As neighbors for the last two years—Windham owns her house and the one next door, which Lucas rents—they are people of different ages with adjacent driveways, of different races with a common walk. They also share a vision rare and strange.

"You'll never meet two people like us. Not in all eternity," says Lucas, stepping from his driveway by his metal sculpture of a boy on a tricycle, past his corrugated-tin horse head entangled in vines, to Windham's side door. "Some people think I'm a little bit . . ." He smiles, eyes crinkling behind wire-rim spectacles. "Crazy."

He jiggles the door. A slight wind moves across the cobalt-blue bottles that Windham stuck onto the branches of a tree to ward off evil spirits.

She steps to the screen and peers up at her friend. He is rumpled, in jeans and a faded purple shirt. She is neat, her white hair smoothly combed. She waves him in.

That Charlie and Kathryn have become buddies seems natural to them. He is a little-schooled folk artist nicknamed "Tin Man," who has shown his work in numerous exhibitions and lectured at Yale University. She is a renowned

Charlie Lucas and Kathryn Tucker Windham in Selma, Alabama. Photo by Bill Starling, courtesy of the *Mobile Press-Register.*

author who tells stories to huge crowds about a friendly ghost named Jeffrey that resides in her house.

The two neighbors share a fascination with stories—the elder woman who has spent her life putting words on the page and the middle-aged man only now learning how to decipher them. "I'm not a readin' person," Lucas admits. But Windham is helping him become one, as any good friend surely would.

To others, their friendship does seem unusual.

"Some folks ask me, 'Charlie, what you hanging out with that old white lady for?'

"'Art and love, it's a beautiful world,' I tell them."

Inside Windham's house, there is a rough-hewn portrait of her in paint and wood, created by Lucas. "When I made that for her," he recalls, "she saw it and busted out laughing!"

She shakes her head. "Oh, Charlie," she says. "Charlie." She smiles. "When we going fishing?"

He tells her that they'll go on Saturday, when he's back from Pink Lily, the village about an hour away where his enormous family lives, and his metal art sprawls out on a pasture.

Lucas looks past Windham's volumes of autobiography, folk tales, ghost stories—books he hopes to read for himself one day—and then to Windham, whose face and thoughts he can already read.

"You think about what you got when you combine both of us knowledge together," he says, with his colloquial way of speaking. "It's like the Fourth of July every day.

"And the neighbors," he adds, "still trying to figure out who we is."

They grew up so differently.

In 1918, Kathryn Tucker was born in Clarke County, the youngest child of a large family. She grew up in an ample, lively house, with her father the president of the local bank. She had one professional ambition above all. As she wrote in her autobiography, "When I was a little girl in Thomasville, Alabama, my playmates . . . wanted to grow up to be teachers, nurses, secretaries, or missionaries. I wanted to be a newspaper reporter."

Charlie Lucas, one of fourteen children, was born in a hamlet not found on a state map, a place he calls Sweetening, which sits near Prattville, in Autauga County. As a boy, he says, he joined the others in working in the fields, picking crops, but not for long. When he had a tendency to make toys and dolls for the younger children from the cotton and sticks and other items he found in the countryside, he was told to stay home as the babysitter.

To this day, he professes, "I don't call myself an artist. I just like to make toys."

Windham describes a happy childhood, one she has written about and recorded on tapes and CDs. She tells of swimming in a Thomasville creek, going to the circus, relishing the family meals.

Lucas describes a childhood in which he felt misunderstood. When his grammar school teacher asked the students what they wanted to be when they grew up, Lucas, who enjoyed music, answered that he wanted to dance in the ballet. "The boys took me outside after school and scrubbed my head in the dirt."

When the teacher stood at the blackboard, Lucas became fixated on objects outside the window, making up stories about them. He was bullied.

Windham graduated from Huntingdon College in Montgomery.

Lucas dropped out of school in the fourth grade.

Windham worked as a reporter for the *Thomasville Times,* the *Alabama Journal,* the *Birmingham News,* and the *Selma Times-Journal.*

Lucas, among his various jobs, worked as a janitor.

Today, Windham still lives in the brick home that she and her late husband, Amasa Windham, bought when they married and moved to Selma in 1946. When Amasa died in 1956 from a heart attack, Kathryn raised their three children in that house. A couple of years ago, when neighbors put their house up for sale, she bought it.

Kathryn Windham had gotten to know Lucas' art in the 1980s, when she saw a metal horse head he'd made that was in front of the house of one of his relatives in Autauga County. She had stopped on the roadside and examined it and asked questions about him.

Lucas had discovered Windham when he heard her telling her ghost stories at a folk arts festival outside of Tuscaloosa, the Kentuck Festival. "I thought, 'Listen to this white woman telling stories like I heard growing up.' They pulled me back into my natural self."

In 2000, traveling in France as part of "Artists of Alabama 2000," sponsored by an arts foundation, the two became friends. When Windham longed for a tomato sandwich, Lucas went out and found some tomatoes and made her one.

Although he had little money, Lucas was helping to care, he says, for many family members on several acres of property near Prattville, in Pink Lily. He had also turned five acres of that property into a field of his metal art—old cars and buses transformed into art objects, gigantic African-like masks made from auto hoods, and welded creatures resembling alligators and dinosaurs.

Two cows and his plentiful grandchildren have free run of the place.

Some folks in the vicinity, though, think him strange. "They say I'm a garbage man."

A couple of years ago, the time had come in his life, he says, "to make a shift." His longtime marriage splintering after his eight children had grown, Lucas needed a place to live on his own. He came to look at the empty house that Windham had for rent.

After she handed him the keys, Windham said, "You ever need help, you knock on my door."

"Miss Kathryn, to me, was like a captain on a boat," he recalls. "She said, 'Charlie, get on the boat and ride.'"

To walk through Lucas' house is to take a journey through a place of imagination far beyond four walls. Lucas uses objects he finds and recombines them into lively, figurative pieces, each with a name and a story. One of his favorite objects to work with is a wheel, inspired by the example of his great-grandfather, Cain Lucas, the son of a slave, who had worked as a blacksmith.

The wheel, says Charlie Lucas, symbolizes the wagon wheel—how it enabled the horse to pull many times its weight—and the cycle of life. "In using the wheel," Lucas says, "I'm protecting the tradition of my great-grandfather."

Lucas' grandfather was a basket weaver, and Charlie honors that memory when he takes metal bands and weaves them together to make the heads of elephants and horses and unusual robotic figures. His own father repaired cars.

"I'm constantly amazed," says Windham, meandering through the art-filled rooms. She points to an ironing board hammered to the wall, painted to look like a face. "And everything has a story to it. Everything means something." She shakes her head in wonderment.

"I listen to what the piece tells me it wants to be," Lucas says. "And they go out of here speaking. Not cussin'."

If Lucas shows Windham the mystery of ordinary objects transformed into art, she shows him the magic of words on the page changed to language.

She reads her stories to him, she says. She reads him newspaper and magazine articles.

And she reads him legal documents. She has asked him not to sign any documents or contracts until she has read them out to him.

In the past, Lucas says, he became involved in a deal with someone wishing to represent his art, but it didn't work out happily. He prefers not to talk about it in detail, for legal reasons, he says. "I was treated," he bridles, "like an ignorant man."

Part of Windham's wonderment over Lucas is how he has survived so long—indeed, flourished—without being able to read. She is astonished that he can travel as he has, giving talks about his art, teaching classes, being interviewed, without even being able to decipher the signs in airports.

Lucas says he has a good eye for numbers, and all airline flights have numbers. But Windham knew that Lucas needed to be able to do more.

"Miss Kathryn and I had been in the library one day, and she said, 'You need to meet somebody.'"

He met Margaret "Peggy" Christian, who works in adult literacy in the library, affiliated with Wallace Community College.

In a small office down the library hall, not far from a room with an exhibition of Windham's photographs of Alabama rural scenes, Lucas sits with Christian, slowly reading out primers.

He started out with a basal reader—a textbook used by beginning readers—and has progressed, over the last two years, to the mystery books, the Stormy Night Series, which Christian says are used in second through the fourth grades.

Christian says that her artistic student is unusual in his dedication and progressing well. Many times adults, she says, drop out of the literacy program, frustrated by slow progress.

To show his appreciation for her help, Lucas made his teacher a present, a metalwork with the theme, he says, of a woman "looking ahead."

At noontime on a recent day, Lucas and Windham go out to lunch at Hancock's Barbecue. When they enter, Lucas gazes at the antique saws on the wall being used as down-home decoration. Windham keeps her eye on him. "Don't get any ideas now," she says.

She knows him well enough to realize that those rusting blades of metal would make perfect objects, recombined into different figures, in the Tin Man's work.

Nearly everybody they pass seems to know Windham. Indeed, her picture is on a postcard of Selma that's sold in local drugstores, and many folks have become familiar with Lucas as her sidekick.

In the restaurant Windham hands out fliers, inviting the community to a "comb concert," an event, she explains, in which people make music by humming on wax paper laid against the teeth of a comb. She has a pocketful of combs with her, imprinted with the words: "Making Music Together in Selma, Alabama."

The comb concert, in its small way, Windham explains, shows how people of different backgrounds can mingle in Selma, have fun and laugh. She says she often meets people around the country who tell her they traveled to Selma to take part in the civil rights marches.

"It's a source of pride for them," says Windham, who covered the marches for the *Selma Times-Journal*. "Then I ask them, 'But have you been back since?'" Few say they have.

After lunch, they get into Lucas' truck, and he drives her through the city.

Passing by historic homes, she tells of ladies who lunched there, tales about Civil War soldiers, anecdotes about events great and small. Lucas peers at the rooftops, especially the tin shingles on one old house, saying the day might come when those shingles—torn off—could become material for his art. He makes the shingles into faces.

He slows by a demolition site, a rubble of floor tiles and wood. Once before, he says, he stopped to pick up tiles on the side of the road with Windham's help. A car had slowed, and some ladies looked out, exclaiming, "Look at him making that old lady work like that!"

The two friends, remembering that incident, laugh uproariously.

They turn into Selma's historic Live Oak Cemetery, close to the heart of the town. Windham says she knows where she will be buried; Lucas says he's not ready to let her go. He adds: "When I wake up in the morning, the first thing I do when I look out the window is see if Miss Kathryn's window curtains are open. If they are, I know I won't have to get the jumper cables to get her going!"

Windham says she's on her third pacemaker and feeling fine.

The hoary oak trees, stone angels, crosses and obelisks slide by the cab of the truck as Lucas slowly rolls through the somnolent graveyard.

Suddenly, there is a whirring sound, a tree branch, it seems, caught up under the wheel. Lucas drives a little faster. The whirring rises.

"That's one of your friends, Miss Kathryn, done jumped up into the truck with us!"

"Oh, Charlie," she says, "Charlie."

PART II   THE TELLERS

*A*labama is rich in its tellers—those who invent, others who report; those who put pen to page, others who spin out the story aloud from imagination or memory.

I have profiled many writers over the years and gotten to know many of them personally from participating in conferences like the Alabama Writers Symposium in Monroeville. In writing about writers I have the chance to develop a double-focus—the author him or herself and the author's subject matter.

Conversations with Sena Jeter Naslund and Diane McWhorter show two Birmingham natives who've both written books grounded in the bombing of the Sixteenth Street Baptist Church on September 15, 1963. Naslund's is a novel, McWhorter's a book of investigative journalism framed within a personal story.

After readers are introduced to these authors and others through my journalistic visits, they can read their books, delving more deeply into the worlds rendered up by the remarkable authors of our state.

As always, I try to take the reader along with me as I explore the worlds of these tellers: Mary Ward Brown's farmhouse in the Alabama Black Belt and a drive down country roads; Frye Gaillard's Mobile, both in the stories he recounts and the setting of the interview, Bienville Square, the heart of downtown Mobile.

Eugene Sledge never set out to tell, but he had to. His memoir, With the Old Breed in Pelilieu and Okinawa, *was written, as he explains, out of obsession—the efforts of a WWII U.S. Marine to free himself of the battle memories that plagued his psyche. Sledge's tale became highlighted in PBS's* The War *and HBO's* The Pacific. *This Alabama afternoon provides a quiet, at-home glimpse of the retired biology professor.*

Not every teller puts his or her thoughts down on the page, though. Sometimes interviews blend into oral history, which is the case with Artelia Bendolph. Bendolph became one face of Depression-era Alabama to the nation, an aspect of our home captured by a passer-through. During the hours I spent with Bendolph in Prichard I was captivated by her story of life in Gee's Bend so long ago. I just listened, taped, transcribed, and put her spoken story into the context of the afternoon.

If you sit down and converse with ordinary folks, before long they'll offer up a line or two of natural poetry. Artelia Bendolph offered many.

Mary Ward Brown

BLACK BELT STORYTELLER

Hamburg

Petite, silver haired, and 87 years old, Mary Ward Brown welcomes you to her farmhouse with a big smile, pumpkin pie, and delightful conversation about some of her favorite things: Russian literature, the four Gospels, Greek tragedy, and Bob Dylan.

"I love Dylan," she says, setting out chicken salad sandwiches near a vase filled with jonquils from her yard.

"When I can't remember something, I quote Dylan, who says, 'I had to send a truck back for it.'"

Brown is a keen-eyed observer of the life of small-town Alabama, a deceptively grandmotherly presence who favors cable-knit sweaters and bell-shaped hats while composing in her slow, meticulous way short stories that probe the melancholy heart of the rural South.

While she lives seemingly isolated, giving directions to her house by markers like a bend in the road and an old fence, she dwells at a crossroads of literary recognition. Her phone rings often and invitations come frequently, distractingly, for interviews and appearances.

Nancy Anderson, professor of English at Auburn University at Montgomery, who's directed an AUM series on Alabama's Black Belt, says Brown's work "transcends the geographic settings. She is in a class of writers with national and international recognition."

Auburn's Wayne Flynt, in *Alabama in the Twentieth Century,* writes, "Brown

Mary Ward Brown at her home in Marion, Alabama. Photo by Bill Starling, courtesy of the *Mobile Press-Register*.

proved conclusively that the literary muse could work its wonder at any age." For Brown, who did not publish her first story collection, *Tongues of Flame*, until age 69 and her second, *It Wasn't All Dancing*, until age 85, fame or anonymity seems to be beside the point.

"I love to work," she says, "but I love people, too."

Books line the rooms of her farmhouse, scores of short story collections,

Greek histories, biographies, books by friends. In one room is a half wall of signed first editions.

Nearest the computer in her study is a copy of Strunk and White's *Elements of Style,* a classic work on clarity in writing. On her bed is a copy of *The Consolations of Philosophy,* by the fifth-century Roman Christian philosopher Boethius.

And Brown listens to books on tape. The bedtime stories that she enjoys now are the recordings of the classics of Western civilization.

After lunch, perched on the edge of her bed, she fusses at her own limitations. "I don't feel educated," she says.

Why does an 87-year-old push to make it through a reading list as daunting as that of a graduate student?

"Because I'm in the world," she answers matter of factly. "You want to learn."

Her formal education took place nearly seventy years ago at Judson College, the Baptist women's college whose imposing columns rise in downtown Marion, six miles north of her farmhouse on Perry County 35.

She had been interested in writing since her undergraduate years and worked early on in public relations for Judson. But it wasn't until she was in mid-life that her desire to write stories, to bring to life characters "with the seeds of real people in them," began to deepen.

It was sorrow that took her there.

Born on June 18, 1917, in the house where she lives now, Mary Thomas Ward came of age in the middle of Alabama's Black Belt. Her parents, Mary and Thomas, owned 3,000 acres rich with cotton. "They weren't readers," she says. "They were doers."

About 250 workers tilled the soil, picked the cotton, tended the animals. Mary grew up with her ear attuned to the music and speech of the workers, most of whom were black. To this day, she loves what she calls "the blue note" in music, relishing jazz, even fascinated by contemporary rap. As an author, she would eventually come to create such vivid dialogue from characters of all backgrounds that some readers, before seeing her photograph, wondered whether she was black or white.

Her father owned a sawmill and built their rugged but cozy home from heart of pine. The house maintains a solid, intimate feeling, the rich timber holding not only her countless books but also dozens of paintings of local scenes, many of them evocative watercolors by her late friend, the Selma painter Crawford Gillis.

Mary shares the house with her amiable English pointer, Boudreaux, who is fond of nuzzling company.

After a seemingly sunny childhood, Mary went to Judson, where she boarded, even though it was nearby. Mary's mother was suffering from cancer at the time; the family thought it best if Mary lived in a dormitory. Her mother passed away while Mary was at school.

She recalls those days, when the boys from Marion Institute would come courting the Judson girls, as is still a local tradition. Brown remembers how the young cadets would sit with the girls on the couches in the Judson lounge, the lights turned down low "until the night watchman came through," she says.

But 21-year-old Mary fell for a debonair Auburn man, Charles Kirtley Brown, fourteen years her elder, who was working as public relations director for the university. They married soon after meeting. "I went to Auburn," she says, "as a bride."

"He called himself 'the great lover,'" she says, laughing.

In 1942, while still at Auburn, they had a son, Kirtley Ward Brown. That same year, her father died, leaving Mary the house and 1,500 acres of the land. The young family moved back to the rural hamlet of Hamburg—which can't be found on many maps—in south Perry County.

"Kirtley had never lived on a farm, much less owned one," she says. They farmed cotton and raised grade Hereford cows. Later came soybeans.

As Brown tells of her life with her husband, she shows a photo of the two of them, young and full of fun, strolling through the New Orleans French Quarter; then another of her husband before their life together, "as a young blade," in hat and bow-tie.

She recalls dark clouds gathering as the years rolled on.

Her son, Kirtley, who by then had a law degree from The University of Alabama, headed off to Vietnam in 1970 with military intelligence. He was stationed in the Mekong Delta.

"I thought, 'If I live through that year, there will never be another that bad in my life.'"

Her son came home, but sadness waited around the corner.

Her husband died at 67 from lung cancer, and Mary, at age 53, was alone. Kirtley had run the farm, managed the finances, taken care of business. Mary had raised their son and periodically tried to do some writing.

"When you've been married a long time and lose your mate, you don't really belong to anybody. It's like the biblical 'one flesh.' . . . It was a terrible loss."

She remembers her husband's buoyant humor, his sense of honor. "He was a great man. It was a privilege"—her eyes brim with tears—"to live with him all those years."

She is silent a moment. Afternoon light streams into the farmhouse. "People worried about me out here by myself, that it was 'unhealthy.'" At night, missing her husband, she would "cry like a hurt animal," and during the day learned to take care of the business of the farm, which included leasing out acreage to other growers.

After the deepest grief passed, "I'd get up at 4:30 in the morning and start writing."

She would write in bed by hand, then go to the old typewriter to continue, take a break, and walk down the country road a mile. "It was exciting. I had a real focus."

Her stories revolved around church people, young couples, old men, people facing redemption, hope, loss.

"I knew about the start and end of the story, but the middle was an adventure," she says.

She took writing workshops at The University of Alabama with John Craig Stewart and author Leonard Michaels, who helped place her first stories in literary magazines.

She found a literary agent, but he died.

After her story "The Cure," about an old country doctor, who is white, and his longtime patient, who is black, was published in *Best American Short Stories,* she wrote to a second literary agent, who took her on.

"I'm not prolific," she recounts writing to that agent. "I write only short stories. I'm no longer young."

✳

"Mary is forever youthful," says Eugene LeVert, who teaches literature at the University of South Alabama. LeVert remembers Brown from his boyhood in Marion, when he would visit with her and listen to her stories and play record albums—Bob Dylan and the Rolling Stones—for her appreciation. LeVert still looks to Brown for inspiration.

"She's my best friend," says Samantha "Buffy" Reinhart, a visual artist in Marion who also looks to her much-older pal for guidance. "She's cool. She's a very gracious person. I never go to her home when she doesn't put on tea or have something baked. And she counsels me about being an artist."

Reinhart, who teaches art at Judson College, says she shares with Brown the identity of being a Black Belt artist. "I don't necessarily make art about the Black Belt," Reinhart explains, "but of it."

Reinhart uses the kudzu plant to extract a pigment for staining her canvases. At a party one evening in Reinhart's home, Brown is there with partygoers in their 30s and 40s. She sits among them on a sofa listening to the Kudzu String Band do a bluegrass version of Bob Dylan's "You Ain't Going Nowhere" and sipping bourbon punch.

On the way home, the stubble of winter fields rolls past beneath the clarity of a February sky. This is a stretch of the planet she knows like the palm of her hand.

Brown says she used to be fearful of death but now is calm about the prospect. She says she once watched a calf being born in the fields behind her house, and the act of its being born "was traumatic. But then it was OK."

She suspects the act of dying will be much the same way.

"Part of me is already dead," she says with her stoic humor. "I've already lost part of my sight, part of my hearing."

Not long ago, in Chattanooga, Tennessee, after being honored by the Fellowship of Southern Writers, Brown fell and cracked her pelvic bone. She used a walker during recuperation and keeps it still in her bedroom to use like a calisthenics barre.

All healed up now, she comes and goes about her beloved house with cautious ease.

In the afternoon, she goes out to her back yard by the bird feeder. In the sun-washed yard, she holds up her hand. "Come on, redbirds. Did you think I'd forgotten you?"

Birds begin to alight in the branches of the holly and the mock-orange trees. She stands there, a small woman in the spacious yard. "Birds? Where are you? Hurry. Come on. I've got all of this for y'all."

She spreads the feed, then goes back into the house and waits by the window. The cardinals descend, pecking at the grain, filling her yard with scarlet, like an inspiration.

Sena Jeter Naslund

A STORY DEEP INSIDE HER

The author of the novels Ahab's Wife, Four Spirits, Abundance: A Life of Marie Antoinette, *and* Adam & Eve *is a Birmingham native who resides and teaches in Louisville, Kentucky. On a balmy late summer morning in 2003, I visited with Sena Jeter Naslund at her home on St. James Court, just before publication of her deeply Alabama novel,* Four Spirits.

Louisville, Kentucky

When Sena Jeter was 10 years old in Birmingham in 1953, she sat in her parents' living room on a sweltering afternoon having an out-of-body experience.

"There was no air conditioning," she recalls.

In her hands she clutched a magical object of the most ancient sort—a book. It was a novel, *Little House on the Prairie* by Laura Ingalls Wilder, and the fictional setting was winter. Young Sena began to shiver.

"I realized I was trembling," the grownup Sena, recalling the moment, says at her home in Louisville, where she writes and teaches. "I thought, 'It's these words that make me feel this way. I'd like to do that one day!'"

Fifty years later, Sena Jeter Naslund—a gentle-voiced woman with dark hair and fair complexion—has made good on her childhood yearning.

Her 1999 novel, *Ahab's Wife*, a retelling of Melville's classic through the eyes of the whaling captain's wife, was a critical and commercial success, named by *Time* magazine as one of the five best novels of the year and honored as a Book-of-the-Month Club main selection.

Sena Naslund. Photograph by José A. Betancourt.

Four Spirits flows out of the civil rights era in Birmingham in 1963. Like *Ahab's Wife,* a hefty novel that swept up 19th-century American history, nautical lore, slavery, religion, and perilous sea voyages into its story, *Four Spirits* is panoramic. Running more than 500 pages, it sets out to make Birmingham the subject and backdrop of a novel that brings to life, at Naslund's count, 129 characters.

There are true-life figures such as the black civil rights firebrand, the Reverend Fred Shuttlesworth, and those of Naslund's invention such as Stella Silver, a young white woman coming of age in a traumatized hometown. The novel takes its title from the morning of September 15, 1963, when a Ku Klux Klan bomb blast tore through the Sixteenth Street Baptist Church, killing four girls: Addie Mae Collins, Denise McNair, Carole Robertson, and Cynthia Wesley.

Naslund acknowledges the wealth of nonfiction that has explored the civil rights movement, most notably Diane McWhorter's *Carry Me Home: Birmingham, Alabama, The Climactic Battle of the Civil Rights Revolution,* which won a Pulitzer Prize in 2001.

But Naslund says there has yet to be a major novel to give life to that heartbreaking time. There is, she says, no *War and Peace* of the civil rights movement.

Naslund is too modest to claim her novel attains that lofty position. The critics, reading public, and posterity will make any such evaluation. But as a writer she has been growing toward an evermore expansive vision.

Alabama native Howell Raines, Pulitzer Prize–winning journalist and former executive editor of the *New York Times,* was Naslund's classmate at Birmingham-Southern College.

"As long as I've known her—and before we formally met, known of her—she's been dedicated to the literary life in the most serious, committed way," Raines says.

"I was always aware of her as someone who knew early on that writing was her metier. That's not an unusual aspiration among undergraduates, but sticking to it as Sena has is a rare and wonderful thing."

Young Sena grew up in the Norwood section of Birmingham, the daughter of Marvin Jeter, a physician, and Flora Lee Sims, a musician. Her father's people hailed from Helicon in Crenshaw County about halfway between Montgomery and Mobile. It was a place-name out of a timeless tale.

"In Greek mythology," Naslund says, "Helicon was the home of the Muses."

She remembers her first childhood trip to her father's home community for two principal reasons.

"My father took the whole family down to the rural area where he had grown up, the family place, Helicon. He wanted us to go there to meet old 'Aunt' Charlotte, who had been born into slavery and who had delivered him when he was a baby."

Marvin Jeter, who hunted in the woods as a boy, also wanted to familiarize his children with guns and let them take turns shooting at trees. Sena was included, despite being young and the only girl. (She has two brothers, Marvin, an archaeologist, and John, an engineer.) The Helicon trip would inspire the prologue to *Four Spirits*.

If her father introduced her to the Old South, it was her mother, a graduate of the Chicago Conservatory of Music, who brought art into her life. Flora Lee Sims played violin and piano. Sena's daughter, Flora Naslund, is named for Flora Lee.

"I heard classical music randomly all through the day," says Naslund, who became a serious student of cello and often uses music in her stories. Two of the characters in *Four Spirits* are cellists; a third plays classical piano.

She describes herself as an "unusual" child, prone to fits of temper. "It consoled me that Jo March, in *Little Women,* also had a very bad temper and had this struggle," the author says. "She was a writer."

Naslund became devoutly religious, setting her sights on becoming a medical missionary in Africa. She felt a "strong, moral imperative" to communicate her religious beliefs to others, she says.

When she went to Birmingham-Southern College, "a very liberal, wonderful school," she says, her "fundamentalism and fanaticism" melted away. Among her classmates at Birmingham-Southern, in addition to Raines, was Charles Gaines, the novelist and screenwriter whose two early works, *Stay Hungry* and *Pumping Iron,* helped bring Arnold Schwarzenegger into national visibility in the movie versions.

From his home in Nova Scotia, Gaines says: "I think one of the reasons Birmingham turned out a good many writers of our vintage was that the civil rights movement activity in the city of that time provided a sort of Joycean soul crucible that drove a lot of pens into action. If not in direct response to it at the time, at least in the indirect responses of thinking, on paper, about the nature of the place we were all from."

Gaines also credits the English Department of Birmingham-Southern of that day with "making us feel, rightly or wrongly, that we could slay giants."

✳

The story was buried deep within her.

In 1957, while Naslund was a student at all-white Phillips High School in Birmingham, the Reverend Fred Shuttlesworth attempted to enroll his children. Shuttlesworth was outside the school; Sena was inside but learned what happened.

"Shuttlesworth had called the police and told them he was coming, expecting protection, but they apparently had tipped off Klan buddies and the police were nowhere to be seen," she says.

"A small group of white men were there with bicycle chains, and he was beaten. His wife was stabbed in the thigh. The attackers escaped. I was horrified that this had happened outside of my school, and I felt guilty. I thought, 'If I had known, would I have gone out the front door and told them to stop?' That was clearly the moral imperative for anybody who found out."

Sena turned to a beloved speech teacher, Miss White, to help her understand what had occurred. Miss White leaned across her desk, pointed to the skin of her forearm, and said there were those who believed "the pigment, the color in your skin," determined how smart you were and what you were like. Miss White proclaimed, "'It has nothing to do with it!'"

"That codified the idea for me that there was extreme racial prejudice and it was the result of great ignorance, stupidity, and fear," Naslund says. "As a teacher she was saying to the class that segregation was wrong. I was electrified by her succinct enunciation of that idea."

But the 15-year-old schoolgirl was in for a shock.

"I could hardly wait to talk to my friends in the hall in the few minutes between changing classes. I asked them, 'Did you hear what Miss White said? Let's talk about this. She's right!' They all stepped back; they all receded."

The church bomb would explode six years later.

To research *Four Spirits*, Naslund went to Birmingham's Civil Rights Institute, read books about the era, did "body research" by going to locations and absorbing impressions, went to the public library to read old newspapers and files.

"The library research," she says, "uncovered so many atrocities."

One horror was the Klan's kidnapping and castration of a black man, Judge Aaron, soon after Shuttlesworth tried to integrate Phillips High. The scene found its way into her novel.

In doing her research, Naslund says she had to stop her work by three in the afternoon, "or I couldn't sleep at night. I'd toss and turn and writhe.

"When I say I didn't know things like that were happening, who do I sound like? I sound like an ordinary German citizen when the Nazis were taking over and carting off the Jews."

She explains, "When I was growing up in Birmingham in the early sixties, I promised myself I would write a book about the civil rights movement, especially in Birmingham, because I was a witness and to some extent a participant."

In 2000, Naslund was in Sydney, Australia, promoting *Ahab's Wife* and the announcement rocketed across the ocean that the suspects in the 1963 bombing were to be tried. (Ex-Klansmen Tommy Blanton in spring 2001, and Bobby Frank Cherry in spring 2002, would be convicted of murder.)

Naslund picked up a copy of the *Sydney News*. "There was the picture of the four little girls, which I knew so well by heart. There I was half a world away, almost as far away from Birmingham as you could get, and I pick up the newspaper and it's screaming from my subconscious."

Outside Naslund's study at her gracious home in Old Louisville, magnolia trees frame the bay window looking out to the street.

"Louisville is the Northern edge of the Southern magnolia," she says, taking her place at her computer screen by the window.

Near her is a copy of W. B. Yeats' poetry open on a divan, a painting of a lighthouse with water crashing over rocks, a bookshelf filled with books by friends and editions of her own.

On a chair is a tower of paper—copies of the manuscript of *Four Spirits*.

On the street, visible through her window, is a fountain where water cascades and gurgles, an ornate, 19th-century iron fountain of Venus Rising from the Sea.

Having once wished to live at the sea, especially after spending time on the island of Nantucket researching and writing parts of *Ahab's Wife*, Naslund says the fountain is her "artificial sea."

The fountain, she says, provides inspiration and solace, especially while she had been composing the emotionally charged *Four Spirits*.

Naslund is known to be a gifted teacher. She went on from Birmingham to obtain her master's degree and doctorate in English from the University of Iowa. She has daily responsibilities with the titles distinguished teaching professor at the University of Louisville and program director of the brief-residency master of fine arts in writing program at Spalding University.

She has family, colleagues, and friends to whom she also devotes her time.

Then there is the world of her imagination, one that turns fountains into oceans and can still feel the shiver of winter on a hot summer's day. It brings to her window even the vista of Birmingham forty years ago.

Four Spirits unfolds on the observation balcony at the feet of the famous Vulcan statue. A fictional college couple, Darl and Stella, have gone there on a date. Civil rights demonstrations in Kelly Ingram Park are taking place but the city appears deceptively peaceful on this May afternoon:

"Darl pointed to the rectangular finger of the Comer Building, twenty-one stories tall, Birmingham's lonely skyscraper. Down in the valley, the sweep of buildings was scarved with a haze from the steel mills. After finding the Comer Building, they looked west and north searching for the parks, Woodrow Wilson Park adjacent to the beautiful library (only for whites) and a few blocks away, Kelly Ingram Park, for Negroes (no library). The demonstrations were launched toward city hall from the Negro park. But trees, already in full leaf, blocked their view, even with binoculars, of the violent attack of Bull Connor's police on the freedom demonstrators."

The scene continues with a reflection by the fictional Stella that resonates of the author's own coming of age in a city whose struggle was hers, too.

"Suddenly Stella felt like a coward. If she wanted to see, she should have the nerve to go downtown. *If she wanted to participate* . . . but the idea frightened her too much."

In the course of the novel Stella will meet head-on that sense of being frightened and, like the author, make the story, in a deeply personal way, her own.

Diane McWhorter

TAKING PICTURES FROM THE INSIDE

From Birmingham to Monroeville, I visited with Diane McWhorter over the course of a remarkable year in her life: the publication and acclaim of Carry Me Home, *recipient of the 2002 Pulitzer Prize. The first part begins a few days before her book was praised on the cover of the* New York Times Book Review, *and the second, more than a year later, becomes an Alabama afternoon in Harper Lee's hometown.*

Birmingham

On a chill dusk in her hometown, Diane McWhorter is driving through quiet downtown streets, taking a visitor on what she calls, "my civil rights tour." By the site of the former Trailways Bus Station where freedom riders long ago rolled into an angry community, by the Gaston Motel, where protesters stayed in the spring of 1963, she drives toward a corner where a stately, brown-brick building, Sixteenth Street Baptist Church, looms in the dwindling light.

"Right over there," she says, pointing to the right side of the church and speaking of September 15, 1963, "is where the bomb blew up."

That bomb took the lives of four children and has long been at the heart of a mystery for McWhorter.

"It blew the clothes off the Sunday school girls and stacked them up like cordwood under a blizzard of debris," she writes.

While the identities of the bombers became known, their motivation—and

Diane McWhorter sits in the upstairs gallery of the old County Courthouse in Monroe-ville, Alabama. McWhorter's book *Carry Me Home: Birmingham, Alabama: The Climactic Battle of the Civil Rights Revolution* won the Pulitzer Prize for general nonfiction in 2002. Photo by G. M. Andrews, courtesy of the *Mobile Press-Register.*

the web of events that led to Birmingham's violent summer of 1963—has been shadowy.

"I wanted to figure out not just who they were, but why they were," she says.

The answers to those questions can be found in McWhorter's richly personal and incisively historical book. The 700-page work—*Carry Me Home: Birmingham, Alabama: The Climactic Battle of the Civil Rights Movement*—took her on an emotional roller coaster during the nineteen years it took to complete and to grow to 3,400 pages in manuscript form.

"I left 2,400 pages on the cutting-room floor," she says.

The remainder presents a portrait of her hometown that wins praise and empathy from some and draws anger from others.

"What she has done is a remarkable synthesis of personal history with the city's history," says journalist and Birmingham native Allen Barra.

"You carry a scar if you're from Birmingham," says native son Paul Hemphill, author of the memoir, *Leaving Birmingham.*

Hemphill says that when people hear he's from Birmingham "they go to the 'Birmingham file' of attack dogs and fire hoses. It's like looking at a bad wreck."

In *Carry Me Home,* McWhorter, once again, returns to the scene of that "wreck." Finishing her drive through downtown as night falls, she heads to the rolling lawns and sumptuous homes of a very different part of town—the place where she began her own journey forty-eight years ago.

Until she was well into her 20s, McWhorter, who now has two young daughters and lives in New York City, had never been in some of the black neighborhoods of downtown Birmingham. Only 10 years old at the time of the Sixteenth Street Church bombing, she was a child "of privilege," she says, growing up in the luxurious world of Birmingham's Mountain Brook community.

Her youth was spent at the country club, the Mountain Brook, and she writes of its members: "Theirs was a snobbery so exquisite that an evening over at the Birmingham Country Club—'that roadhouse,' my uncle sneered charmingly—was considered slumming. For us children, the privilege of belonging meant that you knew which of your friends didn't."

In high school, she was active in sports and social clubs. She was president of her high school sorority. After going north to Wellesley College, she devoted herself to magazine journalism, becoming managing editor in her 20s of *Boston Magazine.*

At 29, McWhorter, by then a rising star in the literary field, secured a book contract to write about her hometown during the civil rights era and was on her way. Little did she know, though, that she was only beginning a journey of discovery that would take her two decades.

A suspicion from her childhood had long been haunting her, and as she began to work on her book, she spiraled deeper into troubling revelations. As she writes in *Carry Me Home* of her early years:

"What were 'civil rights'? I knew that they were bad and that my father was fighting against them, and that was why he rarely came home evenings: 'at one of his civil rights meetings,' my mother explained."

Remembering a pistol under her father's car seat, she "worried that he would jeopardize the family's standing by doing something illegal. Soon those sensations of anxiety and shame would crystallize into a concrete fear: that my father was a member of the Ku Klux Klan."

Quick-witted and engagingly friendly, McWhorter seems comfortable in widely contrasting surroundings, from the front porches and living rooms of hometown neighborhoods where she interviewed hundreds of people for her book to the sleek surroundings of Birmingham's upscale restaurants.

This openness—a kind of former sorority girl zest—may well have been what helped put people at ease to talk with her, from Klansmen to community leaders to the foot soldiers of the civil rights movement.

"I can get anybody to tell me their story," she says.

But if McWhorter, in person, is disarmingly easygoing, her book is bracingly tough. Indeed, its radical thesis is that there were horrifying links between those members of upscale country clubs and the grubby street work of the Klan and other racist groups.

"The rich folks," she comments, "were fomenting racial strife to keep the unions weak." The white antagonisms of the 1950s and 1960s toward blacks were born of the opposition to the New Deal of the 1930s, she explains. In her book, she explores the way, she believes, that "some of the industrial families" fomented "anti-Semitic and racist propaganda."

This link between the "social elite" and the violent, hard-core racists is the bomb that McWhorter herself has exploded in Birmingham in 2001.

And how are folks reacting?

Jake Reiss, owner of Alabama Booksmith in Birmingham, says he recently heard of a local dinner party where the table quickly divided into those who hated and those who cheered on what McWhorter had done. In call-in radio shows in Birmingham, McWhorter has been hit with accusations by those who say that all she is doing is digging up a past that would be better left alone.

McWhorter says that even a family member, her uncle Hobart McWhorter, dismissed the book as full of "fiction," but then admitted to her that he had read only the opening pages.

Her father, on the other hand, who has changed his attitudes since the 1960s, has been supportive of her efforts to tell the tale.

The author is proud of her city and feels the story she tells is one of triumph, too.

"Recently someone from Atlanta asked me what Birmingham had ever done as a town. I told him, 'We ended segregation.'

"Birmingham is as important in the second Civil War as Gettysburg was in the first."

Monroeville

On an early May weekend, Diane McWhorter strolls around the town square, speaking with a visitor about the impact of winning this year's Pulitzer Prize in Nonfiction.

"I keep getting reminded," she says, "how the award has made a difference."

There was, at first, her shock at getting the call. "The only awards you think you deserve," she says, smiling, "are the ones you don't win."

There were the accolades, the euphoria. "I went to a book party, and people looked at me like I was somebody new all because of two little words." She sounds them out carefully, as though still incredulous. "Pulitzer Prize."

There were the gifts from well-wishers—champagne, flowers, even cheese straws from a fan in Georgia—and the media spotlight. PBS's *Lehrer News Hour* booked her for an interview; the *New York Times* photographed her at a Manhattan literary party.

CNN turned to her for commentary about Bobby Frank Cherry, on trial in Birmingham for the bombing of the Sixteenth Street Baptist Church.

As she ambles past a plaque near the Monroeville courthouse she reads aloud: "the lasting fame of this building is derived from the Pulitzer Prize-winning novel, *To Kill a Mockingbird*."

"Harper Lee didn't write a Pulitzer Prize–winning novel," she said. "She wrote a novel. Then it won the Pulitzer. But they become inseparable."

She comes to a man standing by the back of a pickup. He says his name is Melvin Foukal, and that he sells, in addition to frozen shrimp and barbecue pork, books signed by his friend, Harper Lee. The cost: $20. A bookseller friend has assured McWhorter that Foukal's endeavor is legitimate—that the signature is authentic.

While buyers crowd around the truck, McWhorter sees one of the signed novels, a fortieth-anniversary edition.

"Look," she says.

On its cover, in addition to the title and author, are those two little words. A Pulitzer Prize can mean many things to many people.

To McWhorter's mother, Betty Biggs, the prize is cause for celebration.

McWhorter says her mother has lain in bed, marveling at it all, telling herself, "'Lassie won the Pulitzer. Lassie won the Pulitzer.'"

"'Lassie,'" says McWhorter, "is her nickname for me."

To McWhorter's friend, Jane Hicks, the Pulitzer was "a life-changing experience" for the woman she had known since grade school in Mountain Brook.

And to another friend, Freddi Aronov, the Pulitzer became an affirmation of the nearly twenty years of work McWhorter had undertaken.

Aronov remembers how McWhorter, living in Boston and eventually New York, would fly into Birmingham to plow ahead with her research: "She had a list of people to interview"—Klansmen among them—"and would go out in the middle of the night. She was always so excited to interview the next person."

But Aronov says there were many in town not happy with one of the central themes of *Carry Me Home:* the links that McWhorter makes between the affluent social strata and the mob action that transformed the image of the "Pittsburgh of the South" into "Bombingham."

At a Pulitzer Prize reception for McWhorter in Birmingham, where her father was in attendance, she praised from the podium his love and acceptance of her book. He politely stepped forward from the crowd and waved, then backed away to a circle of friends.

Not all of Birmingham has been so accepting.

"*Carry Me Home* is the single most divisive book we've ever had," explains Jake Reiss of Alabama Booksmith. "Many whose relatives were mentioned in the book felt vilified. The detractors like to call the book 'fiction.' The Pulitzer Prize gave credibility to the book, but the nonbelievers are firmly fixed."

Reiss, who has championed McWhorter's book from the beginning and watched its sales soar after the Pulitzer, adds of the book's critics: "If they had affidavits, they'd still be firmly convinced their fathers didn't commit these sins."

The afterword of McWhorter's paperback edition of *Carry Me Home* brings readers up-to-date on the new investigation into the Sixteenth Street bombing and the conviction of ex-Klansman Thomas Blanton Jr.

"Mr. Blanton is certainly not a fan of Diane McWhorter," said John Robbins, one of Blanton's lawyers. "He won't be dating 'that bitch'"—the insult, Robbins indicated, was Blanton's own—"when he gets out of prison.

"The Pulitzer? It didn't make his day."

Another Blanton lawyer, Dave Simpson, preferred to be philosophical. "America is ready to come to terms with what happened. A book needed to be written. Whether I agree or not with the book is not important."

Simpson, in fact, admitted delight at being part of the story, his "shaved head and minibeard" captured in the new afterword. "Don't think I don't have a little ego about being mentioned in a Pulitzer Prize–winning book," he said.

As McWhorter continues her walk on the Monroeville square, a crowd is gathering for that evening's performance of *To Kill a Mockingbird,* Christopher Sergel's dramatic adaptation of the novel, whose first act would be performed on the courthouse lawn.

McWhorter has traveled to Monroeville for its yearly literary conference, interviewed during one session by Amilcar Shabazz, who directs the African American Studies program at The University of Alabama.

Shabazz believes *Carry Me Home* to be a "brilliant book. It's not just coming from a white girl on the fringes of a Mountain Brook reality but from truth itself."

Shabazz emphasizes that, while McWhorter's book focused on the events of 1963, the story of race relations, everywhere, is still unfolding. So many of those stories, he says, have yet to be told.

Governor Don Siegelman, in Monroeville with his wife, Lori, and their children, for *To Kill a Mockingbird,* also speaks about McWhorter's book.

Siegelman says he remembers being in eleventh grade in 1963 at Murphy High School in Mobile. "The events of that day rocked us all. Bull Connor. King. Police dogs. It was explosive."

He adds, "You look at history through various eyes to come up with the truth."

Noted Alabama historian Wayne Flynt, also in town for the literary festival, puts McWhorter in the same category with Shelby Foote, Bruce Catton, and Barbara Tuchman, eloquent storytellers delving into history for a broad readership. "The Pulitzer effect is enormous," he says.

And, he adds, when someone "takes a picture from within" a society, that picture is especially hard to ignore.

As McWhorter makes her way to the *Mockingbird* performance, she is approached by a woman who wanted to get her autograph. Then a mother and son walk up. Then a couple. As she signs books she listens to their stories, too—where they had been during the 1960s, and their experiences with race relations, with prejudice, with hatred and reconciliation.

One woman who would find McWhorter in Monroeville the next day was Julia Matson, a language arts specialist in Birmingham, who wanted to tell the author of a childhood experience of her own, going home with a friend who opened up her daddy's hiding place—to find a Klan hood.

If the Pulitzer has launched McWhorter into prominence—making her a heroine to some and a bane to others—it has also deepened her sense of being a sounding board, a confessor, a patient listener.

As dusk arrives and *Mockingbird* begins, McWhorter takes a seat for the show. When the accused, Tom Robinson, is held in jail and Atticus Finch rides out to defend him against a drunken lynch mob, McWhorter is transfixed by the scene and begins, quietly, to cry.

Inside the courthouse for the second act, McWhorter climbs to the balcony and looks down as Atticus defends, to no avail, the accused. After the play ends, its director, Kathy McCoy, asks everyone to turn their attention to the balcony, where Alabama's newest celebrity was sitting.

As the crowd applauds, McWhorter, beaming, looks down on the arena where a play has just taken place on a theme close to her heart—the striving for justice—raises her hands and does a little shimmy.

When she heads back downstairs, she is surrounded by actors still costumed as Harper Lee's characters, Atticus Finch, Scout, Tom Robinson, Mayella Ewell, Boo Radley.

They press close with copies of *Carry Me Home,* eager for an autograph.

Frye Gaillard

WRITING HIS WAY HOME

Mobile

Thirty-five years ago, when Frye Gaillard, now the author of nineteen books, was starting out as a young newspaper reporter, he covered a hometown story that nearly broke his heart.

Fresh out of college, the 22-year-old idealist whose hero had been Robert Kennedy watched outside the Mobile Municipal Auditorium as black protesters, many of them affiliated with the group Neighborhood Organized Workers, and a handful of sympathetic whites tried to picket America's Junior Miss Pageant to publicize demands for what they argued was fairer treatment and employment of blacks in Mobile.

As tempers mounted on both sides, Gaillard worked to maintain a reporter's objectivity, but, he admits today, felt despair at a scene of tension over race relations.

While Mobile, Gaillard explains, had weathered much of the civil rights movement without pitched anger and bloodshed—unlike Birmingham, Selma, and Montgomery—the late 1960s, he believes, found Mobile "caught in a racial backlash."

He scribbled notes for his *Mobile Press Register* story as he watched the confrontation.

"It was like something about to explode," he says. "Every black person outside of the auditorium that day was arrested." Some white clergymen were arrested too.

Frye Gaillard at the fountain in Bienville Square, Mobile, Alabama. Photo by Mary Hattler, courtesy of the *Mobile Press-Register*.

John LeFlore, a civil rights leader in the community, had been present to witness the events. "LeFlore was not part of the protest," Gaillard says, "but he was taken off to jail in handcuffs. The whole scene was incredibly depressing.

"I left Mobile soon after that," he says. "I was feeling more and more out of place."

Apart from visits to Mobile, Gaillard has made his life, largely, in Charlotte, North Carolina. He and wife Nancy, a school principal, raised their children there. He wrote newspaper stories and books in Charlotte and even launched a small book-publishing company.

Now, Gaillard has authored a civil rights history—*Cradle of Freedom: Alabama and the Movement That Changed America*—that has had an impact quite apart from that of the book itself.

Gaillard and his family will be returning to Mobile—for good.

Frye Gaillard has sandy hair and a quietly engaging voice. His surname, pronounced "Gill-yard," still is well known in professional circles around Mobile.

"I was supposed to be a lawyer," says the lanky author, ambling across Bienville Square. "That was going back generations into the family. My grandfather, Palmer Gaillard, practiced law in Mobile until he was over 100 years old. He died at 103, and went to the office until the last year of his life. My dad was a judge. His brother was also a lawyer."

Gaillard grew up in the heart of the Spring Hill community, on a five-acre tract—an entire city block, he describes it—that his family owned. His father, who passed away in 1972, was Walter Gaillard; his mother is Amante Toulmin Gaillard, of the family for whom Toulminville was named.

Although young Frye was an only child, he was surrounded by an extended family that included his grandfather, who lived on the property in what was called "the Big House," an antebellum home purchased after the turn of the century.

"My grandfather was born in 1856," Gaillard says. "When I was a kid, nine or ten years old, he would tell me stories of when he was nine or ten years old, during the Civil War. He remembered the Union soldiers coming."

"These were people," Gaillard says of his family, "who were very much part of the old South. It was drummed into your head that history matters, that family matters, that your connection to a place matters. So I grew up that way.

"These were kind and decent people," Gaillard emphasizes, "but they were also part of what I came to believe was a very flawed social order in the South."

When Frye was only 5 years old, he had been tagging along behind a gardener, Robert Croshon, a black man, who was cutting the lawn. He was riding in Croshon's wheelbarrow and having boyishly good fun.

"It came time for lunch, and all the white people ate in the dining room," Gaillard recalls, "and Robert ate in the kitchen. I remember asking, 'Hey, why can't Robert eat with us?' I was 'shushed' harshly and told I needed to be quiet because I was hurting Robert's feelings."

Gaillard attended University Military School in Mobile, then a boys' military academy. At age 16, having come of age in a segregated, structured society, he had what he calls an "epiphanal moment" during a visit to Birmingham.

On the street, on Good Friday, within an arm's length of the young Gaillard, Martin Luther King Jr. was being arrested.

"I couldn't get that image out of my mind," recounts Gaillard, "the dignity of Dr. King, the sadness in his eyes, as he was being roughly hauled off to jail. When I saw him up that close, my mind took a picture of him. I couldn't escape the question, 'What's going on here?'"

Gaillard took that question with him to Vanderbilt University, where his freshman class in 1964 admitted the first black undergraduate students to the private Nashville institution. "Later," Gaillard says, "we discovered they were very lonely. They were a small group. The embrace was not what they'd hoped for. I say it with a sense of chagrin."

Gaillard wrote for the student newspaper and headed up the campus speakers' program, which invited in, on one side of the political spectrum, George Wallace and Strom Thurmond, on the other, Stokely Carmichael and Robert Kennedy.

When Kennedy was driven to the airport to leave, Gaillard sat next to him in the back seat of the car.

Bobby Kennedy's assassination in the summer of 1968 was "overwhelming" to him, Gaillard says.

His trips home to Mobile became ever more marked by conflict with his family. "I handled that with all the self-righteous immaturity you'd expect," he says, reflecting on his younger self. "I came home and lectured all my relatives about the error of their ways. It was a time of real strain between me and these people I loved."

From a bench in Bienville Square, Gaillard looks out at the iron fountain, the vast trees, the band shell where a tinny recording of sprightly music plays on a loop.

Citizens of all backgrounds, black and white, amble through the park on their way to the bank or the small shops. He is no longer an argumentative youth but a reflective man in his middle years. Casually dressed in a camel hair sports coat, he appears relaxed, professorial.

While he has written books on NASCAR racing, Habitat for Humanity, country music, and a black, semi-pro baseball team (that one got him featured on the CBS television news magazine *Sunday Morning*), the subject of race relations seems to have intrigued him the most.

"The juxtaposition of the unfairness of segregation with the fundamental decency of the people I'd grown up with made me very aware of the ambiguities of human nature.

"That's one of the things that drives you as a writer, looking for that irony and ambiguity. It certainly has me."

Looking out, he says, "I love the oak trees and the crab claws and the people I've grown up with, but I don't think I would have thought seriously about moving back here had it not been for the assignment to write *Cradle of Freedom*."

The book, over 400 pages, chronicles the civil rights movement as it took place in the Heart of Dixie. The dramatic high points of the movement are explored: the Montgomery bus boycott, the bombing of the Sixteenth Street Baptist Church in Birmingham, Wallace's stand in the schoolhouse door of The University of Alabama, the Selma to Montgomery march.

Intended to be readable, accessible to students of history—and those interested in the state's past—the book, says Gaillard, offers a variation on other books about the 1960s.

"I took a look at the major events that come to mind and the role of the leaders, but I also looked at the role of thousands of ordinary folks who'd decided the time had come to make a stand. As a storyteller, I loved sitting down and listening to those stories."

It was those stories from the "ordinary" people, says Gaillard, that brought him close to the core of his home state again.

"What happened in that particular time was that black people in Alabama called up the most basic questions about how we live. What kind of people are we? Do we really believe what we studied in civics, that we are equal in the eyes of the law? And in Sunday School, that we are equal in the eyes of God?

"There was a relentless push behind those questions. All of us who grew up in those times had to give some kind of answer.

"The collective answer we ended up giving has made this a better place and a better country."

An older lawyer stops by and greets Gaillard, saying he remembers Gaillard's grandfather, Palmer. More people pass by, and someone pauses to ask about the book he's holding, the shiny, red-jacketed book with a picture of civil rights protesters on the cover.

"I see it ultimately as a triumphant piece of history," says Gaillard of the civil rights era.

"For white people it might have been a reluctant triumph," he says. But "we were pushed to reevaluate our society in a way that made us all a little more free."

Artelia Bendolph

THE GIRL IN THE WINDOW

A photograph taken in 1937 in rural Alabama became an icon of the Depression-era South. I tracked down Artelia Bendolph, the subject of that photo, in Prichard in 2002, blind but filled with vivid recollections. She has since passed away, but her words remain.

Prichard

Her crisp hair plaited, her large hands folded in her lap, Artelia Bendolph sits in a wheelchair in front of her red-brick house in Prichard, Alabama, telling a long-ago story. Gone blind in recent years from diabetes—"I got a little grandbaby going on two years old, and I can feel her, but I can't see her"—she peers into the past.

In her broad, high-cheekboned face is a trace of that past—the 10-year-old girl who once sat in the window of a clay-and-log cabin in Gee's Bend, a village on the Alabama River in Wilcox County, Alabama.

"She ain't a girl no more," Bendolph says, "she's a seventy-four-year-old woman now."

It was in 1937 that Bendolph, as that 10-year-old, entered the annals of American history as the girl in the window. A New York photographer, Arthur Rothstein, 22 at the time, had been commissioned by the federal government's Farm Security Administration to chronicle the hard times and effects of displacement of American workers. Rothstein had already photographed the plight of farmworkers in Virginia and cattle hands in Montana.

In 1937 the WPA photographer Arthur Rothstein took this famous Depression-era photo of a 10-year-old girl, Artelia Bendolph, in Gee's Bend, Alabama, in the window of a shack. Photo courtesy of the Library of Congress.

Artelia Bendolph in 2002 at the age of 74 at her home in Prichard, Alabama. Photo by Mike Kittrell, courtesy of the *Mobile Press-Register*

According to "American Memory," a website maintained by the Library of Congress, Rothstein had been in Birmingham photographing the steel industry when his boss at the FSA, Roy Stryker, asked him to head to a hamlet about thirty miles southwest of Selma. Stryker, in assembling a report to Congress, wrote, "I realized how lean our file is on good Southern tenancy pictures. We must find families that are fairly representative of the conditions in the tenancy areas."

Stryker had explained to Rothstein that one journalist had reported that the community at Gee's Bend was "the most primitive set-up he has ever heard of." According to "American Memory," another report spoke of the people of Gee's Bend as "living together in this tribal-like settlement, far away from civilization in their habits and manner of living."

In searching for artful images of despair—and in fulfilling Stryker's mission to "show the city people what it's like to live on the farm"—Rothstein found Bendolph, a young black girl looking out from a crude dwelling, next to her the wooden shutter covered with a couple of sheets of newspaper. On the newspaper was an advertisement of a cheerful white woman holding a bountiful plate of food.

That photograph, to the nation, became an icon of the South's Depression-era poverty and the legacy of inequality.

Bendolph says she does not remember the day that photograph was taken, nor was she ever told about it by Rothstein; indeed, she says she did not know of it until the 1980s, when a friend from Connecticut contacted her. Since then, she says, she has been approached to offer commentaries for books and articles.

The photograph hangs in the Getty Museum in Los Angeles. Countless people, surely, have paused before the melancholy gaze of the girl in the window, wondering what might have become of her.

Bendolph figures that while others have "made money off of me," she has made not a penny. "Don't have none and didn't got nothing," she says. "Well, ain't no need of worrying over it."

On a summer's day in Prichard, beneath the pecan tree she planted decades ago, Bendolph seems to worry over little. While the childhood she describes was full of hardship—"It was rough comin' up in the country," she admits—she looks back on those days with fondness, too.

Daily she rises at 5 a.m., listens to gospel music on WGOK and keeps tabs on her blood sugar. She gave herself insulin shots until she "got blind," when her daughter moved in to help out.

"I'm proud of my house," she says, nodding to the wheelchair ramp rising to the front door as though she can see it. "I been here twenty-nine years, this spot. I never missed a month's payment, never was late."

At lunchtime, usually, her son comes over, and the other men who call her "Godmama." She has raised five children and has fourteen grandchildren and several "great-greats." Her married surname was Wilcox, but she's long been on her own, and wishes to say little of the man she wed.

Even borne down by illness, she tolerates no guff. "I tell my children quick, if they come in here talking, 'This is my house. As long as I live here, I do the bossing here.'"

The house where Arthur Rothstein took her picture was her grandparents' home in Gee's Bend.

"It was two rooms: a great big room, that was our room, a kitchen, then my grandmama and grandfather's room. The house was built from log, it didn't have no living room. We had a big old garden in the back, an old okra patch next to the garden. We had two or three chinaberry trees sitting on the side of the house. In the front, we had a sweet potato patch, and down there at the end of the garden, we had another sweet potato patch.

"We plastered the walls with old newspapers."

She explains why she was in her grandparents' house when Rothstein encountered her: "The night I was born, my mother got sick. She stayed lying flat on her back for three years. We had to turn her. Something happened. One of her legs starting drawing up and went all up in her hip, and she couldn't handle herself. My grandfather and grandmother raised me, that's why I was in their window.

"My grandfather was a half Indian. He was the sweetest man who ever wore a pair of shoes."

He seemed almost magical to her in his powers. "He used to have a horn, like a cow horn, and he'd go into the field, and he'd blow that horn."

Although she remembers, after he blew his horn, "people on the other side of the river talking," she does not know what, exactly, was going on, only the mystery created in a child's mind.

She has different memories of her grandmother, whom she describes as hard-nosed but hard-working. "She would cook collard greens, cabbage, whatever they raised in the garden. English peas, potatoes, onions, squash, carrots. There was so much to do, because I was the only girl, and my grandmama didn't do nothing but cook."

Some parts of the house had no flooring.

"My granddaddy used to go to the woods and cut these little trees—willow trees—he used to get them little trees and make beds out of them for us to sleep on. My grandmother used to take the sacks from the fertilizer and make ticks, and we used to shuck the corn and get the shucks off the corn and tear them apart and put them in to sleep on."

Her mother, when she got well, found another use for the fertilizer bags. "She'd wash the writing out of them, and that's the kind of clothes we wore. I wore overalls, just like my brothers did, 'cause she dressed us all alike. And she would make a cap."

Flour sacks were special, though.

"That's what we had for our Sunday school. The way they sewed them, they looked real nice.

"I went to church at thirteen years old with no shoes on, no socks on, stump barefooted. No shoes, no socks 'cause I didn't have any.

"You see, I used to go barefooted all the time, no matter how cold it was. I didn't never wear no shoes. The people where I worked at always fussed at me about shoes, but when I'd stick my feet in a pair of shoes, no matter how cold it was, by the time I'd get in the house, I'd kick 'em out.

"My mother used to fuss at me for walking on the ground barefooted, but I didn't pay it no attention. She told me those days would come, but I thought she didn't know what she was talking about. The days when she told me I'd be sick for going barefooted."

She now believes her mother was right, and she reflects on how times have changed.

"Now, the children got to have two and three pairs of shoes. No need of going to the store to get them no eleven-dollar shoes. They don't want shoes from nowhere."

✳

As Bendolph continues her story, telling of the co-op store with its bottles of cold RC Cola, of maypole dances at the school and country churches with "a lot of singing and good preaching and roll calling and people's shouting," the Prichard morning wears on, and the heat rises.

Although the hard-edged urban neighborhood where she lives is far from rural Alabama, there is a small-town intimacy to her block. A vegetable truck rolls by. Sugar cane and turnips are piled in the back. The vehicle pauses, and residents approach, looking over the produce.

After the truck moves on, a young man saunters down the walk, looking to where Bendolph sits under her pecan tree. "Oh, sister," the man calls out. "Oh, sister."

Bendolph cocks her head. "Who's that?" she says, puzzled, perhaps even wary, at not recognizing the voice.

In the familiarity of her neighbors, she says, is a feeling of safety.

"You didn't never hear tell of nobody getting killed in the country. If they died, they just laid down and died a nice life. Hardly a day goes through, some-body ain't getting killed down here.

"Just like the little boy got killed up the street. Just like the girl got killed—it was on my street—the girl in the car with the four little children. And the little baby was in the car with them. That upset me a lot 'cause I knew her mother."

She keeps close to home.

"I'm in my own house, and I never bother nobody if anything happens, I just come in. These people around here in the neighborhood know me, I been living here so long, I don't think nobody round in this neighborhood will do no damage. If they do, it'll be somebody I don't know."

She gestures to a neighbor's house. "The lady across the street watches over here real good."

In the country, Bendolph says, there was no such person as a stranger. "When you live in the country, everybody up there, even if you aren't kin to them, you think you're kin to them 'cause they're all so close."

There was little privacy, and as far as personal business went, "you didn't have none," she says.

But the divisions between white and black were stark.

"The white people didn't treat you right. They just beat you out of everything, and they was so mean to you. The white people furnished the stuff for you to work with, but they would take it all back at the end of the crop and didn't leave you with nothing. That's why we had to raise our own hogs, own cows. My mother used to tell me the story about how many a night she used to go to bed hungry."

Bendolph says she developed a close relationship with one white family and eventually came to the Mobile area in the 1950s, working as a cook for them. The family, she says, helped her secure her mortgage twenty-nine years ago, contributed to her monthly payments during the early years, and keeps in touch with her still. She speaks of them affectionately.

But Mobile, she recalls, was no utopia for race relations.

"You used to go downtown, and they had a sign where the whites had a bathroom, and the colored had a bathroom. They had it on the water hydrants. And riding the bus, you had to go on the back.

"I didn't ride the bus too much 'cause I couldn't stand it. If you put your money in and I put my money in and I had to give up my seat to you and you was a man, I didn't think that was right."

As noon approaches, Bendolph says she's beginning to feel weak. She insists that, by noon, she will have to eat, otherwise her blood sugar will plummet.

The hour arrives. "Let's talk a little more," she offers.

As though gathering sustenance from words, she talks about the "rolling store" that used to come through Gee's Bend, how the families would trade buckets of blackberries with the traveling salesman for articles from his truck. She talks about the quilting bees at night. "I'd sit there and watch them quilt. I had an aunt who got burned. They had a kerosene lamp sitting in the middle of the quilt. The lamp turned over, and it just burned her up!

"They didn't have electricity," she adds. "Electric came in in '57." She tells about home remedies: "I had my ankle sprung. My mother used salt meat and vinegar and some clay dust. She put the salt meat next to the ankle and took the clay dust and the vinegar and mixed it up together and damped it on a rag and wrapped it around my leg. It healed up. I never did go to the doctor."

She talks about castor oil and Epsom salts for stomachaches and turpentine on sugar to cure stomach worms. She talks about a time when parents were stricter, and children, she says, obeyed.

"When you left my grandparents' yard or my mother's yard, you had to tell when you were going back. They was going to tell you what time to be back. If you didn't come back in that time, you'da wished you had've."

She recalls the simplicity of romance. "The people were tighter on the children. If you had a boyfriend, and he came to see you, they had to sit on the front porch, and they couldn't stay to the house no later than eight o'clock. Then they had to go home. You could go to church; they'd walk you back from church and walk you in the gate."

And she tells of front porch weddings, with parties in the yard. "They'd have homemade ice cream, a cake with berries on it, collard greens, turnip greens, English peas, fried chicken. They'd kill a hog and bake the meat. They did just as good as they do with these big weddings."

But now, as she continues her long-ago story, she is getting perilously tired. She begins to sag in her wheelchair. Family members emerge from the house and one man pushes Bendolph's wheelchair slowly up the ramp. At the top of the ramp, the man rotates the chair in order to back Bendolph in over the threshold. As she faces the yard, unseeing, the Prichard light bathes her face. She seems to be studying a place far away.

Eugene Sledge

"WITH THE OLD BREED"

*His name and book have become famous now, the focus, in part, of Ken Burns'
2007 PBS documentary* The War *and the 2010 HBO drama* The Pacific *produced
by Steven Spielberg and Tom Hanks. In February 2001, with his memoir already
a national treasure, I visited with the reflective and self-effacing WWII veteran
and professor at his home, a month before he passed away.*

Montevallo

After evening chow on 14 September 1944, a buddy and I leaned against the rail
of LST 661 and talked about what we would do after the war . . . As the sun dis-
appeared below the horizon and its glare no longer reflected off a glassy sea, I
thought of how beautiful the sunsets always were in the Pacific. They were even
more beautiful than over Mobile Bay. Suddenly a thought hit me like a thun-
derbolt. Would I live to see the sunset tomorrow?"
—E. B. SLEDGE, *With the Old Breed at Peleliu and Okinawa*

In a sunny bedroom on a wooded street, a half hour south of Birmingham,
Eugene Sledge—Mobile native, retired biology professor, and author of
an extraordinary World War II memoir, *With the Old Breed*—is fighting
his toughest battle. "With prayers, and the Marine spirit," he says, propping
himself up on an elbow, "I'm going to beat this."

Battling stomach cancer, Sledge, whose *With the Old Breed* has become a
contemporary classic, spends part of his waking hours bird-watching out the

Eugene Sledge on Okinawa, 1945. Photograph courtesy of
Auburn University Libraries and the Family of Eugene B. Sledge.

window with binoculars, consulting one of the several bird books at his bedside. When he has energy, he is doing some writing—penning a crystal-clear recollection of his boyhood in Mobile, which began with his birth in 1923 to Dr. and Mrs. Edward Sledge—signing copies of *With the Old Breed* for a constant stream of readers, and fielding questions from journalists who wish to get his perspective, once again, on having survived, improbably, two of the bloodiest campaigns of the war.

Although largely confined to his bed, his body taking a beating between illness and chemotherapy, the world of his mind is still vibrant. Above him is a painting of Georgia Cottage in Mobile—the ancestral home of author Augusta

Evans Wilson—where Sledge spent his teenage years after his parents bought the house and moved there. And underneath the bird books is a Bible, both a testament of his faith and a reminder, in many ways, of the origins of his Marine memoir.

When he was 18 years old and dropped out of Marion Institute in Marion, Alabama, to join up with the U.S. Marines, he was told, when entering combat, that journal keeping was against regulations. (There was a fear of diaries falling into enemy hands.) He kept notes on slips of paper and stuck them between the pages of his Bible.

Thirty years later, driven to get up night after night and take up the pen, he began to take what he describes as "dictation," paying heed to the voice in his head that told the story of his younger self—the man who'd braved assaults on Peleliu and Okinawa in the Pacific in 1944 and 1945.

"That I survived at all is a miracle," he comments, laying his head back down on his pillow. So many, he says, were slaughtered all around.

"One of the men from my company later told me that he thought I'd been spared for a reason—to write this memoir, to tell the world what we had gone through."

Japanese machine-gun bursts made long splashes on the water as though flaying it with a whip. The geysers belched up relentlessly where the mortar and artillery shells hit. I caught a fleeting glimpse of a group of Marines leaving a smoking amtrac on the reef. Some fell as bullets and fragments splashed among them. Their buddies tried to help them as they struggled in knee-deep water . . . I felt sickened to the depths of my soul. I asked God, "Why, why, why?" I turned my face away and wished that I were imagining it all. I had tasted the bitterest essence of war, the sight of helpless comrades being slaughtered, and it filled me with disgust.

—*With the Old Breed*

Although almost everyone who visits Eugene Sledge short of his own family— he and wife Jeanne have two sons: John, an author and historian, and Henry, a businessman—wants to know about the war. "Sledgehammer," as he was nicknamed by his fellow Marines, says he does everything in his power these days not to think about it.

"I don't let myself," says Sledge, who taught at the University of Montevallo for twenty-eight years, retiring in 1990. "When I lie here, I think about my high school years in Mobile, about wandering the woods outside my boyhood home, finding turtles and watching birds."

He has no taste for war movies. "Why would somebody who's been through combat go to see *Saving Private Ryan,* then have to be rushed off to a psychiatrist?" He laughs ruefully.

He also has no affection for fiction writers—among them James Jones, late author of such popular World War II novels as *The Thin Red Line*—who he believes experienced little hard combat, but used their imaginations to spin out fantastic stories.

"The company's always dysfunctional," he huffs of war novels. "In my experience, being functional, and being close, is what helped get us through. The men of the First Marine Division were among the finest, most-disciplined men I ever knew."

But the war still dogs him. At Peleliu island, Sledge's Marine company, Company K, reported 64 percent casualties. "The Old Breed" became his term of honor for Marines of character and toughness.

Even as a visitor asks him to elaborate on his boyhood—his rambles through the swamplands, his recollections of his father's early medical practice, his experiences of Mobile high society (he shunned an elite club when he was told he had to drink a pint of whiskey as part of his initiation)—Sledge keeps returning to his experiences writing *With the Old Breed.*

He shakes his head. "It's still in print after twenty years, and not a day goes by that someone doesn't get in touch with me about it. But why should anybody be interested?" His question is sincere.

The answer, the visitor gives him, is that *With the Old Breed* is a survivor's testimony—in clear, riveting language—of an experience that relatively few men survived to tell.

The book met high acclaim but few sales when it was originally published in 1981 by Presidio Press, a major U.S. publisher of military history. Then esteemed historian Paul Fussel discovered the book, Oxford University Press reissued it in 1990, and sales soared.

Fussel, in the introduction of the Oxford University Press edition, explained: "Few combat veterans have remembered as well as Sledge the effects of fear, and Sledge knows that the fear is not just of being killed or wounded, it is fear of something even worse—fear of not being able to take it and exhibiting the symptoms of cowardice to an audience of men who have trusted you."

Sledge is honored by the praise his book has received and also miffed. "It's just my little scrap of the war," he says.

Whether proud or modest, he was, until unburdening himself of this memoir, deeply private about what had happened.

Jeanne Sledge—attentively going in and out of the room to check on her husband's needs as he talks to his guest—says that she knew little of his wartime experiences until he gave her a handwritten manuscript in the 1980s to type up for him. Before that, she says, one of the few indications she'd had of his traumatic combat years was during the first year of their marriage.

"I remember," she says, "we were in the car and passed a dog that had been hit. When I expressed sadness, my husband said, 'That's nothing. I've seen friends worse than that.'"

My Pacific War experiences have haunted me . . . But time heals, and the nightmares no longer wake me in a cold sweat with pounding heart and racing pulse. Now I can write this story, painful though it is to do so. In writing it I'm fulfilling an obligation I have long felt to my comrades in the 1st Marine Division, all of whom have suffered so much for our country. None came out unscathed. Many gave their lives, many their health, and some their sanity. All who survived will long remember the horror they would rather forget.
—*With the Old Breed*

There are still many stories Eugene Sledge could tell—of his memories of Mobile's hurricane of 1926, of the old ice wagons that rumbled down the street, of the draining and burning of old Wragg Swamp, of the knife wounds he heard his physician father tell about that filled the emergency rooms come Saturday night, when men were drinking moonshine.

Or he could tell about his days at Auburn University after the war, studying biology as an undergraduate, then completing his doctorate at the University of Florida in Gainesville. He would go on, as part of his standard biology curriculum, to teach such courses as History and Philosophy of Science.

"One friend told me, 'I know how you wrote *With the Old Breed* and why it's so clear. Because you were trained as a biologist.'

"A scientist has to write clearly and distinctly," he elaborates, "so the reader has no guesswork."

What seems to buoy him up now, in this difficult time, are family, friends, and faith, and the joys of that natural world out his window. "My wife has the front yard of the house to landscape," he says, smiling. "I get the back yard to remain completely wild."

And there are, of course, his readers—veterans, college students, even school-age children assigned *With the Old Breed* in class. He shakes his head, both sadly and wisely, when he admits that some young people tell him they had no idea of what "the old breed" went through—the struggles, horrors, losses, the bittersweet triumphs of the war.

When Sledge was doing research to check facts of his book, he was taken aback, he says, to discover official reports of battles sometimes quite different from what he had experienced. "You could hardly place the action," he says. "Information would be sent from the front lines to the back, and the messages change. The stories get souped up.

"One of my commanding officers later told me, 'Sledgehammer, I'm glad I didn't know what you were doing'"—referring to the slips of paper he kept notes on—"'because I'd have made you tear those slips up.'"

As he finishes his conversation with his visitor, he begins to rest, wearied now with all he has said, shoring up his strength for the new, hard battle ahead.

As he signs a copy of *With the Old Breed* for his guest, he inscribes it, under his name, with a poem by an anonymous Marine from his First Division, the same verse he inscribes, he says, on every copy of his book:

And when to heaven he goes
To St. Peter he'll tell
Another Marine reporting Sir
I've served my time in hell.

PART III   THE JOURNEYERS

*T*here are travels of place—New York to Alabama, Alabama to New York—transits of career, and, of course, journeys of the self. The journeyers of this section have been engaged, in various ways, in movements physical, emotional, or spiritual from one place to another.

Mel Israel, aka Mel Allen, left Alabama and headed north to take up a perch behind the microphone at Yankee Stadium, becoming a radio personality so famous in his day that his memory is enshrined at the stadium alongside those of Mickey Mantle and Babe Ruth. Howell Raines ultimately made his way from Alabama to New York, too, sitting in the executive editor's chair of the New York Times, *calling plays in a different way, none more famous than his leadership of the* Times *on 9/11 and during its aftermath.*

Gay Talese found his treasure by serendipity, it seems, when stepping off the train in Tuscaloosa, a young man from New Jersey beginning freshman year at The University of Alabama, taking a first step in what would be his spectacular career as a "New Journalist." Winston Groom's journey takes place through the arc of his career and the peregrinations of his most famous character, Forrest Gump.

Of all the nonfiction stories I've written, none has had more impact on readers than the saga of Tommy Tarrants and Stan Chassin. Their journey was the least likely when they first met as teenagers, Tarrants a bully and bigot, Chassin the grandson of a rabbi, Tarrants grabbing Chassin by the throat and calling him anti-Semitic names. Their lives ran on different tracks for four decades, with Tarrants undergoing a profound transformation. When they met up again after forty years, they were different men, and their connection was profoundly different, too. They had taken a journey through time and of the heart.

Mel Allen

"VOICE OF THE YANKEES"

When I went to Yankee Stadium in the Bronx in 2003 to experience the realm where Mel Allen had become famous, I little expected that the piece I'd write would be a look back, as well, on the stadium itself, which was replaced by a new stadium across the street in spring 2009. The new Yankee Stadium, I'm happy to report, has its own Monument Park, with Mel Allen forever part of the pantheon.

The Bronx, New York

Beyond the left field fence in Yankee Stadium there is a site called Monument Park, with bronze plaques paying tribute to Yankee legends such as Babe Ruth, Lou Gehrig, Yogi Berra, and Joe DiMaggio. In addition to the great baseball players, other members of the Yankee family are honored, among them an energetic talker with roots in Alabama's Bibb County. His plaque, in part, reads: "He made pet phrases, such as 'Going, going, gone!' a part of our language and culture. A Yankee Institution, a National Treasure. 'How about that!'" Mel Allen. "The Voice of the Yankees."

"Mel spoke in mellifluous tones," says Tony Morante, who leads tours of Yankee Stadium and pauses during a tour to remember Allen, who broadcast games to radio audiences from 1939 to 1964. "He had that southern drawl. I was working as an usher, but he always had time to speak with me. He was one of the first dignitaries I met."

Morante says the voice of Allen was beloved by many New Yorkers—but

Mel Allen, 1955. Photograph by Al Ravenna, courtesy of the Library of Congress, New York World-Telegram & Sun Collection.

hardly all. In the early days, there were also the Giants at the Polo Grounds in Manhattan and the Dodgers in Brooklyn.

"You associated Mel Allen with winning," says Morante. "He was despised in other parts of New York."

"The Dodgers were the scrappy underdogs," explains Charles Salzberg, a novelist and New York baseball writer who loved the Dodgers. "The Yankees were corporate, and their fans were arrogant. The Giants were in between. You almost got in fights with other kids over it. You associated the announcers with the teams."

Despite his own team loyalty, Salzberg enjoyed Mel Allen's "southern, soothing voice," over the radio at summer camp. "He was the reason I listened to the Yankees."

The era is gone, of course, when radio can make superstars of baseball play-by-play announcers.

As Ed Mullins, former chairman of The University of Alabama's journalism school, says, "Students today want to be a sports editor for a newspaper or a feature writer for *Sports Illustrated* or an anchor with an attitude for ESPN. The idea of being a Curt Gowdy, Mel Allen, or Red Barber, that's ancient history to kids today. But at the time, it represented the pinnacle of sportscasting success. The entry into the royalty of broadcasting in those days was radio."

As Morante leads stadium visitors to the press box, the infield, and to the most storied place of all—the dugout where the Bronx Bombers still chomp their tobacco and stomp their cleats and ready their bats—he remembers Allen, even outside the broadcast booth, a tall man in a straw hat spinning great stories about the game.

Elmo Ellis is Mel Allen's cousin. Ellis' father, Samuel Israel, and Mel's father, Julius Israel, were brothers. The brothers' father, Wolf Israel, was a Polish-Jewish immigrant who ended up in West Blocton, Alabama, a coal-mining town just south of Birmingham. Wolf Israel started a store in West Blocton that became I&N Quality. The Israels helped found the town synagogue and were active in civic affairs.

"West Blocton was a thriving community in those days. Later on, hard times punctured it," says Ellis, who lives in Atlanta and is retired as vice president of Cox Broadcasting and general manager of radio station WSB AM-FM.

Although Ellis' father stayed in West Blocton, Allen's father started to move around as a salesman, and Mel Allen was born in Birmingham and spent part of his childhood in Bessemer. In later years, Allen's family moved to Tuscaloosa. It was there, as a student at The University of Alabama, that Allen got interested in media and communications, writing for *The Crimson White* newspaper and broadcasting Alabama baseball games.

In 1936, Elmo Ellis lived in Allen's father's house and roomed with Allen, who, by then, had completed a law degree at the university.

"He was commuting to Birmingham to do a daily sports show," Ellis says of his cousin. "He loved sports more than he did law. He was always enamored of sports and had an almost perfect memory for sports information."

They had a sports-loving neighbor, too. "Across the street was a young man named Bear Bryant, his wife, and baby daughter," says Ellis. "He and Melvin became very close friends."

While a speech instructor and debating coach at The University of Alabama, Allen cut a 78 rpm record of his voice, which he used to audition for a slot with CBS in New York. "In 1937 they hired him as a staff announcer," says Ellis.

At the time, though, the young Alabamian still had the name Mel Israel. He changed it, according to Ellis, because of prejudices in the broadcast industry.

"In order to go on the air as a Jewish person," Ellis explains, "it was almost mandatory to have an Anglicized name. There was then such strong prejudice, not only against Jews but also against blacks. The owners of these radio stations were sensitive about things like that. They wanted you to sound like the general population."

Elmo Ellis—who had been Elmo Israel—had encountered the same demands when starting out on his own broadcast career after college. Ellis says he took the first two letters of each of his names—"El" and "Is"—and fabricated his new, last name. Allen's younger brother, Larry, who would soon work with his big brother as a statistician, took the name Larry Allen.

In New York, Mel Allen's first ventures with CBS included being the moderator for the game show *Truth or Consequences*, and filling in for another broadcaster by going up in an airplane to report on the Vanderbilt Cup Yacht race. Ellis says that Allen gave such grand descriptions of the race—"he went on for an hour about it," Ellis recalls—that CBS gave him a shot at sports.

According to Yankee historical information: "His first major assignment was to cover the 1938 World Series. The following year, he assisted Arch McDonald on the N.Y. Yankee–N.Y. Giant baseball broadcasts and became chief announcer the next year."

Larry Allen, in Montgomery, says the secret of his older brother's success behind the microphone was his small-town, down-to-earth manner.

"I heard Mel say on occasion that he pictured himself talking to a handful of people, not to millions. Just to those people who had an interest in the sport he was doing but who weren't experts. He was representing them and had the privilege of being at the game, when they couldn't leave their work.

"That's who he was talking to: a family."

Larry Allen used to go to spring training to assist his brother in finding out anecdotes about all the players, and worked at Yankee Stadium as his statistician.

Much of his time was taken up in other ways helping his brother, whose reputation grew like a player who'd just hit a grand slam in a World Series.

"Mel couldn't answer all the letters he received," Larry says, "so I would answer what he couldn't answer. It was unbelievable, the offers from people calling for him to speak. They wrote to Mel about almost anything you could think of. They might write Mel about DiMaggio, asking him how DiMaggio prepares for a game. I would wonder, 'Why didn't you write to DiMaggio to ask him?'"

Mel Allen's friendship with the players was dramatized in the HBO movie, *61**, about the 1961 home-run race between Yankees Roger Maris and Mickey Mantle as they approached Babe Ruth's record of sixty in a season.

Directed by Billy Crystal, the movie shows the Mel Allen character—played by Christopher McDonald—as a clubhouse regular, even giving Mantle a personal reference to see his doctor for a malady that might be cured by a shot. (According to the movie, the shot was a disaster, and Mantle had a bad reaction that seemed to make his illness worse.) Allen was such an intimate of players that he was nicknamed, "The Tenth Yankee."

A 1984 story about Allen in the magazine *Inside Sports*, for example, quotes Allen as recalling the end of Lou Gehrig's career. Gehrig retired when he started to suffer from amyotrophic lateral sclerosis, a fatal degenerative nerve disorder now called Lou Gehrig's disease. According to the *Inside Sports* interview with Allen: "The year after Gehrig retired, I was sitting on the bench, and someone came running up and said, 'Lou's here.' He couldn't walk by then. He shuffled. The players would all greet him as if there was nothing wrong. I found myself alone on the bench with him. He leaned over, patted me on the leg and said, 'You don't know how important your radio broadcasts are to me. They keep me going.' I thanked him, excused myself, walked down the runway, and began to bawl."

Because the Yankees were famous, says sportswriter Rich Marazzi, Allen's own fame was bolstered. "If he had broadcast for the St. Louis Browns, nobody would have ever heard of him," says Marazzi, author of *Baseball Players of the 50s*, with an entry on Allen.

In the course of his career with the Yankees, Allen broadcast twenty World Series as well as twenty-four All-Star games.

Allen became well known for his endorsements of products, too, says Marazzi. When the Yankees hit a homer, he might refer to it as a "Ballantine Blast," in honor of the Ballantine Beer sponsor. To highlight another sponsor, he might say, "the ball was fouled by the length of a White Owl cigar."

"One thing I admired about Mel Allen," says Marazzi, who had Allen on his show, "was that he paid very close attention to the common man as well as the celebrity."

Marazzi still unhappily recalls the World Series of 1964—the Yankees versus the St. Louis Cardinals—when Mel Allen stopped speaking while on the air. "He was so overcome by the Yankees losing that he couldn't talk. He left the booth."

Marazzi believes that Allen was suffering at the time from "a nasal problem" that affected his voice, and "didn't feel well."

It was a pivotal moment in Allen's career, a silence that spoke loudly to millions of fans. "People said vicious things about him," Marazzi recalls, "that he'd had a breakdown."

Ed Mullins speculates that Allen might have had a psychosomatic reaction to the Yankees' defeat.

Elmo Ellis remembers Allen's mother being ill at that time—the Yankees broadcaster, who never married, had lived with his mother, then his sister in Greenwich, Connecticut. Ellis believes that illness may have put a strain on his cousin.

In 1964, Allen was dismissed as an announcer, "cut loose in the prime of life," says Mullins. He was in his early 50s.

Marazzi believes that "the Yankees inner family got tired of Mel and the way he was carrying on over the years." The dismissal, he says, was handled shabbily.

On the Internet site www.BaseballLibrary.com, Allen is quoted as saying in 1996: "The Yankees never even had a press conference to announce my leaving. They left people to believe whatever they wanted—and people believed the worst. The lies that started were horrible, that I was a lush or had a breakdown or stroke or was numb from taking medications for my voice."

Joe Garagiola was his replacement.

Larry Allen believes that his brother's dismissal as Yankees announcer was linked to a series of shifts by ownership in advance of a team sale. Several other prominent members of the Yankee organization had contracts that were not renewed. There was a sale of the team by Dan Topping in 1966, and another in 1973, when George Steinbrenner assumed control.

"I credit Steinbrenner with bringing Mel back into the Yankee family," says Marazzi.

The days of radio broadcasts were over, but Allen hosted a cable show of Yankees games, and on the networks became a host of a weekly highlights show, *This Week in Baseball*. He gave voice to college bowl games, too.

But the spectacular heights of Allen's career had passed, says Marazzi, who suggests Allen's genius was bound up in the medium of a bygone era. "He grew up on radio. He had a tendency to over describe on TV."

Allen, though, had secured his place in sports history.

In 1978, Allen and co-announcer Red Barber, another southerner (from Mississippi), were the first recipients of the Ford C. Frick Broadcast Award at the National Baseball Hall of Fame in Cooperstown.

On Allen's passing in 1996, at age 83, in Connecticut, George Steinbrenner said, "Mel Allen meant as much to Yankee tradition as legends like Ruth, Gehrig, DiMaggio, and Mantle."

Ed Mullins traveled to New York to attend an interfaith memorial service for Allen at St. Patrick's Cathedral. Mullins, who had played American Legion baseball as a youth in southwest Alabama, says that Allen had "a calling. This became his life, the way a minister accepts a calling. He had this incredibly musical voice. It was, for announcing, operatic. It was prima. It was very, very mellow, very smooth. But it also had an edge to it of a fan."

Game night, Yankee stadium. New York versus the Boston Red Sox.

Outside the stadium are beer-and-hot-dog restaurants, booths selling baseball caps, the rumbling elevated train. Inside the stadium, it is packed to the outfield bleachers. The vast, cool Kentucky bluegrass field—serene during a noonday tour of the stadium—is blazing with stadium lights and hot with competition.

To attend such a rivalry is to understand, at heart, what it means to be a Yankees fan: the crowd coming to its feet with every other pitch, the howls and cheers, the hoots and applause.

This is the world that Mel Allen gave voice to, high in his broadcaster's booth, for twenty-five years.

In many ways the players have changed. Some speak Spanish, one hails from Japan, they make millions of dollars for playing the game. But, of course, things are also much the same. Three strikes—you're out. Knock it over the fence—you've hit a home run. The summer evening is rich with the mystique of baseball.

In the bottom of the ninth, score tied, the Yankees win, and the fans go crazy. They have defeated their longtime nemesis.

Out in Monument Park, the bronze visages of yesteryear look on, one of them, as Elmo Ellis says of cousin Mel, may even be broadcasting, happily, to a "celestial audience."

Gay Talese

MADE IN ALABAMA

New York City

Gay Talese, who graduated from The University of Alabama in 1953 and went on to become one of his generation's most-celebrated authors, was once a middling high school student in Ocean City, New Jersey, with dim prospects for college.

"There was nothing very distinguished about me," Talese says of his growing-up years in a loving Italian immigrant family, "except my interest in other people."

At his elegant Manhattan townhouse, Talese, a trim gentleman in a three-piece suit, recalls his despair at being a high school graduate in 1949 with a fistful of college rejections. As the summer wore on, his father, a tailor, had an idea. One of his customers was a doctor who hailed from Birmingham in the faraway South and had pull at the state university.

"No one knew me in Tuscaloosa. No one knew anything about me. It was a long train ride, and I thought, 'I'm going to have a second chance.' That train ride to Tuscaloosa changed my life."

Talese's book, *A Writer's Life,* recounts the pivotal journey—"I was an immigrant from southern New Jersey"—as well as his years covering the civil rights movement in Alabama as a reporter for the *New York Times.*

While the book, in part, is about what Talese, 74, calls "my coming of age in Alabama," it moves through other locales as well, from New York to Beijing. A female Chinese soccer player; the life cycle of a New York City building; his family's ancestral home in southern Italy—divergent topics join together in Talese's flowing prose.

Writer Gay Talese at the Strand Bookstore, New York City, 2006. Photograph by
David Shankbone.

Some of these subjects inspired book projects that Talese never finished, or
pieces he could not get published, such as a story commissioned by the *New
Yorker* on John Bobbitt and his wife, Lorena, who had famously emasculated
him with a kitchen knife.

Despite his literary acclaim—journalist and novelist Tom Wolfe has said
that he learned to write scenes from reading Talese—the author is honest
about struggle and periodic defeat. "I look for the disappointed element of society," he says, "of which I am constantly a member. A writer is always disappointed if he has standards that are beyond reach."

Talese's articles and books often focus on people dealing with setbacks, such as his 1960s *Esquire* profiles of heavyweight champ Floyd Patterson after his battering by Sonny Liston or Yankees great Joe DiMaggio, deep in retirement, watching Mickey Mantle, the new Yankees star, captivate the crowds. Lavishing great time on his research, Talese employs what he calls "the art of hanging out."

Talese's work "showed younger writers the potential of full-immersion reporting," says Howell Raines, former executive editor of the *New York Times*.

Talese, a high school journalist, became a sports columnist for the college newspaper, *The Crimson White*, and a campus correspondent for the *Birmingham Post-Herald*. It was during these Tuscaloosa years that he began to develop his narrative flair, despite professors who wanted straight reporting.

"Since I sometimes resisted their approach," he writes in his memoir, "and might try instead to communicate the news through the viewpoint of the single person who observed it from the sidelines or might adopt some other narrative technique learned from reading fiction, I was not a faculty favorite."

He soon had his admirers, though, for his human-interest tales about campus characters, including the seven-foot-tall north Alabama boy who declined to play basketball because "he preferred devoting his out-of-class time to trimming trees."

Another story was about the football team's elderly locker room attendant, the grandson of slaves, who was "the players' good luck charm; before each game, as they lined up to trot onto the field, they would take turns stroking the black man's head . . . I was describing one of the rare examples of interracial physical contact that then existed within the segregated world of Alabama athletics."

As an Italian-American, Talese understood what it was like, he says, "to feel different, though not as different," he adds, "as in my father's day."

"I was an outsider," he writes, "a token Italian Yankee. On this campus not yet ready to accept blacks, it got its 'diversity' and 'affirmative action' quotas from people like me and other olive-skinned out-of-staters."

His sports column, "Gay-zing," Talese says, helped him gain social acceptance.

Says Raines, who has a graduate degree from Alabama: "Gay was lucky in his choice of universities for a number of reasons. As a northerner suddenly set down in Tuscaloosa, he quickly learned about the diversity of the nation.

That gave him cultural reach as a newspaper reporter and author. Moreover, at The University of Alabama, he saw firsthand the world of segregation at its most repressive, and his later coverage of the civil rights movement had uncommon depth and authority."

Talese acknowledges that many of the turns of his career have been the result of "serendipity" and even titled his first book, in 1961, *New York—A Serendipiter's Journey.*

By lucky chance, for example, Talese had a college roommate whose uncle was Turner Catledge, then managing editor of the *New York Times.* Talese writes that Catledge "hoped the newswriting would become livelier, saying that the era of just-the-facts journalism was insufficient now that television was the first to reach the public with the text and pictures of late-breaking news."

Talese signed on as a *Times* intern in 1953, then graduated to news assistant. After a two-year stint in the Army, he became a sports reporter in 1956. At the behest of Catledge, Talese's mission, with other staffers, was to make sports writing "more diverting, original . . . and more entertaining."

His work as a general assignment reporter, covering the civil rights movement back in Alabama, came later. Even there, he explains, he was not the reporter responsible for the nuts and bolts of the news but often the "sidebar writer," turning up stories that illuminated the personal dimension. He would stay on at the *Times* until 1965.

The college freshman with little confidence had become the professional reporter with a sure pen. "I had bylines," Talese says of his Tuscaloosa years. "That was my Phi Beta Kappa."

In 1998, he would return as recipient of the journalism school's Clarence Cason Award, and in 2001 as the university's commencement speaker with an honorary doctorate of humane letters.

Throughout his townhouse, mixed in with books and paintings, are photographs of Talese with his wife, Nan, a publisher—they have been married forty-six years—and their two daughters, Pamela and Catherine. *A Writer's Life* is dedicated to all three women in his life.

The house was originally an apartment building, and Talese, who moved in as a bachelor in 1958, lived on the third floor, front room, for $60 a month. As he walks up the stairs to that floor, his Australian terriers, Benchley and Barkley, look up from a couch.

Talese tells of a piano teacher who had resided in one apartment, and a "beautiful woman" in another who had an affair with a famous Hollywood producer. When he and Nan married, they lived on the fourth floor, cooked on a hot plate, and washed their dishes in the bathtub. He held onto his original apartment, too, then got hold of a third and sublet it for a while to an author friend, William Styron, who was working on a novel that would become *The Confessions of Nat Turner.*

In 1972, after the successes of his first two books, *The Kingdom and the Power,* about the *New York Times,* and *Honor Thy Father,* about the Mafia, Talese bought the entire building and turned it into a single-family home.

On the fourth floor now, among other memorabilia, are two life-size cardboard cutout photographs of Talese standing. A gift from former *New York Times* editor Abe Rosenthal and his wife, the pictures, Talese says, show him at two stages: age 60, in cashmere vest and coat, when he had published his memoir about his parents, *Unto the Sons,* a prelude to *A Writer's Life;* and at age 18, a freshman at The University of Alabama in a camel hair coat.

At both ages, Talese was a snappy dresser, and he still wears hand-tailored suits, silk ties, and handmade leather shoes.

The wool plaid suit he's wearing was made for him by his cousin in Paris. He takes off the coat and shows the label: "Cristiani."

"Look at the collars," he says of the suit, "the lapels."

He is not boasting of his wardrobe but extolling artistry.

"I wear a tie even when I am alone," he says.

In *A Writer's Life,* Talese recalls that, as a child on Sundays after Mass, he and his sister accompanied their parents "to stroll with them on the boardwalk in nearby Atlantic City, among the casually dressed crowds and roving photographers who usually mistook us (with our fine clothes and familial formality) for a family of visiting dignitaries from abroad, which is, I think, precisely the impression my parents wished to convey."

As a journalist, Talese says, he dresses up not for show but "for the story. I dress up for every story. The most ordinary person, if you're dressing up for them, knows you're paying them respect in your own appearance. You're making an impression. You're establishing the fact you're careful—with your facts, how you treat people."

Talese, who keeps fit by working out at a gymnasium up the street, is not only careful in his dress, but in his prose.

In *A Writer's Life*, he explains he has "a virtual Stone Age method" of writing, which includes printing words by hand on a yellow legal pad, erasing and reworking them, then slowly transferring his material to a typewriter or computer.

E-mail? Cell phone? Blackberry? "I don't do anything," Talese says with a laugh.

This tailor's son takes notes out of his vest pocket—they are made on small ovals he cuts from stiff, white paper. The paper, he says, is from the shirt cardboard that comes from the cleaners. The notes, he says, are his writer's "memory aides."

Downstairs in his study, where there's no phone of any kind, his research files are cardboard boxes on shelves marked with the titles of his best-selling books: "The Kingdom and the Power," "Honor Thy Father," "Thy Neighbor's Wife," about the sexual revolution and free-love movement of the 1970s, and "Unto the Sons."

An anthology was published in 2003 of his short nonfiction, *The Gay Talese Reader*, which includes the *Esquire* profile "Frank Sinatra Has a Cold," judged by that magazine as the best article in its history.

The boxes are decorated with drawings and pictures cut out from publications. "I do that," Talese wryly says of his arduous creative process, "as time-wasting opportunities."

On the shelf marked *A Writer's Life*, his first major book in fourteen years, the subsections are marked by their own file boxes, thirteen boxes in all, including Chinese soccer, the Bobbitts, and Alabama.

He writes extensively about Selma in *A Writer's Life*, reflecting on his coverage, as one of the *Times* reporters, of the Selma-to-Montgomery march over the Edmund Pettus Bridge. He writes about J. L. Chestnut Jr., the black attorney in Selma who was visible in civil rights cases.

Inside the Alabama box, in folders, is a treasure trove of clippings and incidental items. There are specifics about the civil rights movement, but there is also an old homes tour booklet of Selma—the perfect vehicle for an author to remember the beauty of the antebellum homes at a time of social strife.

There are files on an interracial marriage, a black-on-white rape, Governor George Wallace, the Selma public school system, all of which show up in the book. *A Writer's Life* offers many of Talese's first impressions of these stories and what it's like to revisit them decades later.

For all of Talese's absorption in stories of the civil rights movement, he emphasizes, "I wouldn't buy into the northern liberal viewpoint that the South was the only place with racial problems."

He remembers the Klan not only in Alabama but as a boy growing up in New Jersey. He says his Italian-Catholic father told him of a cross-burning in 1922, across from his tailor's shop. "He thought that had to be for him."

These days, he says, he might find more blacks and whites eating in the same restaurant in Selma than in Manhattan. "This is still a segregated city, this liberal New York," he says.

On the wall of the study are dozens of pages pinned to a corkboard, on which Talese has written notes to himself on the progress of the book. "This is a writer," he explains, waving to the pages, "talking to himself."

The last page is dated August 26, 2005. In bold letters is printed: "Book finished!" It goes on: "I completed Page 605 this afternoon. The book ends as it more or less began: It tells the story of a Chinese soccer-playing woman, Liu Ying . . . But it is not about her, nor is it about anything in a singular sense. It is a book about writing a book. It is a book about not writing a book. It is about the process of writing, the hopes and setbacks and meanderings that infuse a manuscript."

When Talese leaves his townhouse for an evening on the town, he heads to his favorite haunt, Elaine's, the Upper East Side restaurant presided over by Elaine Kaufman, a longtime friend of Talese's and other regulars.

"I take care of him," says Kaufman, as Talese sweeps into the establishment and takes his place at a dining table across from the bar. Along the top of softly lit restaurant walls, with their motif of Venice canals, are hundreds of photographs of writers, several of Talese with friends. Mixed in with the photographs are framed book jackets, including Talese's.

Younger writers, passionate about their craft, soon join Talese, some by invitation, others because they pass by, know someone, and are waved over to have a chair.

Talese speaks with them in his poised and knowledgeable manner, excitement also in his voice as conversations unfold.

Manny Fernandez, a *New York Times* reporter at the table, who says Talese's writing "has had one of the biggest impacts on how I write," admits to being in awe of the author, who is his elder by forty years. "I'm like a high school basketball player meeting Michael Jordan," he says.

Murray Weiss, criminal justice editor at the *New York Post* and an author, comments that Talese "is one of the great writer-reporters of our time."

Sridhar Pappu, a young journalist, passes by and is beckoned to take a chair.

The circle of writers grows. Elaine, the proprietress, settles into a chair and joins in.

Talese, the literary lion, unmistakable in his tailored suit, his red tie, his urbane style, is the center of attention, but he asks questions, too. Where are you from? Where did you go to college? Tell me about your family. He's hanging out.

By 11 p.m., with the younger generation enjoying the company and ready for dessert, for one more glass of wine, Talese bids good-bye and rises from the table.

Hat on, overcoat thrown over his shoulders against the chill, he is out the door—the vitality of the Tuscaloosa college freshman still in his step—and hailing a cab home.

Howell Raines

COMING FULL CIRCLE

Before Howell Raines left the New York Times *in 2003, I visited with him at the* New York Times *offices in Manhattan, a place of energy, dynamism, and push. In 2006 I caught up with him again in a far more relaxed, and reflective, setting.*

Oxford, Mississippi

On a breezy afternoon at Rowan Oak, Howell Raines, his wife, Krystyna, at his side, saunters beneath the whispering cedar trees leading to William Faulkner's historic home. The former executive editor of the *New York Times,* on book tour for his new memoir, *The One That Got Away,* has not always moved at such a leisurely pace.

For forty years as the Birmingham native spent workdays chasing stories as a reporter or presiding over publication from an editor's chair, he was fueled by what he calls "the adrenaline" of daily newspapers, a cycle he likens in his book to building a house "every day, for time everlasting, amen."

In 2003, however, in a saga played out before the nation, Raines lost his job as executive editor in the aftermath of a scandal involving plagiarism and lying by a young reporter, Jayson Blair.

"My career ended in the most unexpected way," he says.

Raines is now, he says, "getting a chance to visit the road not taken."

At age 62, the newspaperman who won a Pulitzer Prize in feature writing and later presided over seven Pulitzers for the *New York Times* after the terror-

Howell Raines, author of *The One That Got Away*. Photo by Bruce
Newman, courtesy of the *Mobile Press-Register*.

ist attacks of September 11, 2001, finds himself, in the traditional sense, unem-
ployed. In his light-beige linen suit, open-collar shirt, and Panama hat, he is
contemplative—"I'm no longer addicted to stress," he says—looking through
Faulkner's house not as a tourist or journalist, but as an aspiring author.

That aspiration is not just to be published, as he is already an author of a
novel, *Whiskey Man,* an oral history, *My Soul Is Rested,* and a first memoir,

Fly Fishing Through the Midlife Crisis, but "to climb the mountain" of a new novel about the Civil War.

"Newspapers were the love in the second chamber of my heart," he says. In the first chamber, from the days he was an undergraduate at Birmingham-Southern and did his master's in English at The University of Alabama, was the love of books. "I've come full circle," he says.

As Raines enters the room where Faulkner's typewriter sits near the window, he is captivated by the Nobel laureate's eccentric method of outlining the novel, *A Fable.* Faulkner scrawled the outline on the wall. Raines peers closely. "I can use help with my plots," he says, laughing.

Rowan Oak curator William Griffith has brought out a Faulkner treasure, though, that entices Raines even more. "Can I hold it?" he asks. Griffith nods. Raines picks up Faulkner's fishing rod as though handling a sorcerer's wand.

Griffith tells Raines he is a fly-fisher, too. The men talk about bonefish versus carp. "Carp," says Griffith, "are much spookier than bonefish." He asks Raines questions about Faulkner's rig. Raines balances it in his hands.

Fishing is a powerful theme in Raines' life, and *The One Who Got Away* devotes much of its text to Raines' fly-fishing adventures from islands in the Pacific to rivers in Russia. One of the two biggest fish that got away in the memoir is a blue marlin that Raines fights for seven and a half hours on an expedition in the company of his best friend from Birmingham days, Tennant McWilliams. The other, metaphorically speaking, is the *New York Times.*

As Raines looks around the property outside the author's home—the stable, the cookhouse, the cabin where Faulkner's "Mammy," Dilsey, lived—he converses comfortably on topics ranging from fishing, to religion, to Faulkner's understanding of race relations, to the inspiration for him of "late life" artists who continued to do dynamic work into old age like W. B. Yeats and Pablo Picasso.

And he talks about roads not taken, and detours, too.

Raines says he had gotten a contract to write *The One That Got Away,* several years ago, intending it to be a sequel to *Fly Fishing Through the Midlife Crisis.* But he ultimately gave the money back and started over.

Two occurrences befell him that altered the course of this newly envisioned version. On his own for many years after a divorce—he and his first wife have two sons, Ben, a journalist, and Jeff, a musician, and two grandchildren—he fell in love with Krystyna Stachowiak, a Polish citizen working in New York City. On March 8, 2003, their family and friends, as he writes in the memoir, toasted "the first Silesia-Alabama nuptials in anyone's memory." His memoir thus became, in part, his love story with Krystyna.

Then, on June 3, 2003, he was fired by *New York Times* publisher Arthur O. Sulzberger Jr. As he writes in *The One That Got Away:* "Newspapers are hierarchical. When the ship hits a rock, the captain may have to walk the plank. Such was my fate. Some people thought I got a raw deal. Others were glad to see me go."

Raines spends the first two sections of his memoir, though, on life, love, and fishing. The final third, only 50 pages or so of a 308-page book, delves into the back-story of what befell him at the *New York Times*.

"This is a good place to talk about time and its passage," says Raines, as he and Krystyna finish their tour of Faulkner's domain and rest on a bench near an arbor.

What Raines set out to do, he explains, is write about "the universal experience of loss. When I was younger, I thought that what was most interesting was regret. Now I realize that it's loss. When you get older you realize that loved ones are taken away from you, that things are taken away from you, not of your own volition.

"We've all got it coming. We just don't know when."

Oxford's town square is a picturesque place, with its county courthouse, Civil War monument, student-lively restaurants, and upscale boutiques. On one corner is Square Books, whose owner, Richard Howarth, is mayor of the town, a testimony, surely, to the visibility of literary culture in Ole Miss' hometown. As Raines arrives at Off-Square Books for the Wednesday event—a roomy annex to the bookstore down the block—he tells a fitting anecdote. When he and Krystyna rented a car at the Memphis airport for the drive to

Oxford, the rental agent told him: "Breathe the air down there and you might become a famous author."

The bookstore begins to fill with folks from the community and a good number of students, several from the university's journalism department.

Raines' old friend, Curtis Wilkie, author and former southern correspondent for the *Boston Globe,* is in attendance. He says that he believes Raines' values, his "journalistic conscience," was forged like others of their generation of southern journalists by "being exposed to the civil rights movement. It is reflected in what he writes, whether international affairs or national politics."

Raines includes some short chapters in his memoir, labeled "Snapshots," which depict signature moments in his life. For his reading, Raines chooses a selection from *The One That Got Away* entitled "Snapshot V: Legion Field, in Birmingham, 1964, Enrollment Day, the Paul W. Bryant School of Journalism."

Raines, who's five feet eight inches tall and has curly, salt-and-pepper hair, and moves with a bit of a swagger, takes his place at the podium and projects his southern storyteller's voice into the crowd. He reads about his first newspaper assignment from the *Birmingham Post-Herald*—to cover the Auburn-Alabama game. He reads of Alabama player Raymond Ogden running the ball to the goal line as "behind me the Alabama stands released a gush of sound that crashed like a tsunami upon the sideline jubilation."

Raines tells of how he jumped into the air himself but then realized he was there to cover the game, not cheer: "Almost thirty years later, in 1993, William Safire in his *Political Dictionary* would credit me with inventing the term 'defining moment,' which went on to become one of the clichés of American political reporting. I suppose if you invent a cliché, it is all right to use it. This was my defining moment as a journalist. I leapt into the air as a fan, and, as Raymond Ogden passed on his journey into obscurity, I came down as a reporter."

After Raines' reading, the audience asks questions about Jayson Blair, the future of newspapers, and today's politics. Raines, who throws in zingers in his memoir criticizing the *Wall St. Journal* editorial page, Fox News, and the current administration, wryly answers that the only thing that might make him return to journalism would be "a third term for George Bush."

He adds, as well, that "the Democratic party is in collapse."

Raines' defining moment, as on Legion Field with Bear Bryant nearby, has come again.

In the memoir's "The Last Editorial: On Bear," he writes that Bryant, after losing a game and "watching a nasty replay," said, "I had my chances to win. That game is over."

Raines has his new mountain to climb.

Winston Groom

THE HOUSE THAT GUMP BUILT

Point Clear

The objects in Winston Groom's study in the elegant Point Clear home he shares with his wife, Anne-Clinton, and their young daughter, Carolina, provide insight into the work and sensibilities of the author of *Forrest Gump* and thirteen other books of fiction, memoir, and narrative history.

On the table is a six-hundred-page manuscript for a novel, *El Paso,* about Pancho Villa and the Mexican Revolution, which Groom's been working on for ten years. Across the computer screen unfolds the text for a history that he's on schedule to complete this summer—a narrative of the Battle of Vicksburg together with his argument "that the war should have ended there."

On the fireplace hangs the cavalry saber that belonged to his great-grandfather Fremont Thrower, who rode with Gen. Joseph "Fighting Joe" Wheeler. Thrower provided Groom with a personal connection to his Civil War history, *Shrouds of Glory.* The sword, Groom speculates, also likely belonged to his great-great-great-grandfather, Elijah Montgomery, a major in the War of 1812. Groom wrote eloquently of Major Montgomery in his book, *Patriotic Fire: Andrew Jackson and Jean Laffite at the Battle of New Orleans.*

While his military histories—his focus in recent years—are epic narratives, he often finds a way into them through his family's past. As he explained in the opening of his World War II book *1942,* "I was not born into a family of warriors, although practically every generation of it has served in one Ameri-

Winston Groom, author of *Forrest Gump*, in the study of his Point Clear
home. Photo by Mary Hattler, courtesy of the *Mobile Press-Register*.

can war or another, from the War of Independence and the War of 1812, to
the Creek Indian wars and the Civil War, to the Spanish-American War and
the First World War."

Over his desk is a *Forrest Gump* movie poster—Forrest sitting on a bench—
autographed by cast members. "Dear Mister Groom," reads one inscription, "I
can only thank you and hope you'll forgive my irregularities in this Forrest.

Very respectfully, Tom Hanks." "Mr. Groom," reads another, "thanks so much for Mama Gump!! Yours forever, Sally Field."

Then there are the cabinets filled with countless research books that Groom pores over for his histories. After publishing thousands of pages, he is an author who's still intent on mastering new topics.

And, leaning against the cabinets are the guns. Shotguns, he specifies.

Although, like Groom, I grew up in Mobile, went to the same high school, and also had a distinguished lawyer dad, I never toted a gun of any kind through woods or field. So I look to Groom, whose father raised him hunting, to tell me about the seven double-barreled shotguns leaning against his library shelves.

He lifts each and sights down the barrel, then, handing one to me, he explains they are all bird guns, though each has a different use—waterfowl, quail, pheasant, or skeet. "I'm not a collector, but I do like fine guns," he says, "especially old ones, since the craftsmanship was so much better then." Then he recounts their stories.

One is a 28-gauge Arietta, a Spanish gun made in the 1960s that he won in a lottery at his sporting clays club in Cashiers, North Carolina, where he and his family spend the hottest part of each summer in their cool mountain retreat. Another is a 12-gauge Guyot, a 1910 French gun that he got from a man who'd been in the American embassy in India and claimed it had belonged to the Maharaja of Jodhpur.

Then there is the 20-gauge L. C. Smith, a Crown Grade American sidelock built in 1926, with engravings of dog and quail scenes on the locks and extra fine checkering on the black walnut stock. His newest, an Italian Beretta 20-gauge, a versatile gun fashioned to make left-handed shooting easier, was acquired for Groom by the president of Beretta after he lost sight in his right eye. "He took pity on me," Groom says.

In a long row above the sofa are the framed dust jackets of his books. His mother-in-law, Wren, who doubles as his researcher, made the display starting with his first novel, *Better Times Than These*, which he wrote after serving in Vietnam as a lieutenant with the Army's 4th Infantry Division. During the war, while in combat, Groom took notes; when he returned stateside and took out his notebooks, they still had dirt, clay, and bits of blood on them. He says they helped jog his memory for the novel, which was inspired by James Jones' *The Thin Red Line*. Jones became his mentor and, soon, his close friend.

While living in East Hampton, Long Island, and New York City, Groom also became friends with, among other luminaries, Willie Morris, Joseph Heller, and Peter Matthiessen. "They showed me many kindnesses," he says.

I ask Groom if, after the violence of combat, he found it difficult, or even absurd, to wield a gun for sport. No, he says. He didn't go hunting until two years after returning from Vietnam, and one of his first forays was duck hunting in the Mobile River Delta. As he recounts the pleasures of that hunt, and others, seeking out duck, quail, and dove (he has just returned from a turkey hunt in piney south Alabama, though he jokes, "I generally don't like to hunt anything that gets up earlier than I do"), he talks of the delight of being in the woods, marsh, or open fields. He decries real estate development despoiling rivers and paving over fields, selling out nature's beauty for the quick buck.

But even more than the hunt, he says, "I enjoy the après-hunt. It's about camaraderie." Besides, he adds, "Hunters are great liars." At a hunting camp, storytelling becomes the stock-in-trade, and telling stories, is, after all, what Groom likes to do best.

The night is rainy, and as Groom and I head to his car to go out to dinner, we walk through his beautiful, spacious home—"the house that Gump built," he says, acknowledging how the novel and movie turned him from a hard-working, well-regarded author into a hard-working, well-regarded, and well-compensated one.

On the carport wall in front of Groom's car is a handwritten sign that says, "*Reserved Winston Groom (wrote some book). Will work for gumbo.*" Groom tells me it once designated his parking spot at the blessing of the shrimp boat fleet at Bayou La Batre. Several years ago he was grand marshal of the event in recognition of Bayou La Batre being, in *Forrest Gump*, the place where Bubba Gump Shrimp came into being, and afterward they gave him the sign.

Groom is lanky, with a somewhat formal bearing and flashes of dry wit. If you ask how tall he is, he says, "Five feet seventeen inches. Don't count on your fingers."

At The University of Alabama, where he had enrolled in ROTC knowing that the Vietnam draft was on, he was editor of the college humor magazine. He began his career, though, writing serious, dramatic novels, not only about Vietnam but also about the tangle of race relations, money, and old families in the Deep South, such as *As Summers Die*, which became a television movie with Scott Glenn, Jamie Lee Curtis, and Bette Davis. But the rollicking humor of Gump was waiting to surface, and the chance came.

His dad, Winston Groom Sr., sowed the seed for Gump when he told him a story about a mentally disabled boy in Mobile who was teased by other children, but who, as Groom recalls, learned to play the piano in three days. "Gorgeous music," he says. The character got his name by serendipity, when Groom, just home from Vietnam in 1967, was on the West coast, amidst the rising clamor against the war. He quickly discovered that walking into a San Francisco bar in his Army uniform was not a good way to meet girls, so he went out and bought a civilian suit at a big department store called Gumps, at the time the city's largest. The curious name stuck with him through the years and found its soul in Forrest.

Like Groom, Gump, too, would go to Vietnam, though Groom has written overtly about the war only on a few occasions, including his nonfiction book *Conversations With the Enemy*. Still, Groom admits, in terms of his understanding of warfare and how humans hold up under fear and pressure, there is a little bit of Vietnam in much of his work.

We arrive at Lakewood Restaurant, across the Grand Hotel's Robert Trent Jones Trail golf course. I order a vodka tonic, but Groom asks for a Virgin Mary, telling me he's cut back to an occasional beer. We talk about the tradition of writers and heavy booze—and writers destroyed by it. Although he has enjoyed his share of hard partying, at 64 and with a young child—his first—he has different goals. These days he enjoys working out at the health club, playing tennis with his daughter, and staying in shape. Too often, he laments, he picks up the *Mobile Press-Register* or the *New York Times* to find the obituary of a friend. He is determined to stay healthy, and to maintain what he calls "the same level of writing."

He continues to find a source of inspiration in the early models of his parents. His mother, Ruth Knudsen Groom, a high school teacher with a master's thesis on Shakespeare, died while Groom had his first job as a reporter at the former *Washington Star*. Looking back on it now, he says, her passing became a linchpin in his decision to leave the job and write his first book. How would she feel about his accomplishments now?

"I'm not a big church-goer," he says, "but I think she's seeing it."

Now this son of a teacher, a man who has spent much of his life educating himself on new topics—the structure of a novel, the history of America at war, how to shoot a shotgun left-handed—feels the responsibility to be a conscientious teacher to one beloved pupil of his own. At an age at which many men have young grandchildren, Groom is concerned about ensuring that his grammar-school-age daughter doesn't grow up any faster than she has to.

"But we don't want to hold her back, either," he says.

Although many of Carolina's classmates have seen the movie *Forrest Gump*, Groom has kept her from seeing it. He has worried about some of its violence and language. But she is curious.

This summer, he figures, will be the time for the two of them to sit down together and watch it.

Tommy Tarrants and Stan Chassin

DELIVER US FROM EVIL

Mobile

Walking slowly across the grounds of Murphy High School, Stan Chassin looks for the spot where "the most violent thing I'd dealt with in my life" happened. "Here's where it took place," he says, coming to a covered walkway by the auditorium. He touches his chest. "I can feel my heart racing again."

It was spring 1964, not long after the court-ordered desegregation of the all-white school. Law enforcement was present to keep order—Chassin remembers a sheriff's posse riding horses around the quadrangle—but Murphy had returned to relative calm.

Chassin's days were otherwise nothing out of the ordinary: classes, sandlot baseball, an after-school job, and youth group meetings at the synagogue where his grandfather had been rabbi.

Then one day on the way to the auditorium for an assembly, an older student named Tommy Tarrants approached. At six foot three, he towered over the five foot, six inch Chassin.

With thousands of students at the school, Chassin knew Tarrants only by reputation: "He was tall, gangly, violent. He was a hood."

"He did not know who I was," Chassin says, thinking back, "but what I was."

Tarrants passed closely and said: "Kike bastard."

"Hood bastard," Chassin returned.

Tommy Tarrants at the C. S. Lewis Institute in Springfield, Virginia, 2007.
Photo by Louise Krafft, courtesy of the *Mobile Press-Register*.

Newspaper headlines from the *Mobile Press-Register* detailing the criminal career of Tommy Tarrants. Photo by John David Mercer, courtesy of the *Mobile Press-Register*.

Stan Chasin on the grounds of Murphy High School, Mobile, Alabama, 2007. Photo by John David Mercer, courtesy of the *Mobile Press-Register.*

Tarrants grabbed Chassin by the throat and slammed him against a wall. "If I see you again, Jew bastard, I'll kill you!"

"He held me like this," Chassin says, leaning against that same wall and clutching his own throat, a 59-year-old man hurtled back in time. "I was shaking."

Chassin did not report the confrontation to school officials, but it was all the talk among students. "You're sixteen, seventeen, you try to be tough."

The next day, Chassin was in English class when the principal, R. B. Taylor, summoned him. "Stay away from Tommy Tarrants," the principal told Chassin. "He's dangerous. He could kill you."

Chassin stayed away, but Tarrants cast a shadow.

It was around that time that a swastika was painted on Chassin's synagogue, and hate calls were placed to the two rabbis in Mobile and to black civil rights leaders in the area. Tarrants, it was later discovered, was the perpetrator.

That summer, Tarrants was pulled over by Mobile police late one night while driving through a black neighborhood with a sawed-off shotgun. He was convicted of a federal firearms violation and placed on probation until his twenty-first birthday.

But Tarrants was not to be stopped. In 1967, he was picked up in a stolen car in Mississippi with a .45-caliber submachine gun—and in the company of Sam Bowers, leader of the White Knights of the Ku Klux Klan.

Tarrants returned to Mobile on bond, but soon dropped out of sight. In the spring of 1968, Tarrants returned to his house in Mobile one afternoon to find FBI agents waiting. A car chase ensued. Tarrants got away, and fled on to Mississippi. Chassin, by then a student at the University of South Alabama, followed the news.

On July 1, 1968, Chassin picked up the *Press-Register* to see a shocking story datelined Meridian, Mississippi: "Mobile machine gunner is shot, woman companion dies in firing: Thomas Tarrants and 2 others critical in Meridian hospital," shouted the headline.

The story explained, "A commando squad of policemen, defending the home of a prominent Jewish businessman, sprang a trap on suspected nightriders early Sunday, wounding a young Alabama man and killing his woman companion."

Being chased by police, according to the article, Tarrants fired a 9mm submachine gun, wounding one officer. Tarrants, in turn, was shot in the arm, leg, and abdomen.

Police found a notebook in Tarrants' pocket that vowed: "Gentlemen: I have committed myself to totally defeating the Communist-Jew conspiracy which threatens our country—any means necessary shall be used."

Chassin remembers what he felt at the time: "I hope the son of a bitch dies."

As a Jew in Alabama, with its predominantly Christian culture, Chassin says he grew up feeling different—"in school you were known as the Jewish child"—but he had never encountered harsh anti-Semitism, until Tarrants.

He describes his boyhood as "pleasant," and liked Mobile so much that he stayed put. He married, raised two daughters, and kept on as a member of Ahavas Chesed, Mobile's conservative Jewish congregation.

His confrontation with Tarrants had been an isolated case, but it continued to shake him. "I saw the evil, the hate, in his eyes."

Tarrants was sentenced to thirty years in Mississippi's Parchman penitentiary, a prison farm surrounded by a high fence and barbed wire. He was convicted, the news accounts said, of attempted bombing, referring to the twenty-nine sticks of dynamite he had intended to leave at the home of Jewish businessman Meyer Davidson.

On July 24, 1969, while doing a work stint in the prison hospital, Tarrants escaped from Parchman with two other inmates.

Two days later, the three were ambushed one hundred miles away by the FBI, and one of them was shot dead. The inmates had in their possession five hand grenades, two rifles, two pistols, and a bayonet.

Tarrants was hauled back and put in solitary confinement.

In the late 1970s, Tarrants' name came up again, this time in the most improbable way. Experiencing what he would later describe as a powerful religious conversion, Tarrants became, or so it was said, a changed man.

He had started reading Greek philosophy, immersed himself in scripture and soon gained the support of both a black inmate and a prominent lawyer in Mississippi—who was Jewish—in getting early parole.

After eight years at Parchman, Tarrants was released, went on to the University of Mississippi, took courses, and in 1979 published a book: *The Conversion of a Klansman: The Story of a Former Ku Klux Klan Terrorist*. In Mobile, Chassin felt doubtful, he says, of what he heard about the new Tarrants.

Tarrants moved to Washington, D.C., became a minister, and ultimately president of the C. S. Lewis Institute. In his capacity with the institute, Tarrants was invited to Mobile to speak at Spring Hill Presbyterian Church.

A friend of Chassin's, Erk Ashbee, knew of Chassin's history with Tarrants and got him interested in attending the event.

"A flood of impressions of Tommy Tarrants came back to me," Chassin says. "I began to think about it in an aggressive manner, my feeling of watching his career."

Chassin was in the synagogue on Yom Kippur, the Day of Atonement, fasting and praying when "Tarrants' name came up in my mind."

That High Holy Day, Chassin says he heard a voice trying to speak to him. Chassin believes the voice was God's.

The voice told him, "I want you to perform a mitzvah," Hebrew for "good deed." The voice went on, "I want you to forgive Tommy Tarrants for what he did to you, and I want you to ask Tommy Tarrants to forgive you for hating him all these years.'"

Still, Chassin was uncertain.

❇

Washington, D.C.

Soft-spoken, humble of manner, Thomas A. Tarrants III leans back in his office chair in suburban Washington, D.C., surrounded by books on religion and philosophy, and looks down at a newspaper headline from November 28, 1968: "Tarrants Found Guilty, Sentenced to 30 Years."

The 60-year old sees a mugshot of himself at age 21 next to the story: "A self-styled guerrilla waging a 'holy crusade' against a 'Communist-Jewish conspiracy' was convicted Wednesday night of the attempted bombing of the home of a Jewish businessman."

He is silent a long time. "I feel shame and disgust. You can see what a head case I was."

Today, he is president of the C. S. Lewis Institute, a nondenominational organization with the motto "Discipleship of heart and mind." His life is a stark contrast to the violent bigotry of his youth.

He explains that his work includes mentoring the C. S. Lewis Fellows, men and women who come to the institute to deepen their understanding of spiritual matters.

In his initial lecture to the fellows, he says, he uses his own trials as "an example of the life-changing power of God's grace." He tells them about his boyhood in Mobile, the sin of hatred that consumed him, and his salvation in a jail cell.

His listeners must surely find it hard to envision him as a kid raising his hand to grab the throat of a Jewish classmate or a gun to blast into homes of black families.

"I was filled with rage," Tarrants says.

In his 1979 memoir, *The Conversion of a Klansman,* Tarrants sketched out his slide toward vehement hatred of Jews and black people.

While he was aware of Jewish people in Mobile—he describes a grammar-school crush on a Jewish girl and says his grandmother worked for a jewelry store owned by Jews—he knew nothing of Jews personally, nor the tenets of their religion.

As a teen he became a loner, he says, alienated from his family—"I hated my father"—and was adrift. He relished firearms and bought a handgun, a sawed-off shotgun, and a machine gun with money from after-school jobs, and stored them in his bedroom.

In recent years, he says, when seeing stories of alienated kids who explode, such as the massacres at Columbine and Virginia Tech, he glimpses something of his own youth. "I was a problem waiting to happen."

It was the anti-Red fervor of the 1950s and 1960s, and a conviction that the Jews were behind an international communist conspiracy, that focused Tarrants' rage.

He devoured propaganda literature about an alleged Jewish plot to control the world, such as *The Protocols of the Learned Elders of Zion*. He listened to tapes by Wesley Swift, a Klan expositor who gave rise to the neo-Nazi Aryan Nation.

He eventually linked up with a racist political outfit named the National States Rights Party. "A lot of our meetings took place in cars, walking, talking. There was a great paranoia about tapping of the phone," he says.

Spurred on by those connections, he says, he set out on several drives through Mobile's black neighborhoods, shooting into people's homes. "Our hope and dream was that a race war would come," he says.

He hung out with members of a secret paramilitary troop, the Minutemen. He became versed in guerrilla warfare.

"I thought I was a Christian fighting against the communist-Jewish conspiracy," he says sadly. "It was a noble thing. I was doing it for God and country."

In the fall of 1963, the integration of Murphy High School proved to Tarrants that his world was being turned upside down.

He agitated at the school for resistance. Then, when not enough resistance came, he angrily called the office of Governor George Wallace and left a message asking for intervention. A response came from the FBI, which called his home looking for him.

He was convinced, at the time, that his home telephone had been tapped. He was suspended from Murphy for ten days.

"'The Jews were behind it.' The message sells in times of social upheaval," he says, thinking back.

By 1967, Tarrants was arranging meetings in Tuscaloosa with Robert Shelton, imperial wizard of the United Klans of America. Tarrants also headed to Mississippi and met with the imperial wizard of the White Knights of the Ku Klux Klan, Sam Bowers, and joined up with him.

An application for the White Knights of the Ku Klux Klan stated, in part: "We do not accept Jews, because they reject Christ, and, through the machinations of their International Banking Cartel, are at the root center of what we call Communism today.

"We do not accept Papists, because they bow to a Roman dictator. . . . We do not accept Turks, Mongols, Tarters, Orientals, Negroes, nor any other person whose native background or culture is foreign to the Anglo-Saxon system of government by responsible, free individual citizens."

He had been grievously misdirected, he says now.

Even in the midst of committing violent crimes, he says, he felt certain that he would go to heaven. "I went about feeling like I had had my ticket punched," he says. "I had made a profession of faith. But I had no change of heart, of life."

He was unbowed in that arrogance, even after being convicted in 1968 of the attempted bombing of the home of Meyer Davidson, a Jewish man in Meridian, Mississippi.

Placed in solitary confinement at Mississippi's Parchman penitentiary following a brief escape, Tarrants began to plumb his soul.

It was in a six-by-nine-foot jail cell—"reading was the only thing that kept me from going crazy . . . cra-zi-er"—that he began to reflect on the meaning of his life. He took to heart the words of Socrates: "The unexamined life is not worth living."

He embraced Matthew 16:26: "For what is a man profited, if he shall gain the whole world, and lose his own soul?" He says, "I fell on my knees and prayed and felt a thousand-pound weight lifted from me."

Thus began what he describes as "a startling transformation."

Others came to believe that Tarrants was a changed man and spoke on his behalf, including Al Binder, a Mississippi lawyer who was Jewish and influential in political circles. In December 1976, Tarrants got out of Parchman on a work-release program that enabled him to enroll at the University of Mississippi. Three years later, he published his memoir.

Knowing that the Klan would call him a traitor and possibly try to harm him, Tarrants moved to Washington, D.C. He completed a master's degree in divinity and a doctorate in ministry, and became a clergyman and spiritual counselor.

When he looks back over his life, he realizes that he had close calls along the way. "In every one of these situations, I deserved more than the other person to be the one who died, but I was spared," he says.

In his memoir he wrote: "By God's grace I was protected, despite my vile behavior. It was a miracle. . . . Truly the living Christ was active to redeem me and work out his plan for my life."

That plan, Tarrants explains, includes his dedication to help people reconcile their differences: race, religion, differences of the heart.

He would find himself facing the need for a reconciliation of his own.

Mobile

It was the week before Thanksgiving, and Stan Chassin had been nervous all day.

Tarrants was to be the guest speaker at a dinner at Spring Hill Presbyterian Church.

"My father always taught me to confront my fears," Chassin says. "I had a chance to unload my demons. But the closer I got to that day, I wondered, 'Do I have the internal fortitude to go through with this?'"

He drove alone to the church and entered the Fellowship Hall. When he walked into the room and saw Tarrants, he had a flashback to high school. "I thought, he's not so big, I could have taken him!"

Tall and slightly stooped, Tarrants had no hint about him of the long-ago teenager's swagger or ranting anger.

As Tarrants was introduced by the Reverend Norman H. McCrummen III, Tarrants seemed to Chassin "almost frail."

Tarrants began by speaking of his pleasure at visiting his hometown and noted a task he had accomplished this trip—buying a cemetery plot for himself.

He did not say so during his speech, but Tarrants bought the plot next to his late father's grave. He had a difficult relationship with his dad while growing up, even hated him. But the father and son had made peace at the end, and there had been forgiveness between them.

With his gently modulated voice, and touches of a dinner speaker's humor,

Tarrants spoke of his mission at the C. S. Lewis Institute and the importance of faith.

Tarrants told of his slide toward militant bigotry, how he learned to despise blacks and loathe Jews. He talked about sin as "a cancer" that had come into his body and heart.

He told of being in a prison cell, of reading classical philosophy and scripture, of a profound change in his heart as he came to understand the true meaning of God in his life. He spoke of grace, of forgiveness.

In the audience, Chassin listened and watched.

Now he believed that what God had asked of him on that Day of Atonement was to be fulfilled.

Tarrants finished his speech. He asked for questions.

Chassin hesitated. Then he stood. "It's hard facing you," he told Tarrants.

Chassin began to recount his story of when Tarrants had grabbed him by the throat and threatened him.

His voice got stronger; he grew calmer. As he spoke, he saw a look of pain on Tarrants' face.

Chassin told Tarrants that he had been in synagogue on Yom Kippur—"praying very hard"—when he heard God speak to him.

"God told me," Chassin said, "'You have to forgive him for what he did to you. And then, for all the hatred and disgust you felt toward him, you have to ask Tommy,'" Chassin's voice was breaking now, "'to forgive you.'"

The Fellowship Hall fell silent.

Quietly, Tarrants answered: "I appreciate you being so gracious and forgiving. I'm very grateful, Stan, for your having the courage to come and share your forgiveness."

Tarrants addressed the audience: "Isn't it amazing," he went on softly, "what God can do? God spoke to him."

Chassin walked forward and held out his hand to shake. The two men embraced. Chassin was weeping.

Tarrants, who had never had anyone approach him from his past like this, felt anguished to know of the pain he had inflicted on Chassin all these years. He wondered who else from his past might still be carrying old wounds, whom else he must still reconcile with.

McCrummen came back to the podium, crying, and said he had just witnessed an extraordinary event, that God's mercy and the presence of his intervention had been made evident.

"In the fullness of your love, you give us a heart and a mind, to recognize this," McCrummen prayed. "Thank you for seeing us and hearing us and not giving up on us."

Samford Turner, executive presbyter of south Alabama, who was in attendance, wrote up a long letter recording what had transpired and e-mailed it to local pastors, who forwarded it throughout the community.

In coming days, Chassin was approached by numerous friends, even relative strangers, who told him that in reading of the event, they had started crying.

Chassin says his life has been changed.

Tarrants says that this event "raises questions that may lead to a new phase" in his own life, "a new journey." What more can he do, Tarrants wonders, to combat racism and anti-Semitism? "Where will this lead me?" he wonders of the reunion with Chassin.

It is several weeks later that Chassin returns to their old high school, Murphy, to walk the grounds and remember the violent encounter "that joined our lives."

Chassin has the feeling, he says, that he has "entered a new phase of my life."

He talks, too, of reconciliation, of God's presence, of moving ahead into the future.

Then he turns a corner on an alley of the school, near Carlen House Museum, and on a wall is spray-painted a swastika. Under it is written: "DIE."

For a moment, Chassin is taken aback. "It makes me so sad," he says.

Then he realizes what lies ahead for him. His mission now, like that of Tarrants, is to further education about hatred, about forgiveness.

"The ignorance," he says, "never goes away."

PART IV WITNESSES TO THE MOVEMENT

You could fill whole libraries with the literature of the civil rights movement—memoirs written by participants, works of journalism and art inspired by the heroic efforts of participants, documents of the tumultuous era. Indeed, one of the through-lines of this collection is the shaping influence of the movement, and of black-white relations, in a changing South.

Many of the people I've profiled are old enough to have experienced the movement in some way. Born in 1953, I have an Alabama memory that my daughter, born in 1987, never will—"colored" and "white" designations for public restrooms and water fountains. Those artifacts of history are just two of the myriad outward expressions of a culture divided within itself, and at war with itself. How did we get through that time of conflict and anguish? How did we, to quote civil rights activist Fannie Lou Hamer, "keep on keeping on?"

I don't pretend to offer definitive answers—Diane McWhorter, Sena Jeter Naslund, Frye Gaillard, and Howell Raines are among the authors profiled in this collection who have deeply explored the topic—but I do keep asking the questions. In this section, those who ponder the questions were involved with the movement in a deeply personal way.

Neil Davis was editor of the Lee County Gazette in Auburn during the height of the struggle. With Davis I used one of my favorite interview styles—taking a drive. While I'm at the wheel asking questions, my subject holds the tape recorder, answering, reminiscing, and philosophizing as meaningful locales roll by. Through Alabama's political past, and down its highways, from Auburn to Tuskegee, Davis tells his stories.

Johnnie Carr, 89 when I interviewed her, was a direct link back to the era of the Montgomery bus boycott. Vivian Malone and James Hood re-created, through their points of view, that day when they arrived at The University of

Alabama in Tuscaloosa, and Governor George Wallace was making his infamous "stand at the schoolhouse door."

A different perspective on Governor Wallace comes from Wallace's son, George Wallace Jr., with whom I visited only a year after Governor Wallace's passing. Wallace Jr.'s story offered me an intimate, family perspective on a man controversial to the world.

In the course of my journalism career in Alabama, I've walked Edmund Pettus Bridge on an anniversary of the Selma to Montgomery march, following behind Reverend Jesse Jackson, Reverend Joseph Lowery, and Congressman John Lewis. I went to Marion on the day that Coretta Scott King died to interview people in her hometown, and talked to friends and relatives of Rosa Parks for a story about her after she passed. When Reverend Fred Shuttlesworth came to give a talk in Mobile, I ambled with him through his old neighborhood. But these titans of the civil rights movement have had volumes written about them, or written their own monumental books. The figures in this section have not had quite so much exposure on the page.

Theresa Burroughs, for example, is a beautician who once gave refuge to Dr. King in Greensboro, and later opened up a small museum dedicated to the era on a back street of town. Burroughs' story reminds us how many people, in individual ways, were impacted by the movement; how many stories of regular folks, in each community in Alabama, are yet to be told.

Neil Davis

A few years before he passed away in 2000, I spent a memorable two days with Neil Davis, exploring the home region he loved and believed in passionately, despite all.

Auburn

L ate one night in the early 1950s, the telephone jangled in the home of Neil Davis, owner and editor of the *Lee County Bulletin.*

"Davis?"

"Speaking."

"Is it true you're a pinko, nigger-lover?"

Last time, Davis had hung up the phone. Now, he answered: "Yeah."

The receiver on the other end clicked down, but Davis had recognized the voice.

Next morning, with the steeliness and civility he maintains still at age 82, Davis went to pay a visit.

"He was in business downtown," Davis recalls. "I told the man, 'I feel sorry for you and the way you let your family down. I knew some of your antecedents. Good, decent, upstanding people. They would have been so embarrassed if they'd heard what you said last night.'"

Davis shakes his head, chuckling. "Boy, did it get away with him!"

Bald, bespectacled, injured from a recent fall, Neil Davis, publisher of the *Lee County Bulletin* (later the *Auburn Bulletin*) from 1937 to 1975, looks back

Neil Davis in March 1997. Photo by William T. Martin.

on countless enemies. With courtly manner, and brutal pen that reached far beyond Alabama, he often got their goat.

"Back in the thirties and forties, if you were liberal that wasn't the currency of the day. It was 'pinko.' And now they mean pretty much the same thing when they say liberal. It didn't take much to be a liberal in those days. If you just believed in a modicum of civil rights, justice, and equality of opportunity, then, in today's jargon, you were a liberal."

A 1935 Auburn graduate, he went to Harvard University in 1941 on a Nieman fellowship, a prestigious grant that allows working journalists to further their studies for a year. It was rare for the editor of a weekly to receive this honor.

Rather than continue on to the glamour of a big-city paper, Davis decided to deepen his commitment at home. In his Nieman class was Harry Ashmore, who returned to the South, too, to edit the *Arkansas Gazette* during the Little Rock school crisis of 1958.

As a white liberal, Davis daily confronted the fact that old ways die hard. With gentlemanly grit he worked to change these ways. George Wallace's administration, Davis says, "had a black-list of their opponents. I was told my name was on it, and the name of the then *Lee County Bulletin.*"

But Davis' editorial opinions in the small-circulation Bulletin, reprinted for legions in the *New York Times,* the *Washington Post,* and the *St. Louis Post-Dispatch,* joined the often-isolated voices of other liberal southerners and coursed through a turbulent nation.

Governor Patterson might as well stop pretending to be shocked. So had some of our newspapers. They piously have talked of preserving the law while simultaneously they have assumed a most provocative position. When public officials and papers use inflammatory language, urge last-ditch stands and fighting every inch of the way, what do they expect?
—Neil Davis, 1961, commenting in the *Lee County Bulletin* on racial violence in Montgomery, reprinted by the *Washington Post*

German shepherds, fire hoses, billy sticks, the images of civil rights confrontations in Alabama, violent and graphic, are burned into America's consciousness.

But there are other images, of hard-working men and women bearing not guns, but ballpoint pens; of editors churning out papers deeply engaged in local issues. These issues took on epic dimensions when the subject was voting rights, or Klan activity, or Governor George Wallace, or the Reverend Martin Luther King Jr.

But weekly papers like Davis' were far more than broadsides. As he sits with a visitor and leafs through yellowing pages of fifty-year-old *Bulletins,* a chronicle unfolds: church suppers, school pageants, Little League baseball games.

Writing community news was Henrietta Worsley Davis, Neil's wife. Neil and Henrietta had met as college journalists at the *Auburn Plainsman,* the university's student newspaper. They went to work together at a Georgia weekly until the publisher directed Neil to endorse the U.S. Senate candidacy of Eugene Talmadge. "Talmadge," Davis explains, "was the devil incarnate in the eyes of people interested at all in racial justice." It was time to move on.

Even a progressive boss, though, might not have suited Davis' spirit. "I didn't want to be working for somebody who said, 'This is the stance we'll take,' and I was supposed to stand and salute and click my heels together."

Neil and Henrietta married, returned to Auburn, and founded the *Bulletin,* nurturing the newspaper and rearing three children. Davis even toyed with personally jumping into politics, but knew the publisher's chair was the best bully pulpit.

"Besides," he explains, "contemplating a run for office was incompatible with being an honest writer of editorials. It made me too temperate."

In 1987 Neil lost his wife, and lifelong colleague, who had endured cancer.

In the view of Jerry Brown of the Auburn journalism department, the kitchen-table appeal of Henrietta's articles on schools, and other local doings, was part of what made the *Bulletin* a must-read for Auburnites. Neil's editorials might have rankled some townspeople, but readers lined up on Thursday for the paper chock full of news about people down the block.

An angry mayor, in the 1950s, ceremoniously canceled his subscription to the paper, but was later seen slipping to the newsstand to buy a copy.

Even the *Bulletin,* though, reflected an era of deep racial segregation. During the 1930s, news about Lee County's black residents was confined to the column "Colored People."

As a liberal editorialist, Davis took heart from other writers around the state, many of whom had cut their teeth at the *Plainsman* or *The Crimson White* over at The University of Alabama.

He found kindred spirits in Grover Hall Sr. of the *Montgomery Advertiser;* Charles Dobbins, who founded the *Anniston Times* and went on to the *Advertiser;* and Gould Beech of the *Southern Farmer.*

Carrol Kilpatrick became White House correspondent for the *Washington*

Post and kept close contact with Davis. Kilpatrick had been editor-in-chief at the *Crimson White* the same year Davis had headed up the *Plainsman*.

Make sure . . . that these promises are not merely bait to catch suckers.
—Neil Davis, 1938, on politicians who guarantee tax cuts while promising improvements in education, roads, and health

On the wall of Neil Davis' study is the inaugural address of President John F. Kennedy with a personal inscription. The *Bulletin,* Davis says, was one of only four newspapers in Alabama that had endorsed Kennedy.

Alongside it are portraits of other of Davis' heroes, men who were also his readers, men like Hugo Black and Alabama senators John Sparkman and Lister Hill. "To Neil Davis," reads the Hill inscription, "friend and comrade in 'the Cause.'" "The Cause" was Hill's term for the New Deal.

In the Deep South, Davis explains, it was not always easy for politicians, or journalists, to communicate their concerns about racial equality. In order to be persuasive, they first had to survive. Davis explains the dilemma for Hill and Sparkman. Committed to progressive agendas, they would vote for bills that relieved the plight of poor Alabamians, black and white. At the same time, in order to assure reelection, they wouldn't touch civil rights. He recalls Hill's convening young business professionals in Alabama to enlist support for "the Cause." At that meeting, some men complained to Hill that he and Sparkman could be counted on by the Dixiecrats to vote against civil rights bills. Why, they wanted to know, wouldn't the senators dare vote the other way?

"Hill's reply was, 'It would be easy for me to do that. The result would be that I might as well just resign, because the next election I'd be defeated. What you have to choose between is whether I do what you think I ought to do, or whether I go along with this awful business and get reelected and continue to fight for federal aid to education, health care, hospitals.'"

Davis says that his longtime friend, the late Ralph McGill, editor of the *Atlanta Constitution,* was caught in much the same quandary as the politicians. It was not until the last years of McGill's life that "he shook off all restraints.

"McGill was like most liberals of the day who were homegrown and had a feel for the situation. He was criticized by some liberals for not being bolder on the discussion of racial matters. But he was like most of the liberal members of the Congress and state legislatures down this way. You didn't talk about liberating the Negro. You didn't face the issue head on, so much as you talked about education.

"We would never work ourselves out of the doldrums of the economic and social policy of our state, our region, until we made educational opportunities available to the entire population."

Voting rights was another explosive issue. One battleground was the poll tax, $1.50 per year to cast your ballot.

"The idea was, 'Don't corrupt the process by letting all this so-called riff-raff vote. As long as it's in the hands of us privileged class, good, God-fearing, church-going people who pay their bills and don't run around on their wives these are the chosen; chosen by God.'

"On my paper, we probably drove people crazy talking about the abolition of the poll tax. If you couldn't abolish it, at least get rid of the accumulated feature of it. If you didn't vote for four years, then you owed six dollars. Poor people didn't have six dollars!"

If we're to spend $150,000 as a memorial to wearers of the gray, why not put it into scholarships in the field of Alabama and Southern history?
—Neil Davis, 1949, editorializing on expenses for a Confederate monument in Vicksburg, Mississippi

In his family's white-frame Presbyterian church in Hartford, Alabama, down near Dothan, Neil Davis, as a boy, read the words on a wall: "God is love."

These words, he says, "are imprinted on my psyche."

Taking a long drive with his visitor through Auburn, and on to Tuskegee about twenty miles away, Davis reflects on the role of religion in his own life, and that of the civil rights movement.

Active in his Presbyterian church's effort to provide housing for the poor, Davis explains how religion, to some people, justified segregation: "They'd say, 'If God meant us all to be the same, he'd have made us all white.'"

He relishes the memory of that Sunday when the Reverend John H. Leith stood before his Auburn congregation. A White Citizens Council chapter had formed in town a few days before.

"In the long prayer after the sermon, he asked for forgiveness of people of prejudice no matter what they were based on and then he said, 'Heaven help us when a lot of us get to heaven, and see all those black faces.'"

Davis laughs uproariously. "I thought that was just colossal! How are you going to argue with somebody who puts the message in prayer?" He wonders if George Wallace, in his changed stance on racial issues, has spiritual concerns in mind. Davis speculates: "He's thinking about going to the front gate in Heaven and St. Peter recognizing him and not letting him in."

In past years, the former governor, defeated and worn, has made personal overtures to Davis. Once, Wallace called Davis at home and ended up chatting with Henrietta for a half-hour. "I forgive Wallace," Davis says, "but I can't forget.

"He could have said, 'I'm opposed to desegregation.' He didn't have to defy it. He didn't have to stand in the schoolhouse door. He didn't have to threaten to call out the National Guard, and even after that happened he kept the thing fanned to such a fever pitch . . .

"I've watched Wallace go through this process of trying to make amends. He got a big black vote last time he ran. Who knows? He might have had a change of heart, but I still see him as the opportunist. He did some dreadful things, and we're still paying for it."

He looks out at the passing landscape, the run-down houses, and scrappy yards as Lee County changes to Macon County. "Still paying for it."

Sanitary conditions in the colored community are deplorable . . . hardly any colored housing is served by sewerage systems . . . a majority of families have to depend on shallow wells, many of them near open privies.
—Neil Davis, 1949, commenting on neighborhoods unfamiliar to his white readers

Besides the *Lee County Bulletin,* Davis was publisher of the *Tuskegee News* from 1963 to 1975. As his visitor drives him by the courthouse and square, then out by vast, crumbling homes, like antebellum dinosaurs, Davis looks back on this place, too.

Before Davis came to town as publisher, the newspaper had offered little news of black residents, despite Tuskegee's being home to one of the premier, historically black universities in the nation. "We waited until about three months of publication before we ran a major story that involved a black, and ran the story on the front page and his picture with it."

Davis gazes at the verandah and rocking chairs of Booker T. Washington's home; at a banner, hung near the Lincoln Gates, printed with Washington's creed of self-reliance: "Cast Down Your Bucket."

He recalls two Tuskegee Institute professors in the early 1960s who were refused the right to vote by white registrars, even after being made to answer complex questions about the U.S. Constitution. He recalls the day, as publisher of the *Tuskegee News,* that the story about the syphilis experiments on black male patients broke.

"Good gracious alive. The leap from the 1930s to the mid-1960s, '70s," he says, sighing with amazement. "Unless I make a point to recall those days, I just don't deal with it."

Out on the roadside, he spots the sign, "Tuskegee Senior Citizens Program."

"I don't know what's going to happen to all these programs," he frets, "as Congress gets on this balance-the-budget binge and starts cutting out things. We haven't gone too far with federal programs, we haven't gone far enough! In jobs, in education, in child care, in transportation."

With the road back to Auburn winding through the early afternoon, Neil Davis talks like a man starting a journey, rather than concluding one. Still courtly, and tough, he challenges: "When you talk about humane, you're talking about human beings, aren't you? I don't know anybody who wouldn't like you to be able to say to them, 'You're humane.' But when it gets over into human beings, it's a mystery how people don't always go from one thing to another."

Vivian Malone and James Hood

THE STAND IN THE SCHOOLHOUSE DOOR

In 2003, I contacted by phone Vivian Malone and James Hood prior to the fortieth anniversary of their enrolling in The University of Alabama. The occasion seemed right to turn back the clock, to capture their remarkable memories. Two years after these conversations, Vivian Malone passed away at age 63.

On a sweltering day forty years ago this week, Vivian Malone of Mobile and James Hood of Gadsden set out to enroll for classes at The University of Alabama at Tuscaloosa. With U.S. attorney general Robert Kennedy orchestrating the event from Washington under the watch of President John F. Kennedy, and with Alabama governor George Wallace blocking the students' way, the registration assumed an epic scale, a confrontation between federal and state governments, a standoff between a chief executive with a civil rights agenda and a state leader defiant of one.

Malone and Hood, both 20-year-old black students at the door of an all-white university, had stepped, jarringly, into history.

Vivian Malone Jones these many years later says she had anticipated, sadly, what might occur that morning but hoped her home state could do better.

She knew of the racial antagonism that Charlayne Hunter and Hamilton Holmes had been met with on January 9, 1961, when they enrolled at the University of Georgia in Athens. The following year, on September 30, James Meredith's matriculation at Ole Miss in Oxford, Mississippi, had been the catalyst for riots, tear gas, and gunfire.

"I figured by the time Alabama integrates, everybody else has done it," Malone says from her Atlanta home, her warm, reflective voice summoning yes-

Vivian Malone, one of the first African Americans to attend The University of Alabama, walks through a crowd that includes photographers, National Guard members, and deputy U.S. attorney general Nicholas Katzenbach. Photo by Warren K. Leffler, courtesy of the Library of Congress.

teryear as though it were today. "Surely, Alabama won't raise up the flag of hatred or denial. That's when the governor came in with his stand on 'segregation now and forever.' I knew we weren't going to be in for a smooth transition."

She spent the night of June 10, 1963, with family friends in Birmingham—Hood stayed in another home—and the two linked up to ride in a government car to Tuscaloosa, accompanied by Assistant Attorney General Nicholas Katzenbach and John Doar of the Department of Justice. The car was hardly alone. "We had a caravan," she says.

Along the way, the cars came to a halt, and she remembers officers communicating by two-way radio with the White House. "They didn't have sophisticated communications like they do now. We had to make sure the presidential proclamation was being delivered," Malone says, referring to the "cease and desist" order being signed in Washington by Secretary of State Dean Rusk. Katzenbach would give a copy of that order to Wallace.

When they arrived at the Tuscaloosa campus, Malone was startled by the presence of armed guards on the front lawn. "And I had never been around that much press before—cameras everywhere."

What happened next was broadcast throughout the country and seared into the national consciousness. Katzenbach got out of the car and approached Wallace and offered the presidential proclamation, demanding admission for the students according to court order. Wallace, stalwart in front of the doors of the university's Foster Auditorium, refused.

Malone watched the proceedings from the car.

Looking around at the sea of officials, Malone remembers thinking: "It is such a shame that the government has to spend this kind of money for these two little black students to go to school!"

She adds, though, "I wasn't the reason the money was being spent. I really did have a right to be there. I was not imposing on anybody."

Her religious upbringing helped sustain her, the lessons of faith she learned growing up in the Emanuel AME Church in downtown Mobile, she says. "I attended that church from age six until I moved away. I still consider myself a member."

The support of her parents in Mobile, Willie and Bertha Malone, both now deceased, also gave her heart. "Now that I look back, they were amazingly strong. They were right there the whole way. They never wavered in the least."

In the car, with the tension building in front of Foster Auditorium, she felt becalmed. "I wasn't afraid at that point. I was praying. I was thankful I was being allowed this opportunity."

That was a watershed year in American history, especially for the civil rights movement.

"In the annals of civil rights history, the 'Stand in the Schoolhouse Door' is a close fourth after Alabama's Montgomery-Birmingham-Selma trifecta," says Pulitzer Prize–winning journalist Diane McWhorter. "Although it did not keep African Americans out of the university, it did launch George Wallace's national political career—which demonstrated that the South's race problem was a national one."

To talk with Vivian Malone and James Hood today is to converse with two of the ordinary citizens of 1963 who not only stepped into history but were forever shaped by it.

While Kennedy and Wallace were powerful elected officials, Malone and Hood were only college kids—transfer students, respectively, from Alabama A&M in Huntsville and Clark College in Atlanta.

"I grew a lot," Malone reflects. "I had the experience of living in and around people who didn't want me to be there. I learned to live with that and come out a whole person."

Malone went on to graduate from The University of Alabama in 1965 and worked for the federal government in positions such as employee relations and personnel specialist with the Veterans Administration; most recently she has worked for a life insurance company in Atlanta.

Hood left UA after the summer of 1963, returning in 1995 to complete a doctorate in interdisciplinary studies. A resident of Wisconsin, he retired as dean of the protective services program at Madison Area Technical College.

Hood despairs that a younger generation does not always take measure of the challenges and triumphs of the past.

"Not even today do they understand what I went through," Hood says of his five grown children. "Their world was totally different. When I try to explain the differences they say, 'Dad, nothing could have been like that.'"

Hood's own recollections of June 11, 1963, are vivid.

"I looked up and saw military people on top of buildings with guns. Ah! We had been told it would happen, but just seeing it! The president had told us things would be OK. I didn't question it. I didn't challenge it.

"Our instructions were to sit in the car until Nick (Katzenbach) went up, heard what the governor had to say. The governor was supposed to step aside. Then Nick was supposed to come back and get us. The walkway was lined with reporters, U.S. marshals, military people."

When Wallace did not relent, Katzenbach returned to the car. "Nick said we'd go to Plan B," Hood remembers.

"Plan B," Hood explains, meant that Malone and Hood would go to their dormitories, then wait for the head of the Alabama National Guard, Gen. Henry Graham, to receive orders to federalize and fulfill his military duty.

As E. Culpepper Clark writes in his searching and dramatic *The School-*

house Door: Segregation's Last Stand at the University of Alabama: "At 3:30, General Graham, in combat fatigues with the Confederate battle flag of the 31st Dixie Division stitched on his breast pocket, came forward and saluted the governor. Snappily, Wallace returned the salute. Graham then said, 'It is my sad duty to ask you to step aside, on order of the president of the United States.'"

Clark, a former dean of The University of Alabama's College of Communications and Information Sciences, continues in his book that Wallace begrudgingly complied, but proclaimed, "'Alabama is winning this fight against federal interference because we are awakening the people to the trend toward military dictatorship in this country. I am returning to Montgomery to continue working for constitutional government to benefit all Alabamians—black and white.' With that, Wallace and his entourage walked quickly toward waiting patrol cars . . . As the governor's motorcade pulled away, Wallace kept repeating a warm 'Come back to see us in Alabama' to a bank of reporters."

Hood recalls how he and Malone were directed to return to Foster Auditorium, then fill out their registration forms. By then it was close to dinner time.

"I walked into the cafeteria," Hood says, "and one whole area was isolated. I sat at that table alone."

The University of Alabama avoided the physical violence that had erupted at Ole Miss. In part, according to John L. Blackburn, the university's dean of men in 1963, that relatively calm transition was due to advance planning. Frank Rose was the university's president.

Blackburn says he had arrived at Tuscaloosa in the summer of 1956 after the unhappy experiences of Autherine Lucy, the first black student to enroll. According to Clark's book, Lucy had been met with an angry mob screaming taunts. She left after only three days.

As the summer of 1963 approached, Blackburn and other campus officials met with student leaders to discuss possible scenarios in response to the Malone and Hood registrations.

"I told the students," Blackburn recalls, "we were not going to have an Ole Miss.

"Everybody had worked on the scenario of how it would happen, but nobody was sure what George Wallace was going to do, and nobody was sure what the federal government was going to do. As a university administrator, we had studied these things and decided: when an institution lost control of its destiny, it was a disaster."

Blackburn believes Wallace thought that once he had defied Katzenbach, Malone and Hood would be taken from the campus.

Leading them to their dorms instead, Blackburn says, helped defuse the opposition.

"It was late when I went home that day," Blackburn says. "I remember walking across the campus and, oh, I had such pride at what we had done that day. That it got through. That nobody got hurt."

Malone remembers her first evening on campus.

"That night I went to bed there was a bomb threat. In the morning, when I woke up, I found out that Medgar Evers had been killed," she says of the civil rights leader murdered in Mississippi.

"You don't go through thinking it's not a potentially dangerous situation. You can't let it take you over."

Vivian Malone had found early inspiration in her ambitions from Mobile civil rights leader John LeFlore, a friend of her uncle Joe's, who was also active in the movement, she says. Her parents had raised their children on St. Anthony Street in downtown Mobile.

In 1961, Malone had just graduated from Central High with a nearly perfect grade-point average, but had not been accepted to all-black Alabama A&M in Huntsville on the first round application because her high school had failed to forward her transcript. She took a summer job working at Little Realty in Mobile.

"LeFlore decided we needed to go down and integrate the extension (campus) of The University of Alabama," she recalls, referring to the former Mobile institution of higher learning. "He came by and asked if I'd be interested.

I said, 'It can't be true. It's what I've wanted to do for a long time.' Somewhere in my heart I felt I might just go to The University of Alabama.

"I did go down and took the exam. Of course they didn't accept me. The only letter I received said, 'Due to the pressures of enrollment we cannot accept you.'"

She then went on to Alabama A&M and was in touch with the NAACP legal defense fund.

She remembers vividly the call, in 1963, concerning her acceptance to The University of Alabama in Tuscaloosa: "I worked at the A&M switchboard. I received the call directly from my attorneys that I had been accepted in June. I was excited about it—an eager anticipation as if you're about to celebrate something big. You know you're going to do something that will make a difference. I felt as if it wasn't a matter of choice at that point. It was something I had to do."

Hood says his determination to go to all-white Tuscaloosa came in part from a reaction he had to reading a well-publicized study by a white academic, Professor W. C. George of the University of North Carolina. George, as Hood tells it, had fashioned an argument that black people did not have the mental capacity of whites. Hood wrote George a letter rebutting the argument, and says he received a disdainful reply scrawled on a piece of napkin.

Arthur Dunning, who is black and grew up in the west-central Alabama town of Sweet Water, matriculated at Alabama in the summer of 1966 and became a vice president at the University of Georgia. "There's an extraordinary amount of political capital you use when you exclude people," Dunning says. "All you do is help a group of people to develop long memories. You imprint, over the generations, the lack of credibility and trust.

"Faulkner writes that, 'The past is not dead, it's not even the past.' I think when you're in a region with a deep sense of place, you also need to emphasize, to an extra degree, a vision of the future."

The schoolhouse door, Dunning suggests, presents a threshold leading there.

"I think the stand in the schoolhouse door was the symbol of transition that had been in place for generations, and what was unraveling in front in 1963 was a dramatic change in status quo in the South, not just Alabama."

❈

For Vivian Malone Jones' part, the story of June 11, 1963, does have a conclusion, however somber. She has thought much about the nature of that story as she is in the midst of penning a memoir about her experiences.

In 1996, she was honored by the George Wallace Family Foundation with the Lurleen B. Wallace Award in Courage. George Wallace was there for the occasion.

"I had been places where he was speaker," Malone says of Wallace in the years since 1963. "I had never been face to face with him. It was something I had been waiting for for a long time.

"I always wanted him to say that it was just wrong what he did. It wasn't until the 1970s that I heard he made a statement to that effect. When I met with him, it was a gesture, my being able to say to him that I forgive him.

"And I forgave him. It was an ending to a story—especially an ending for him. And a beginning for me."

Hood says he was with the former governor in the final stage of his life.

"I remember talking to Governor Wallace before he died," Hood recalls. "'What is it you would like me to write about you?' I asked him."

According to Hood, Wallace answered: "'That I was wrong when it came to race.'"

"What's the second?"

"'Everybody is a child of God.'"

George Wallace Jr.

THE LOYAL SON

A year after his father's death in 1998, I visited with George Wallace Jr.—then in public office—to talk about fame, family, loneliness, and his famous namesake. He also shared excerpts with me of a memoir he was working on.

Montgomery

I can recall as a very young boy my father coming through our front door at our spacious home in Clayton, Alabama, and telling us that he would be a candidate for governor of Alabama . . . That was a moment when we were embracing a life that would have an impact on our state and country but also embracing those twins of joy and pain which have become our constant companions to this day.

—GEORGE WALLACE JR., from a memoir in progress

In his office high up in a stately, red government building downtown, George C. Wallace Jr., a public service commissioner for the state of Alabama, is remembering the man he calls "truly my best friend." He has just returned from a hunt in Africa, where he shot an impala and read Hemingway, an author who inspires him as he works on a book, he reveals, about his family.

A lean 47-year-old with his father's arching brows and dimpled chin, he looks out at the capitol, where his father took the oath of governor four times,

George C. Wallace Jr. stands by a window in his office with an autographed photo
of his father. Photo by Mike Kittrell, courtesy of the *Mobile Press-Register.*

and his mother, Lurleen, once. In a voice reminiscent of his dad's, although
not as driving, he hearkens back to a year ago.

It was Saturday night, September 12, and he'd tuned the television in his father's hospital room to CNN's *Larry King Live.* On the show taped a few weeks
before, George Jr. had been a guest, along with the Reverend Jesse Jackson and
CBS news veteran Mike Wallace. The guests were discussing the legacy of the

80-year-old political figure who now languished in the bed, in chronic pain since his legs were paralyzed in 1972 by an assassin's bullets, now progressively deaf and, with Parkinson's, barely able to speak.

The men debated whether George Wallace, in the 1960s, had truly been a racist, or, in fact, a populist attuned to a segregation-minded electorate. Interspersed were clips from Mike Wallace's *60 Minutes* interview of October 22, 1968, where the governor, both combative and funny, had teased the newsman as "Cousin Mike." To communicate with his father, George Jr. had written out on a legal pad what everyone was saying on the show that Saturday night. ("Mike Wallace talked about how much he always liked George Wallace personally," George Jr. says, thinking back. "Dad smiled and watched it.")

The next day, Sunday, after visiting his father again and heading home, he had a premonition. He'd sensed loss before: On a night in May 1972, he'd dreamed that his father, campaigning for the Democratic nomination for president, had been shot in the throat. Two days later, in Laurel, Maryland, three bullets ripped into Governor Wallace's abdomen and arm, one lodging in his spinal cord. "It was a Secret Service man, Nick Zorvas, who was shot in the throat," George Jr. says.

Driving home that Sunday, September 13, 1998, George Jr. got the call on his car phone from a nurse to hurry back. He was with his father when he died.

"Someone told me that when you lose your last parent, you have a real sense of being alone. Even at forty-seven, I understand what they mean," he says. "I really have that sense of being alone."

I recall moving to Montgomery while in the fourth grade and the trauma this caused as it meant leaving all the familiar places and people behind.
—George Wallace Jr.

On the walls of Wallace's office—"I'm actually 'the 3rd,' but I've been called 'George Jr.' all these years"—are photographs that tell the story of a family, and of a time: Lurleen, as a toddler, standing next to her brother Cecil in Tuscaloosa, Alabama; George Wallace as a tough young boxer at The University of Alabama; George Jr., at age 12, dancing with his sister, Peggy Sue, at their father's 1963 inauguration party ("My mother, Bobbie, Peggy, and I took lessons in the auditorium of Clayton High School," he writes in his memoir. "We worked to become proficient in the fox trot, waltz, and other dances whose names thankfully slip my mind.")

On his desk he keeps a picture of his dad, who is dressed in a red sweater. "To my son, George," reads the inscription, "for whom I have much admiration & respect, but more than this, love. Daddy."

When he was 7, George Jr. first campaigned for his father. "The 1958 governor's race," he writes, "found me most of the time standing on a chair to reach a microphone asking people, to 'vote for my daddy.'"

He's still taking up for his father, defending the man, and his legacy, against all nay-sayers.

"He was a product of his time," he explains. "He was advocating the positions of the people who supported him. And to suggest, as some do, that those positions were synonymous with ill-will, ill-feeling, hate, or malice is simply not true. It was a system, segregation, that the people of the South grew up with and they accepted like they accepted their religion. Clearly it was wrong, but to suggest that all people of the South had hate in their hearts is simply not true."

He emphasizes that "the totality" of his father's 80 years be told, not just a chapter like the one when he stood defiantly in the schoolhouse door in Tuscaloosa. When, for example, the director Spike Lee came to Alabama to make the 1997 film, *4 Little Girls,* about the deadly bombing of the Sixteenth Street Baptist Church in Birmingham, Wallace encouraged him to portray his father in a balanced way. Lee, he believes, did not. "My father was devastated by the bombing of this church. He was just torn up," he says.

He repeats a claim he made on *Larry King Live* that his father in no way ordered violence in 1965 against the voting-rights marchers at the Edmund Pettus Bridge in Selma. "You probably think he ordered the troopers on horseback to knock women and children down," he says, anxiously.

The years of chronic pain his father suffered, he believes, had "a purifying effect," enabling him to feel "a tremendous empathy for others. I know he believed he was spared, that the Lord kept him here for some reason. I'd like to think it was to bring people together."

On the office wall is a framed condolence letter of September 16, 1998, from President and Mrs. Clinton. It states, in part: "George Wallace was one of the most dynamic political figures of our time. Over the course of his long life, he came to symbolize reconciliation in our society and was a vital part of our national journey away from divisiveness."

The pictures in the office tell a light-hearted story, too, as in the picture of *The Mike Douglas Show* in 1971. George Jr., age 20, has neatly combed, long hair and holds a guitar. Next to him, laughing, is Governor Wallace. George Jr. had just handed the talk-show host a gift, a wristwatch with the governor's face as the dial, and the arms of a boxer as the clock hands: "I told him, 'It keeps time, but runs to the right.'"

As a guitarist and singer, Wallace performed rock and country music at his parents' political rallies and professionally. At age 15, his group, Governor's Four, cut a record on the Be-Bop label at Muscle Shoals, "Papa Was Governor Until Mama Moved In."

That both "Mama" and "Papa" were governor made for a unique childhood. Wallace believes he's the "only man" in American history to have both parents take the oath. In Texas, he says, Ma Ferguson became governor after her husband, but he's heard they had daughters.

While George may have overshadowed Lurleen in life, on these walls she dominates. There is a spectacular photo of the calm-eyed, fair-haired woman dressed in hunting garb, holding a shotgun and a luckless turkey. Taken in April 1967, the picture betrays no hint of the cancer that would overtake her by May 1968. ("As a middle aged parent," Wallace writes, "I often reflect upon the loneliness she felt as she began to comprehend the seriousness of her illness.")

A group photograph recalls more recent loss—George Wallace Jr.; a political aide, Scott Whiteley; Governor Wallace in his wheelchair; and John Kennedy Jr., who had come to Montgomery in 1995 to interview Wallace for the inaugural issue of *George* magazine.

George Jr. and John-John—their namesakes, he says, were "on different ends of the political spectrum"—had lunch together at Auburn University at Montgomery. They talked, he said, about their fathers.

You must understand that one of the main reasons for my father's success as a politician was his one dimensional approach to life. He lived for politics to the exclusion of all else . . . When we would go to our lake home at Lake Martin for some relaxation, mother and the rest of us would enjoy the water and the tranquility which comes with the lake. Now on the other hand, when Dad would go with us he never could seem to relax.

—George Wallace Jr.

For several years, Wallace has been typing out what he calls "reflections." Although he is reluctant to term it a memoir, the excerpt he shares has all the markings of that genre.

In the pages he looks back, with longing, to the simple, secure world of his childhood in Clayton, "the small Southern town in southeast Alabama" with its "summer afternoons which seemed to last forever." The large pecan trees, the swimming hole, the dancing lessons with his sisters and mother—he recalls, for the reader, an idyllic world. He also remembers, with deep affection, the farm of his maternal grandparents, Henry and Estelle Burns, in Greene County, in the western part of the state.

But he turns melancholy: "How interesting," he writes, "that our feelings about such things as swimming, running, laughing, and innocence should be so drastically altered by the accumulation of years. Is it not sad that while we gain some wisdom as we grow older we lose the yearnings of youth and the wonderment and curiosity the tender years encompass."

The public spotlight grew harsh: "This constant being looked at and stared at as though we were some kind of carnival exhibit I believe took its toll on all of the family, some more than others."

The spotlight turned cruel: "As my father's profile became more pronounced nationally it became more difficult for us as our family received threats and the mansion itself was fired upon by passing automobiles, and you could see the holes where the bullets had struck the front."

And there was loss: "My mother's death at age forty-one was a traumatic event for our family made even more so because her illness and very personal battle with cancer had been on the front pages of the paper for months."

No wonder he writes: "I do know that when I have had the opportunity to travel out of state over the years it has been a relief to have the anonymity to relax and not feel as though you are on display."

Wallace is not certain whether his writings will be finalized as a book. Public office has kept him busy with other demands. "And so much has happened in the last year," he says, "there's a whole other dimension to it in terms of my thoughts and reflections."

If he does see his manuscript through, his insights may be of value to those still puzzling over one of the most controversial figures of the 20th century.

"While he loved his family dearly," he writes of the governor, "he was not a father figure in the sense that other fathers were."

Defining that father—not only to the world, but also to himself—remains a heavy task for the son.

Johnnie Carr

SUSTAINING THE DREAM

Johnnie Carr was about to turn 90 when I drove to see her in 2001. She was still president of the Montgomery Improvement Association, formed in 1955 at the time of the Montgomery bus boycott. She kept on longer, too, living to age 97.

Montgomery

Oak Park, across the street from Johnnie Carr's house in Montgomery, is a pleasing refuge of winding walks and inviting benches, a place full of light and innocence. When Johnnie and her husband, Arlam Carr, moved into their house in 1943, however, Oak Park might as well have been a thousand miles away.

"Back in those days Montgomery was completely segregated," says the petite, 89-year-old president of the Montgomery Improvement Association, standing on her porch across from the park. "This was a black neighborhood. The whites were from the other side of the park, and we couldn't go into it. The only black people allowed were maids nursing white children.

"My brother-in-law came to visit us from Chicago while he was on furlough from the Army. He decided, while I was fixing dinner, to walk out there into the park to look at some animals they kept in the park, and a fellow saw him and ordered him out."

She shakes her head. "He was wearing his uniform!"

The sight of the park stirs other memories, too, especially about the opposite side, where Jackson Hospital rises from a parking lot.

Her son, Arlam, named for her husband of fifty-six years, was born in 1951

Johnnie Carr holds a photograph of Rosa Parks in the living room of her home in Montgomery, Alabama. Carr was a leader in the civil rights movement in Montgomery, which began with the Montgomery bus boycott. Photo courtesy of the *Mobile Press-Register.*

and needed an emergency hernia operation. The Carrs' family physician recommended a surgeon, a white doctor, who ordered Arlam be taken immediately to Jackson Hospital.

"At the time," Johnnie Carr remembers, "there was a black hospital around the corner and that's where you had to go to recuperate."

After the surgeon performed the operation, though, "He walked out and told the nurse, 'I want a room for baby Carr tonight.' The nurse said, 'Oh!' and almost flipped 'cause she knew it was a black baby. The doctor told her, 'Baby Carr's going to stay at this hospital tonight!'"

The white doctor got his way—a heroic act, Carr says. He, however, did warn her: "The only thing I want you to do is stay in the room with him and don't let any of these folks see you."

Arlam would go on, as a teenager, to serve as the litigant in the lawsuit against the Montgomery school system that forced desegregation of formerly all-white schools. Today, he is a producer at WSFA television station in Montgomery.

On this bright, cold Montgomery morning, Johnnie Carr leaves the porch and enters her home. It's a home filled with photographs of old friends—one of Rosa Parks sits on a table—and honors and medals praising Carr for her work as president of the Montgomery Improvement Association, the organization formed in 1955 to orchestrate the Montgomery bus boycott.

Turning 90 at the end of this month, Carr has endured long enough to see the south change dramatically. Indeed, only last Sunday a bus pulled up in front of her house—parked on the street between her porch and Oak Park—and she was invited to step aboard and say a few words.

The bus, she says, was part of a civil rights tour being taken by visitors to Montgomery. Carr was one of the tour's attractions.

"I've seen a lot of history," she says.

On the cover of the juvenile book *Johnnie* by Randall Williams, the author and publisher of Montgomery-based Junebug/New South Books, there is a drawing of a black woman and a white woman together. The white woman is tasting the cake mix of the black woman. The scene is gentle, sisterly, harmonious.

It is a picture, Carr explains, of her mother and a white lady who admired her cooking, in the rural area outside of Montgomery. "My mother was a cake maker, an A-1 cook," she explains. "White women would come out to our home and bring her material to bake a cake.

"In the country, you didn't see segregation on the order that you did in the city when you saw it taking place in recreation, in the library, when you went into an establishment and saw colored and white fountains. That's when you noticed what segregation was really like."

If the city made segregation more visible, though, it also provided opportunities for young Johnnie. When she was a child, her parents enrolled her in the Montgomery Industrial School, a private school for black girls, as she describes it, "started by whites from the North.

"Those white teachers came from the North, and they dedicated their lives to teaching black girls. You were always taught to think positive, and well of yourself, never that you weren't as good as anybody else because of the color of your skin or the texture of your hair. It was the content of your character."

At Montgomery Industrial young Johnnie became friends with a classmate, Rosa Louise McCauley—who would later take on the married name Rosa Parks.

"Rosa was such a quiet person," she says. "If you asked her a question, she was ready to answer, but she wasn't talkative."

Did they talk about politics in those days? Carr laughs at the question. "It was the farthest thing from our minds!

"I became more aware of politics in Roosevelt's administration. He did so much to bring up the citizens all over."

It was at her church—Hall Street Baptist, down the block from where she now lives—that she first got involved, in the late 1930s, in the National Association for the Advancement of Colored People.

At the time, she recalls, the NAACP's mission was to reverse "the stigma of segregation. On the railroad train, for example, you couldn't get first-class accommodations. You had to go all the way to Cincinnati to get them. In the dining room you had to sit behind a curtain. We worked to tear down the curtain. Our ministers who were going to conventions around the country, they were crowded in Jim Crow facilities."

Other issues arose, too—police brutality, an unfair judicial system; she lists problems and the efforts of the NAACP to address them.

She had thought about leaving Alabama for good—"friends were going to New York for 'sleep-in jobs,'"—but at the time she was divorced from her first husband and had two young daughters. Her responsibility to raising her children prevented her from leaving her home.

It was an NAACP meeting that put her back in touch with Rosa Parks. "I was secretary of the NAACP, and Rosa Parks saw my name in the paper—

we hadn't seen each other since 1927, when we left school—and she said, 'I'm going to the meeting to see if that's who I went to school with.' I don't think, since then, we've let six months go at a time when we weren't in contact with each other."

The day was December 1; the year, 1955. About 9:30 that night, Carr says, her phone rang and a friend, E. D. Nixon, told her: "They've arrested Rosa. They got 'the wrong woman.'"

By the term "wrong woman," Johnnie Carr says, Nixon meant that Rosa Parks was someone who would not back down from challenging the system of bus desegregation. She was a figure of quiet strength, someone willing to take the pressure of being arrested and to hold up under the force of public scrutiny.

According to Carr, two other women had formerly been arrested for refusing to give up their seats to whites in Montgomery. Parks, however, was the first that the NAACP believed could serve as a "test case" for the bus boycott to come.

"We were going to boycott the buses on December 5, the day of Rosa's trial."

The news went out. JoAnn Robinson, a professor at Alabama State University, mimeographed and distributed flyers. Ministers spoke of the boycott from their pulpits. Phones rang and people went from porch to porch with the news.

"The buses ran empty that Monday," Carr says.

"When they first started, they knew people would need help to stay off the buses. Everybody couldn't walk. The first thing they asked was black taxi cabs if they'd ride people. You'd take the whole group for the fare. People were willing to do anything they could. They were fed up with the treatment they'd been getting. As soon as the authorities learned what the taxi cabs were doing, though, they threatened to take their franchises. We organized churches with station wagons, people with private cars. When the authorities learned what we were doing, they said we were running transportation without proper licenses."

At Holt Street Church, on December 5, Johnnie Carr remembers, the first "mass meeting" took place for the formation of the Montgomery Improve-ment Association, the organization that would orchestrate what would be-come the year-long boycott of the Montgomery buses. The first president of the MIA was chosen: the Reverend Martin Luther King Jr.

King had not been in Montgomery long. Carr remembers his having ap-peared at an NAACP meeting after his arrival. "When he got up to be pre-sented at the meeting and made a few statements, Rosa Parks and I happened to be sitting together. I said to Rosa, 'He's something else!'

"We weren't dreaming about any movement. We just recognized from his making a few remarks that he was a little bit different. When things moved on and he was president of the MIA, he'd make speeches on breaking down walls, and how to do it with nonviolence. With love in your hearts.

"Those were concepts that people had to learn.

"I heard King speak often. We had mass meetings every Monday night."

She describes the fervor of those meetings—the crowds, the speeches, the inspirations—all critical to keeping the boycott alive.

When the boycott succeeded after a long year, King was very specific in how black Montgomery was to conduct itself, Carr says. "Dr. King would not let you 'over-excite.' You had won, but you wanted to be calm. 'Now I've got the right to sit where I want,' you'd say, 'but I'm not going to do it in an ugly way. I'm going to be courteous.'

"Dr. King said, 'When you start bothering with the foundation of any-body's building, they're going to try to retaliate and not let it happen.' It's why I feel Dr. King's teaching is something I'm glad to have known. Something I could be involved with in my life."

Arlam Carr Jr., 50, is a producer of the morning show, *Today In Alabama*, at WSFA in Montgomery, a television station a few minutes from Sidney La-nier High School. "When I was a boy," he says, sitting in a conference room at the station, "we'd be in the car and pass Lanier. It was pretty, it was big! 'Mama,' I'd say, 'I want to go there.'"

Soon he learned that, being black, he was prohibited from attending Sidney Lanier.

When he was 13, though, and a student at a middle school attached to Alabama State University, his parents, Johnnie and Arlam Sr., sued the schools to force desegregation. U.S. district judge Frank M. Johnson Jr. would ultimately rule on the case.

"My friends told me, 'Do you realize what you're doing?'" the younger Arlam recalls. He shakes his head. "We were not doing it to make history. We were doing it because it was right."

He remembers how his parents moved their bedroom from the front of their house to the back, worried about a bomb being hurled through the front window. "Friends called and said, 'We'll stand guard.'"

When Johnson's decision came down to desegregate the schools, he says, it specified that the first black students begin by entering the tenth grade. That year, Arlam Carr Jr. was in the ninth. A year would pass before he realized that boyhood yearning to attend the "big, pretty" school.

He describes a chilly reaction from the white student body when he finally did get to enter Sidney Lanier. The black students were asked to come in late the first day of school, he says—to avoid confrontations—and when his homeroom teacher introduced him to the class, he was waiting in the hallway as she announced a new student. Then he stepped forward. "All eyes hit me and it got quiet."

There were awkward moments, as when he refrained from eating fried chicken in the school cafeteria because he did not know whether he was expected to eat it with his hands or knife and fork—and did not want to stand out as being different from the other teenagers. There were bizarre episodes, too, as when a classmate asked him if black people's feet were like their hands.

"Dark on one side and light on the other. He had never seen a black person's foot!"

He was in the same class, he says, as George Wallace's daughter, Peggy Sue. The tragic night that Martin Luther King Jr. was killed, he had been at home, watching the news. When he arrived at Lanier the next morning, the flag had not been lowered to half-staff.

"That angered me!"

He says that when he complained to the administration, they told him that the ROTC was responsible for the flag. "I was in the ROTC," he explains. He went to the ROTC office and made sure the flag was lowered right away in memory of King.

As president of the Montgomery Improvement Association, Johnnie Carr is a busy woman. Raising money for college scholarships, helping with voter registration, commemorating the Montgomery bus boycott, and helping celebrate the birthday of Martin Luther King Jr.—these are some of the ongoing missions of the organization.

"We may not be on the front page with news," says the Reverend Leon Ross Sr., pastor of the Weeping Willow Baptist Church, "but we're very active." Ross's church will hold part of the celebration—an afternoon of song— on King's birthday.

The phone rings continuously in Johnnie Carr's house—calls from other MIA members, invitations for speaking engagements, journalists wanting her to tell her version of the story, once more, of the boycott.

"They look at me as a mother," she says of the members of her organization. "The way I carry myself, and the way I've led—they see it is how I can have a relationship with ministers, politicians, anybody. I've never had any apprehension about my gender as a woman or my color as an African American. I've felt I was as good as anybody else, and if I applied myself I could do anything I wanted.

"I don't hate anybody. If you're a Ku Klux Klan or a skinhead or somebody who wants to murder people, I just feel sorry for you because it's really bad for you to have that sort of thing in your life.

"For you to hate me is worse on you than it is on me."

On the verge of becoming a nonagenarian, she is like a young woman still— dedicated to the spirit of the civil rights movement, full of energy and hope. Although race relations are "far better," she says, "than in the past, we still have to make it better. It's not all on the white race. Not all on the black race. There's still some of us who don't understand how we need to live together.

"I feel like the community is going to be better than it is. That's my purpose in life. To make it better."

Theresa Burroughs

IN BEAUTY'S CARE

Greensboro

I f you were to meet Theresa Burroughs, 75, at her beauty shop in this serene Hale County town, you would hardly guess she had been deemed
an agitator during the 1960s, gotten hauled off to jail a few blocks from
her house, and been knocked down and trampled on crossing Edmund Pettus Bridge in the Selma-to-Montgomery march.

With her friendly smile and hair in a style she calls an upcurl, she does
not seem like a woman who harbored famous men behind these walls, keeping watch as hooded nightriders eased down her block brandishing shotguns.
Even the drawing of the Reverend Martin Luther King Jr. on her wall, near
the curling irons and hair relaxers, seems ordinary, since the street outside is
named for him.

But linger with Burroughs as she's washing Dora McQueen's hair, and you
realize that the longtime cosmetologist is a political activist at heart, and that
the beauty shop, as McQueen says, "is where it all happens." Political candi-
dates have entered here to seek support; celebrated visitors have stopped in to
relax and pass the gossip.

Burroughs refers to King as "Doc."

Ask about the yellow cottage across the street, a small black history museum called the Safe House, and you will hear Burroughs talk about how she
conceived of it several years ago and led early efforts to fill it with artifacts em-
phasizing civil rights leaders from Greensboro and the surrounding Alabama
Black Belt.

Theresa Burroughs stands in front of the Safe House Black History Museum in Greensboro, Alabama. Burroughs is a hairdresser who was a civil rights marcher and was on the Edmund Pettus Bridge in Selma when the marchers were beaten. Photo by Bill Starling, courtesy of the *Mobile Press-Register.*

While she works shampoo into McQueen's hair, she explains why the museum, which opened in 2002, is named the Safe House. She recalls a summer night in 1965, when the gentle lanes outside her beauty salon seemed on the brink, as she tells it, of becoming a bloodbath.

That night there had been a voting rights rally at St. Matthew AME Church in Greensboro—a "mass meeting" energized by speeches given by King and the Reverend Ralph Abernathy. Afterward, while people visited in the church basement, Burroughs says, a man ran inside to announce that the Ku Klux Klan was driving toward town. The Klan was looking, she says, for King.

Fearing a passage out of town might be blocked, Burroughs took King and Abernathy to her mother's home in the old Depot neighborhood of Greensboro. Adjacent to her mother's house was the beauty shop that Burroughs had opened a few years earlier.

One man, recalls Burroughs, told others: "Go get your guns. The Klan is coming, and they want to kill 'Doc.' We're not going to let them kill him in Greensboro."

Before long, Burroughs says, the Klan procession reached the end of her street. "They had their headlights off, but the lights on inside the cars. They were wearing their hoods and holding up guns."

With her friends, Burroughs crouched in the beauty parlor, vigilant at the window. "The night was black, and we were black," she says.

The Klan cars passed slowly, menacingly down the street, reached the end of the block, then turned around and rolled back through.

Later that night, Burroughs recalls, she got access to an empty house across the street from her beauty shop and made sure that Abernathy and King could spend the night there. In peace. In safety.

"It's why we call it 'the Safe House,'" she explains, a name given it by the late Samuel Mockbee, a famous architect from Auburn University who, with his students, helped in initial efforts to restore the building.

At four that morning, King and Abernathy departed the house and were spirited away to another destination.

Beauty and politics: Through much of her life, the two concerns have intertwined for Burroughs.

Born in 1929 to Mattie and Napoleon Turner, young Theresa grew up in what she describes as a nearly all-black community. "The only white people I'd see were when we went to the store or when the mailman came."

She thought little of divisions between the races, though. A mixed-race couple resided down the block. "I grew up thinking whites and blacks live together."

The white man of the couple, whose name was Jim, would pay Theresa and her friends a nickel or dime to "scratch his head and wash his hair."

Soon Theresa found herself earning change washing the hair of other people in the neighborhood. "I wanted things to look pretty," she says.

After marrying Kenneth Burroughs, a mechanic, and starting their family of four children—Kenneth has since passed away—Theresa practiced fixing hair on children in her neighborhood, then got a degree in cosmetology. Part of her training included a stint, she says, at a beauty school in Mobile run by Bestida Brothers on the former Davis Avenue, now Dr. Martin Luther King Jr. Avenue.

Opening up her own salon back home, Burroughs Beauty Bar, she had a thriving business, bringing her scissors and combs and gels to bear on a procession of hair trends.

Then came the Afro. "People said, 'We ain't gonna straighten it no more. We're growing it out, and lettin' it fly!'"

Burroughs, who says the Afro was the most political of all the hairdos, acknowledges that the style was not good for a hairdresser's bottom line.

While Burroughs never wore an Afro, she expressed her politics in other ways. She describes her politicization as having two stages: The first was the shock she experienced as a child, sitting at the roadside, when she failed to say "Yes, sir" to a white man asking her a question from his truck.

"Don't ever say 'Yes,' to a white man!'" she recalls him raging. "Look at me. Say it—'Yes, sir.'"

She grows agitated these many years later as she completes the story. "He told me, 'You know what? I could snatch you off that bank and kill you, and nothing could be done about it.'"

She was a young woman before the next event occurred that seemed to push her fully into activism. Civil rights leader Albert Turner Sr., who hailed from her home area and worked with King, was heading up the Hale County Improvement Association. "He was organizing the Black Belt," she says.

Galvanized by Turner's vision, Burroughs started going to the meetings at local churches and soon was working to enlist the help of others, many of whom were already coming to her shop.

Burroughs remembers that some of her customers—employees at a nursing home in town—were instructed by their white boss not to have their hair done at Burroughs Beauty Bar. "He told them, 'She's an agitator,'" Burroughs says.

One of her friends today, Sarah Teacher Fields, remembers Burroughs as an inspiration—as well as her first hairdresser. As a girl in junior high, Fields got arrested during a voting rights demonstration and was thrown into what she remembers as a filthy jail in Selma for two days. "When I got home, my mother had to scrub me with Clorox," she says.

Burroughs lives a couple of miles from Fields, and the two women visit often. Down the street from Burroughs is another friend, Adelaide Hearns, who also participated in the voting rights meetings. When Hearns got married, it was Burroughs who styled her hair.

Hearns was deeply involved in voter registration. The soft-spoken woman describes that era as a time of "focus." People were outdoors together, on the street, talking to one another, sharing ideas and convictions.

Now, says Hearns, there is a greater sense of isolation.

Hearns and Burroughs lament how young people dismiss, or are oblivious to, the valiant efforts of a past generation.

One reason that Burroughs started The Safe House museum was to engage children in stories too quickly fading.

Burroughs makes vivid her own story of the march across Edmund Pettus Bridge in March 1965. She remembers the law enforcement officers shouting, "Get the hell off this bridge!"

The marchers, she says, kept on.

When the Alabama state troopers came sweeping through the throng on horses, wielding billy clubs, setting off tear gas, one of the horses knocked Burroughs to the ground. Above her was chaos—troopers running, swinging their sticks, marchers scattering, falling. Bloody Sunday, as March 7, 1965, came to be known, was captured by *Life* magazine photographer Charles Moore.

In The Safe House museum, Burroughs keeps a copy of the book, *Powerful Days: The Civil Rights Photography of Charles Moore*. In the collection is the scene at Edmund Pettus Bridge. Visible in the melee is the face of Albert Turner Sr., his white cap among the helmets of the troopers.

Turner is leaning toward a woman on the ground. In the photo, you can see only her sleeve and her purse.

Burroughs points to the image. "That's me," she says. "That's my purse."

Within the walls of the Safe House are succinct displays on black history—artifacts of slavery, replicas of "colored" and "white only" signs, an overview of the *Brown v. Board of Education* desegregation case. The collection, says Burroughs, reflects the input of her museum board, including Amilcar Shabazz, who has served as director of the African American Studies Program at The University of Alabama.

On one wall are photographs of Greensboro residents arrested for their voting rights activities. The photos were taken by the Alabama Department of Public Safety and found only recently by Burroughs and the museum board. Like enemies of the state, each person arrested holds a sign with his name scrawled on it, along with his date of birth.

A woman in her 30s, with an intense gaze and neatly brushed hair, looks out from one of the photos. The name on the placard: Theresa Burroughs.

Burroughs has made sure that her daughter, Toni Love, knows what she went through. Whereas Toni, in her 30s, seems to have had little political drive as a young person, she was one of the few blacks to first attend an all-white school in town.

Her mother, she says, insisted.

When her high school put on a Shakespeare play, she says, blacks were not allowed to have roles—there were anxieties, she says, about romantic pairings on stage between blacks and whites. In protest, Toni led a boycott of the play. Her mother had encouraged her to do so.

And when Toni did not seem to have a career direction, her mother started paying her to clean the beauty shop and taught her to wash hair.

Toni went on to receive degrees from Stillman College and the University of West Alabama and has become a successful cosmetologist with a school of her own—the Cosmetology Continuing Education Center in Moundville, a half hour away.

After her mother finishes washing Dora McQueen's hair, Toni, on a visit home, offers to give McQueen a trim. A tall woman with a full head of hair, Toni takes her place behind the hydraulic beauty chair, takes McQueen's locks between the fingers of one hand and begins to work the scissors with the other.

Burroughs uses the moment to get off her feet and perches on the sunsplashed windowsill. Out her window is the street sign, Martin Luther King Boulevard—the street she had renamed, from Depot Street, for the man she protected here.

On the opposite corner is the yellow house, "The Safe House," of her making. In this safe house of her own, with the familiar music of scissors snipping and women talking, she relaxes into the afternoon.

PART V DOWN BACK ROADS

*O*ne of the great joys for me of journalism about people is discovery—
whether in what a person has to say, is thinking and feeling, or the
physical discovery of what's down a country road. That road may lead
to a place of historical interest, like the rural crossroads near Demopolis, where
a group of people remembers—and is attempting to restore—the Rosenwald
School they attended as children. Or it may take me to a site where folks muse
and meditate on simple pleasures, like the old men beneath the ragged tree in
southeast Alabama engaged in a perpetual domino game in "The Oak Tree Social Club," or the cousins in northwest Alabama philosophizing about hounds
and raccoons in "Visiting Old Pals."

I have long been interested in the ethnic diversity within southern culture, a
dimension of the South too often overlooked by mainstream media. Down back
roads and along city streets I find this diversity: Sara Hamm, of the last Jewish family in Eufaula, who tends the synagogue's fading cemetery; Bessie Papas, a 96-year-old woman who arrived in Alabama as a child from Greece and
watches satellite television from Athens while residing at Malbis Plantation, a
Greek Orthodox settlement near Spanish Fort, a short drive from Mobile Bay.
In the national imagination Alabama is usually characterized by our majority,
African Americans and white Protestants or, along the Gulf Coast, Catholics.
But there are other ethnic and religious groups, including growing Asian and
Hispanic populations, who blend other traditions with southern sensibilities.

I've included "Driving Mr. Bellingrath" here because that friendship between
Edward Carl, butler and chauffeur, and Walter Bellingrath, the wealthy owner
of the glorious gardens, came about in their many sojourns together down Alabama roads. While I spent an Alabama afternoon with Carl, I never had the

chance to do so with Walter Bellingrath, gone well before my time. But I like to think of their own Alabama afternoons together in the 1940s and 1950s. Separated by class and race through most hours of the day, they sat side by side in Bellingrath's Packard limousine, Carl behind the wheel, Bellingrath in the passenger seat, a couple of fellows swapping stories as they rambled down back roads.

Sara Hamm

KEEPING THE FAITH

Eufaula

Facing east toward Jerusalem as religious tradition prescribes, the old Jewish cemetery, scored by weather and battered by vandals, sits high on a bluff over Lake Eufaula. The headstones—the ones still standing— look toward the peaceful water below and the pinetops of Georgia beyond.

The inhabitants of these graves journeyed far during their lives to settle in this once-cotton-flush town on the Chattahoochee River. Their births, many from the 1800s, took place in Poland, Russia, Bavaria, and Alsace.

Their descendants moved away for better opportunities or intermarried and converted or just forgot their family history.

"This is all that's left of these people here," says Sara Hamm, who, with her son and daughter, comprise the entire Jewish population of a town that a century ago had a synagogue and a main street thriving with Jewish merchants. "When this happens," she says, picking up a cracked headstone and trying to drag it onto its base, "it makes me so angry!"

With the help of her husband, Lee Hamm, a Eufaula police detective, she has been clearing the brush from the cemetery, putting stones back in order as best as possible, and seeking help to restore the burial ground to its solemn grace.

The restoration's new benefactor has proved to be an Atlanta man, Richard Katz, who discovered the Jewish cemetery while on a drive south with his wife, down a popular corridor from Columbus, Georgia, through Eufaula, to Florida.

Sara Hamm and her son, Chad, stand beside a grave marker in Eufala's old
Jewish cemetery, which came to be part of Fairview Cemetery in the 1800s.
Photo by Roy Hoffman, courtesy of the *Mobile Press-Register*.

The Katz Foundation, says Sara Hamm, is committed to contributing funds.
She is taking bids now—consulting with a friend, a Christian undertaker—
from those who wish to have the contract for gluing, resetting, re-pinning,
and replacing the monuments.

She has also started the process of locating descendants, both to support
cemetery care and to find out more about the long-ago Jews. Some current

generations, she says, live close by but show little interest. "It's sad how some people can turn their back on their heritage," she says.

Sara Hamm is devoted to maintaining her own heritage.

Once a week she takes a break from her job as business manager of Reeves Peanut Company, a large wholesale shelling operation in Eufaula, and drives her 9-year-old son Chad an hour away to Hebrew School in Columbus, Georgia, and twice again for religious school and Saturday morning Sabbath worship. Her home is the only one in town where Menorah lights burn during Hanukkah, and she makes visits to the local schools to talk to classes about her religion, often surprised at how eager the children are to hear her.

Her daughter, Jennifer, understands herself to be among a handful of Jewish students at Troy State University in Troy and travels to religious services in Montgomery, fifty miles away. Inspired by her mother's example, Jennifer says, she is trying to organize a Jewish student support group.

While Sara Hamm says she is entirely comfortable being "unusual" in her religion, she admits that, at times, it is hard to keep up steady worship at a congregation far away. The High Holy Days of Rosh Hashonah and Yom Kippur, for example, always come in early fall, and often on weekdays, during the height of the peanut season, when the Eufaula factory demands sixteen-hour workdays.

"The High Holy Days are special to me, I'm always aware of them," says Hamm, stepping across the broken monuments of the cemetery. "But I can't leave for so long."

The talkative, energetic 42-year-old with curly brown hair and a ready laugh is silent as she steps across a fallen column imprinted with "Isaac Bashinsky, Orchowa, Prussia, February 28, 1812, Troy, Alabama, April 3, 1892."

She comes to a grave with a crumbled base, "Henry Oppenheimer, Gronau, Hannover, July 28, 1807, Cuthbert, Georgia, May 26, 1870."

She steps over another marker, "Simon Lewy, July 27, 1839, July 31, 1898, Co. G, 6th Georgia Infantry C.S.A.," and comes to a granite headstone broken into three pieces, "Faust Strauss, June 12, 1831, November 1, 1893."

Many of the headstones have Hebrew lettering, in ancient contrast to the Christian graves on the other side of the wrought iron gate, with their crosses and angels. But all the souls hereabouts share the shade of the cypress and sweet gum trees, the wind moving through the moss, the light dwindling at the end of the day.

In the late 1800s, the old Jewish cemetery became part of the newly named Fairview Cemetery, which also swept into its province, according to a historic sign, the old Presbyterian, black, Masonic, and Oddfellows cemeteries.

Hamm takes a small, broken headstone—a 1-year-old child's remaining claim upon this world—and tries to balance it back on its base. "When people come here to visit," she says, "I want them to feel proud."

Hamm's religious identity came by way of her Jewish mother; her Baptist father is descended from Cherokee Indians, she says. But it was her maternal grandparents, Avarum Moshe "A. M." Rudderman and Jennie Turner Rudderman, who deepened her sense of pride in her faith.

She grew up as Sara Gulledge in the town of Clayton, about a half-hour from Eufaula in rural Barbour County, where the first knowledge many folks had of Jews came from reading about them in the Bible. Because she went to the Baptist church with her father sometimes, she grew familiar with the Old and New Testaments. "When people said to me, 'If you don't believe in Jesus Christ, you're going to hell,' I told them, 'If you're a true Christian, you won't be judgmental.'"

On Saturday evenings, her parents would drive from Clayton to Eufaula to have dinner with the Ruddermans, and Sara and her two sisters would spend the night with their grandparents.

On Sunday mornings, Grandfather Rudderman carted the girls to synagogue religious school in Columbus. On Passover, the family gathered at the grandparents' home.

Both Ruddermans were born in the United States and started their life together in Atlanta but moved to Eufaula in the late 1930s, opening a store called Ruddy's—"Ruddy's Got It!" was the slogan—with shoes for sale on one side, dry goods on the other.

About the time of their arrival, says Hamm, other Jewish stores were closing down, such as Lewy Brothers, with the new generations heading to Birmingham, Atlanta, or beyond, and leaving their ancestors behind in Eufaula's cemetery.

Lee Hamm, who is not Jewish, remembers his wife's grandfather well: "He always had a cigar in his mouth, wore a white shirt, checkered pants, and drove a yellow Cougar."

He remembers Jennie Rudderman as always upbeat and optimistic.

The Ruddermans lived in one of Eufaula's grand homes: a white, large southern colonial with sixteen-foot ceilings, marble fireplaces, and wide porches on Randolph Street. The house is still owned by the family and fully furnished, though no one has lived there since Jennie Rudderman died four years ago, Hamm says.

When Hamm visits the empty home, she communes with the memories of her grandparents—their Bible, in English and Hebrew, sits open on a bookstand; in one glass case is a plate with Hebrew lettering used during Passover seders. In the front doorway is a mezuzah, a tiny scroll with biblical commandments, commonly marking the entrances to Jewish homes.

Hamm remembers that, on Sunday afternoons, she and her grandmother would walk the few blocks to Fairview Cemetery, then go down the path to the old Jewish graves.

In 1987, her grandmother finished a restoration of the old Jewish cemetery. It has taken less than twenty years for the rough company of the weather and the cruel hand of man to bring the place to near ruin again.

In her commitment to restoring the cemetery, Hamm is making good on the promise of her grandmother, to keep the past alive, to honor the dead.

A. M. and Jennie Rudderman are buried in a new part of Fairview Cemetery, in a tiny new Jewish section with, to date, only their own relatives laid to rest there. There are, after all, no other Jewish families in town.

On a bright winter day, Hamm takes Chad to stand over the markers for her grandparents and shows him that rocks have been left on the headstones: a sign in Jewish cemeteries that loved ones have visited.

She tells Chad, "Our faith is as strong as these rocks."

Restoring Rosenwald

THE OAK GROVE SCHOOL

Demopolis

Almost eight decades have passed since Charles S. Foreman Sr. entered the first grade in Gallion, Alabama, a Black Belt farm community in Hale County, about a half hour east of Demopolis. At first, he went to school in a church—Oak Grove Baptist, where his great-grandfather, a former slave, had been the first minister—and the church pews and aisles, he recalls, were the crowded classroom.

As was often the case in the South, rural blacks went to school where they could—churches, shacks, barns, tumbledown schoolhouses—learning their ABCs in the months between planting and picking. And young Foreman, the son of tenant farmers, was no exception.

As Booker T. Washington lamented in 1914 in *Outlook* magazine: "More money is paid for Negro convicts than for Negro teachers in Alabama," offering up Wilcox County, Alabama, as an example, saying that "per capita expenditure for education in 1912 was $17 for whites as against 37 cents for Negroes." In the state of Mississippi in 1912, Washington had said, 64 percent of the black children in the state had attended no public school whatsoever.

By 1925, when Foreman was 8, though, he looked across a field next to Oak Grove Church and saw an edifice being erected with tall, white-washed walls, high windows to gather the sun, and a shiny tin roof.

It was a Rosenwald School.

"It was nice," Foreman, 85, recalls with a smile.

Oak Grove would become one of nearly 400 Rosenwald schools in Alabama

Charles Forman Sr. sits in an old school chair inside Oak Grove School, a Rosenwald School near Gallion, Alabama, in rural Hale County. Foreman attended the school in the 1930s from the first to sixth grades. Photo by Mike Kittrell, courtesy of the *Mobile Press-Register.*

and more than 5,000 throughout the South and Southwest. Built along strict specifications and varying by size, the grammar schools took their name from Julius Rosenwald, president of Sears, Roebuck & Co.

Today, the remaining Rosenwald schools are considered among the nation's most endangered historic sites.

In 1925, while Foreman did not know what "Rosenwald School" meant—his school continued to go by the name, Oak Grove, as it does today as a historic site and museum—he did know that his community had played a large part in creating it.

Land that had come down from his minister great-grandfather, Darby Willis, had been donated for the school. Funds had been raised, in part, by his family and others in Gallion. They sold chickens and eggs and used part of their income as tenant farmers to invest in the school.

Soon, after traipsing the roadside every morning with dozens of other children, Foreman entered not the church but the new building. "It was so different," he says. "It even had doors, so you could close off different rooms!"

In one room were the first through third grades; in the other, fourth through sixth.

There was a kitchen, a cloakroom, even, he remembers, a stage.

The school day began with "a prayer circle," then proceeded to lessons taught by women teachers—graduates, he says, of Alabama State. To back up the teacher's word, a switch waited on the wall.

One day, he says, the county agent came and gave a talk, and Foreman began to learn of the origins of the school and the two strikingly different men whose friendship had given rise to it: the black educator Booker T. Washington and the Jewish philanthropist Julius Rosenwald.

Foreman would go on to his own successes, including graduation from Tuskegee Institute, which Washington founded in 1881. Foreman studied agriculture, attaining a position as a county extension agent, and later earned the distinction of becoming Marengo County's first registered black voter and serving as a local school board chairman.

"It's important for me to preserve Oak Grove School," he explains, echoing the sentiments of other family members from Gallion. "It was my start."

The National Trust for Historic Preservation, headquartered in Washington, D.C., named the Rosenwald schools, as a group, one of the eleven endangered historic sites in the United States for 2002–2003.

Five of Alabama's remaining Rosenwald schools, including Oak Grove, are listed on the National Register of Historic Places.

As National Trust president Richard Moe has stated: "In a time of great racial inequity, Julius Rosenwald worked with communities across the South and Southwest to improve educational opportunities for African Americans. We can't risk losing the tangible reminders of this great collaboration."

The National Trust explains the threat to the remaining structures: "The schoolhouses were originally owned by the individual school systems, but when schools were integrated, those constructed under the Rosenwald Fund were often closed. Many of the Rosenwald schools were destroyed, while others were simply abandoned."

✳

The heyday of Rosenwald school construction occurred between 1914 and 1932.

"Many Rosenwald schools continued in operation until the 1954 Supreme Court ruling against racial segregation in *Brown vs. Board of Education of Topeka* was implemented during the 1960s," states a pamphlet called "Rallying! for Rosenwald School Buildings," published by the Alabama Historical Commission and the Cahaba Trace Commission.

Laura Adams Phillips, an architectural historian from Mobile who lives in North Carolina, emphasizes the importance of documenting the remaining schools.

In North Carolina, Phillips has, in the course of doing research for architects and builders, discovered rural schoolhouses, some of them Rosenwald schools.

There were so many Rosenwald schools built in the South, she says, that "it makes you realize the magnitude of the project. It's mind-boggling. It had a huge impact on black education in the South."

Phillips explains the larger role of schools. "Like churches, they were community magnets.

"But Rosenwald didn't just come in and pass out the bucks," she says. "Local people had to put up part of the money, too. It was a joint venture."

In Gallion, Edmonia Borden, a cousin of Charles Foreman Sr., says that calling the schools by the Rosenwald name, she believes, is deceptive.

"They were community schools," says Borden, who has taken the lead in preserving the Oak Grove School as a museum for visitors and maintains it as a cultural center for the neighboring church.

A graduate of Oak Grove from the 1950s, Borden went on to graduate from Alabama State and to work as a teacher in Illinois for thirty years before retiring and moving back South.

Julius Rosenwald, Borden argues, put in money for the schools, but the largest contribution was made by the black citizens in villages near the schools.

"In 1910," says Peter Ascoli, "my grandfather read Booker T. Washington's *Up From Slavery* and was greatly inspired by it." His grandfather, Julius

Rosenwald, had not finished high school and was impressed by Washington's spirit of self-reliance and independence.

The Rosenwald schools, Ascoli says, were completely the idea of Booker T. Washington.

Washington, he explains, had earlier approached a Standard Oil Company executive for support. He discovered Rosenwald through the Sears, Roebuck president's support for the YMCAs in the South and his position on the board of trustees of Tuskegee.

Tuskegee president R. R. Moton said in his eulogy for Julius Rosenwald in February 1932: "Here was a man . . . who wasn't a Christian as we think of the term, yet who had as much of the Christian spirit as anybody, I think, in building Young Men's Christian Association buildings—not simply for Christians who represented another creed, but for a race not his own race."

Ascoli said his grandfather's philanthropic mission had its own religious origins.

As the son of German Jewish immigrants—Rosenwald's father began life in America as a peddler—Julius grew up in Springfield, Illinois, near the home of Abraham Lincoln's family. As a young man in Chicago, he attended the Reform congregation Temple Sinai, where he was moved, said Ascoli, by the sermons of Rabbi Emil Hirsch.

The basis of those sermons was the importance of "tzedakah," the Hebrew word for charity.

Rosenwald's charity, which reportedly would exceed $60 million, took the form of large gifts, including the founding of the Chicago Museum of Science and Technology, and small ones, such as the thousands of "challenge grants" for Booker T. Washington's black rural schools.

In 1949, the president of the Julius Rosenwald Fund, Edwin Embree, explained in a report, "The work of the Fund in Southern education stressed four programs: the building of schoolhouses for rural Negroes, the provision of library services, the education of teachers and the development of strategic centers of higher learning for Negroes."

Ascoli describes pilgrimages his grandfather took from Chicago down south on the train, to Tuskegee, in the company of other Chicagoans interested in the conditions of the Deep South, among them Jane Addams, founder of Hull-House, which provides social services and health care.

Because Rosenwald schools often included an element of practical education—sewing, gardening, shop—some critics today contend that Rosenwald simply wished to deliver a service-oriented education to the black population, while assuring they would have the earning power to supply a market for Sears, Roebuck products.

"Total rubbish," Ascoli responds.

There is no Rosenwald Fund today, Ascoli explains, because it was set up to disperse all of its money within a set length of time after his grandfather's death in 1932. Unlike the Ford and Rockefeller Foundations, the Rosenwald foundation eventually closed its books.

On a sultry summer day in Gallion, on a bright green lawn off of a red-dirt road, the Oak Grove School stands, baking in the sunlight. Edmonia Borden is walking a visitor through the museum—the potbellied stove in the corner, the schoolteacher's desk, where her mother had given instruction, the faded photographs of children, posing in front of the school.

Her cousin, James Dawson Sr., shows the visitor around the grounds. At the edge of the woods is a decrepit outhouse. In a corner of the field is a cemetery, where church members are still laid to rest. Dawson touches a splintered windowsill of the school. "We need to get all this fixed up!" he says.

Like Foreman and Borden and other family members, Dawson wants to keep history alive by shoring up the walls of this old schoolhouse.

For him, though, it's not just about preserving America's history; it's about saving a big piece of his own history. He remembers how he and the other children used to play outside of the school on pretty days. Although he is 74, he becomes a boy again, recalling the games.

"We used to shoot marbles," he says, "right over there."

As he looks across the lawn, one almost expects him to hunker down, the tall windows of the grammar school overhead, produce a shooter, and flick it into a circle filled with other marbles—immies and aggies and puries—and claim his shining bounty.

Bessie Papas

A MALBIS LIFE

In 2005, when she was 95, I spent several afternoons with Bessie Papas at her Greek Orthodox plantation home in rural Baldwin County. Billy Scourtes, half her age and the great-nephew of Jason Malbis, also resided there. Papas lived to age 98. That same year, 2008, Billy Scourtes passed away at age 49.

Malbis

Tucked away off noisy Baldwin County 181 and U.S. 90 is a pale-pink plantation house with ironwork balconies, where Bessie Papas, 95, lives in a world that whispers of another time. Although the jazzy new shops of the Eastern Shore Centre are only five minutes away, here, at the nearly century-old Malbis home, the calendar seems to turn more slowly. Down the long, quiet hallways, portraits of Greek ancestors look back like journeyers from the past.

A native of Greece, Papas came to this community of Greek Americans eighty-five years ago and has been here since. Of all her generation—those who first inhabited the close-knit realm created by Jason Malbis—she alone remains.

If this fourth daughter born to George and Stamata Papas in the village of Pikerni, near Tripolis, Greece, had instead been a son, her family might never have come to America.

"In the old country," explains Papas, sitting at a long, mahogany table in the main room of the plantation house, which is a private residence, "a girl was a calamity."

An old family photo of the residents of the Malbis home. In this photograph of Bessie Papas' family, taken in front of the Malbis home around 1935, Bessie is on the front row, far left. Photo by Bill Starling, courtesy of the *Mobile Press-Register*.

A painting of Jason Malbis, wearing the garb of a Greek Orthodox monk, hangs in Bessie Papas' home in Malbis. Photo by Bill Starling, courtesy of the *Mobile Press-Register*.

Her father, a laborer, could not provide dowries for four daughters from his wages in Greece. So he headed to Chicago, where his brother Philip had a restaurant, and George worked there for nearly a decade, sending money home.

"I didn't know my father for the first nine years," Papas says.

While in Chicago, George Papas had met another Greek man, Jason Malbis, who had bought land far to the south, in Alabama, in 1906. For $5 an acre, Malbis and his friend William Papageorge had made a first purchase of 120 acres of fertile soil in Baldwin County, thirteen miles east of Mobile, on a rise above Mobile Bay. Eventually, the community that Malbis was building would purchase thousands of acres in that area.

Papas says her father went south to the Greek colony because Malbis contracted with him to transport some mules there.

When Bessie's father arrived on the verdant stretch of land with a flower nursery and the newly built plantation house, he decided to stay and work, she says. "He asked Mr. Malbis if his family could join him there."

Jason Malbis, a former monk and lifelong bachelor, said he would welcome them.

Papas shakes her head in wonderment. "My mother would say, 'Where did I get the courage to bring my family?'"

As Papas, a cordial, elegant woman, tells her story, she makes 1920 seem like yesterday: the trip with her mother, brother, and two unmarried sisters from Tripolis to Piraeus, outside of Athens, to catch the steamship for America; the twenty-one-day voyage during which, she recalls, a woman died onboard, and the Papas family celebrated Easter; the arrival at New York harbor, where they spent two or three days on Ellis Island.

"I didn't speak a word of English," she says with her clear, gentle voice, faintly accented with the Greek she still uses to converse with others in the household.

Then came the long train ride south to Alabama and their final stop, Bay Minette.

"It was dark," Papas recalls. Outside the train window were small fires. "They were burning stumps."

The family was taken by car to Malbis, where they met up with George Papas. To Bessie's mother, the locale seemed bleak.

"I remember my mother asking, 'Where have you brought my children? To nowhere? To starve to death?'"

Papas pauses, a catch in her voice, remembering her parents and the good life they made for their family in Alabama. They lie in graves near the church on the Malbis grounds, along with the rest of her family, and many others from the plantation world of old.

Bessie's birth in 1910 might have seemed like the final "calamity," which tore her family from Greece, and transplanted them to Alabama. Now, it strikes her as a blessing.

"I was," she says, "my father's lucky child."

There are many ways to measure the luck of Bessie Papas.

At 95, she walks without a cane, sees well enough with a pair of eyeglasses, and has a clear memory.

When young Bessie arrived at the Malbis plantation, she met two other girls her age, Nafseka Mallars and Antigone Papageorge.

A teacher from North Dakota, Marie Starkey, was brought south by the families and became the teacher at the nearby Spanish Fort school. Papas remembers walking to the one-room schoolhouse with her close friends.

The plantation house itself rang with the voices of children and was crowded with families. The men, she says, had a room of their own.

"We slept outside on the porches in the summer," Papas recalls, saying the intense heat did not bother them as children. She says eighteen to twenty people were living in the plantation house, and, at meals, as many as seventy-five filled two dining rooms, sitting at tables set up through the main room and at the long table where she lingers now.

"No one can understand how so many people lived together and so peaceful," she says.

She describes a world in which Greek ways and beliefs were principal. A Greek Orthodox priest would be brought from Pensacola, she says, to perform christenings, baptisms, and weddings at the plantation. Often the families would take the bay boat to Mobile and attend Greek Orthodox religious services there—held in a room, she recalls, before the construction of the church on Ann Street—and visit with relatives who owned the Metropolitan restaurant downtown. When Papas was 15, she worked as a cashier at the Metropolitan.

In 1927, she recalls, the Causeway road over Mobile Bay was opened. She depicts a realm of hard work on the Malbis plantation, with the men fixing breakfast and making bread from a small bakery out back, then working in the fields during the day. She remembers her mother slaughtering a hog, making sausage. Bessie helped out in the canning plant, where okra, beans, eggplant, and others foods were preserved.

The original bakery on the plantation grounds, long since demolished, became the source of a growing enterprise. After Jason Malbis took over Yuille Bakery in downtown Mobile, Malbis Bakery expanded to a large facility on Broad Street in the city, near the railroad tracks.

According to a *Mobile Register* story in 1951 about the Malbis enterprise, "The bakery could make 100,000 pounds of bread a day; 20,000 pounds of cake, and 85,000 pounds of crackers and cookies per day."

Bessie Papas, her brother, and one of her sisters began working at Malbis Bakery and lived in Mobile during the week, returning to the plantation on weekends. "We had over three hundred employees," she says, "and seventy-five different varieties of cookies and cakes."

The grounds of Malbis, she says, were filled with flowers—camellias became a big export—and there were attempts, Papas says, to grow olive trees, develop grape arbors, and cultivate silkworms.

After her stint at the bakery, Papas was given a job back at the plantation as secretary and bookkeeper at the nursery, where she worked for years.

One of the artifacts of that era still on the property is the ice plant, now a tumble-down brick structure with long-dormant machines rusting beneath cobwebs.

Papas recalls bountiful food at the plantation dinner table whatever the occasion, including the Greek dishes of dolmades (grape leaves) and plaki (baked fish).

Even now, the sizable kitchen of Malbis hums with activity. Eugenia Eftaxa, one of many orphans brought to Malbis after the 1940s from war-torn Greece, now in her 70s, is busy making Greek cookies for guests. The next evening there will be a birthday party, and, as always, the long table will be set, and dinners will be served. When Eftaxa, a smiling woman with short gray hair, steps out of the kitchen to serve the cookies and coffee to visitors, she chats with Bessie in Greek. On a table near the sofa is a Greek magazine.

The Greek language is dying out among the youngest generation here, Papas acknowledges, in part because the older generation is passing on. "What keeps the language alive," she says, "is the grandmothers."

While she never married—"It was my choice," she makes clear—she says she helped care for many children at Malbis over the years. Family and religion, she emphasizes, are at the core of her being.

She shares the Malbis home now with William Scourtes, who is half her age and the great-nephew of Jason Malbis. He heads up the Malbis Corporation, which owns all of the remaining landholdings. Another descendant, Tommy Malbis, also lives there.

Around Bessie's neck is a medallion with a cross and Greek writing alongside. It reads, she says, "Jesus Christos Nika"—Jesus Christ is Victorious.

"We were taught one book for all people. The Bible."

Indeed, the possession she speaks of with fervency is a gift brought to her from the Holy Land.

"I have a cross that Mr. Malbis brought from Jerusalem. It has," she says, with a hush in her voice, "a piece of the original cross."

Mega Spileo is a monastery high on a mountain near Kalavrita, Greece. Built in the 4th century A.D., it has been the rugged home to generations of Greek Orthodox monks who have committed themselves to the ascetic life. Among them was Antonios Markopoulos, from a poor family in the small town of Doumena.

But Markopoulos decided to leave the monastery. He cut his beard, traveled to America and took the name Jason Malbis. When he arrived in Baldwin County in 1906, according to the booklet "The Faith of Jason Malbis," published by Malbis Plantation Inc., he pronounced, "The Almighty has revealed to me that this is the land for which we are looking, and here is where we shall stay. I saw a brilliant sign on the horizon descending from heaven and brightening the area around us with untold splendor."

As Papas walks about the plantation house today, she passes a portrait of Jason Malbis as a monk—wearing the tall black headgear, sporting a flowing beard, and his dark eyes looking out with a sad calm. Near the entrance to the house is another painting of Malbis—clean-shaven, a businessman of the 20th century with civic responsibilities.

In the bedroom where Jason Malbis resided in the house—now William Scourtes' room—there's a photograph of Mega Spileo, its stone buildings seen from a distance, a large cross marking one of them. Near the photograph are artworks with images of the apostles.

When Papas talks of Jason Malbis, she does so with reverence. Even in his life after the monastery, she depicts a spiritual man. "He was a great and visionary person."

He headed up the plantation, and when Malbis was incorporated and the first families joined in what "The Faith of Jason Malbis" terms "the brotherhood"—a community of stockholders—Jason Malbis was elected president.

Shortly before World War II, Jason Malbis traveled back home to see his sister. According to the booklet the war "soon overshadowed the poor little land of Greece, which was invaded by the Italians and Germans, who cut off all communications with the outside world." Jason Malbis fell ill, and word was sent back to Malbis plantation in January 1943 by the American Red Cross that he had died in Greece on July 22, 1942. His remains were eventually transferred back to Malbis, and placed in a shrine in the Church of the Presentation of the Theotokos, "which was built on the grounds in accordance with the instructions he stated in his last letter from Greece."

At the community center at Historic Malbis—a housing development across U.S. 90 from the plantation home, with streets named for Jason Malbis and Papageorge and others—William Scourtes shows a visitor a display of panels on the life and times of Jason Malbis.

On these panels the progress of Malbis plantation is vivid: the creation of the ice plant, the development of the nursery, the rise of the bakery. Jason Malbis even designed a towering office building for downtown Mobile, though it was never built.

Scourtes envisions the old ice plant near the Malbis home as a museum one day, open to the public to tell the history of the area. Scourtes says that there were times in the history of the area when outsiders wondered if the plantation was a kind of monastery. But the people at Malbis "were not monks or nuns," he says, shaking his head.

He interprets Jason Malbis' vision as one in which the monastic life "was more elevated but more practical." He says it was meant "to be a utopian society."

Scourtes, who feels the weight of history on his shoulders—"I had twenty uncles and twenty aunts raising me"—says he's determined to extend the vision of Jason Malbis as he can. He heads up a corporation with seven members on the board and fifteen stockholders. "It's closely held," he says.

The corporation, which at one time controlled as many as 10,000 acres of Baldwin County land, he says, has selectively sold off properties over the years, though it still retains 3,000 acres. Jason Malbis' land became the subdivisions of Lake Forest and Timber Creek and now the sprawling complex of stores at the Eastern Shore Centre.

Scourtes is also looking to develop another Malbis subdivision, and, among other outlets, to advertise to Greek communities in Chicago, looking for northerners wanting to retire in the South. Perhaps one day, he says, there will be enough Greek residents in the area to sustain a church in addition to the one in Mobile. The church on the Malbis grounds today is used only on special occasions.

"I'm carrying out what I feel is important," Scourtes says. "I feel I'm carrying out the tradition of the settlers."

Because Jason Malbis was a monk, Scourtes says, there was some question raised in the old country at the time of his death as to who would acquire his holdings, since monks were supposed to give their worldly possessions over to the monastery.

But a law was passed in Greece, Scourtes says, that stated that Malbis' acquisitions after he left the monastery were his personal holdings.

In time, the value of those holdings has increased considerably.

Baldwin County land that sold in 1906 for $5 an acre, says Scourtes, has recently sold "for 50,000 to 75,000 dollars an acre."

It's late afternoon at Malbis plantation, and Eugenia Eftaxa, finished in the kitchen, is going home for the day. Bessie Papas is tired from having visitors, although she has been tireless in her hospitality. She has shown off the paintings of old friends and ancestors and countless photographs on tabletops of loved ones and well-wishers. The television is filled with news of another hurricane on the way—Dennis—but the old plantation house has withstood them all.

She walks out the front door and leans against the railing, looking out on the rolling yard, the lane heading back to the old dairy, the giant oaks and magnolias. It's hard to imagine that, just across Interstate 10, there's a Dillard's, a Bed, Bath and Beyond, and a Williams & Sonoma. Down U.S. 90, the Malbis Motel, once a hot spot for travelers, is empty and marked for demolition to make way, says Scourtes, for a Lowe's.

One expects a horse and buggy, a bearded worker, a wagon filled with camellias, to rumble by.

Across the yard is the Malbis church, built after Jason Malbis' death—and open to visitors, unlike the house—and the cemetery. Near the gravesites of Papas' family members and the Papageorges and the Mallars and others from her first years at Malbis, are the two women she met as little girls when first arriving with her mother—Antigone and Nafseka, who also enjoyed long lives at the plantation house. Between them lies their teacher, Marie Starkey.

"I never thought I'd be the last one," Papas says.

She admits she would like to go out and walk around the grounds, but she's not up to it. Instead, it's time to go in and rest. By early evening, thanks to a satellite dish, her favorite show will be on television, a soap opera, and she will watch it eagerly.

It comes from Athens.

Edward Carl and Walter Bellingrath

DRIVING MR. BELLINGRATH

Theodore

Tall, deep voiced, and elegant of manner, Edward Carl, 80, was certainly not to the manor born. Although he learned early on to set a formal table with china and crystal, serve a four-course meal, and navigate a Packard limousine, he grew up down a dirt road in the south Mobile County community of East Fowl River. Carl's family worked in the satsuma and pecan industry. Kerosene lamps lit his family's home.

A tan-complexioned gentleman—"I had one grandmother considered white," he says, "and her sister's family is considered white"—Carl grew up going to a local elementary school. For high school, he'd catch a ride to Bayou la Batre, where he boarded a bus to Mobile to attend Most Pure Heart of Mary. The school was founded in 1902 by the Sisters of St. Francis of Philadelphia for the purpose of educating African American children.

"I rode on a bus that was carrying seafood into town," he recalls.

But he was getting steeped in another education, as well.

Not far from his home, a Mobile businessman, Walter Bellingrath, had purchased a plot of land in 1918 for a fishing camp—"Belle Camp," he called it—and over the next two decades that "camp" flourished into Bellingrath Gardens and Home. Edward Carl's uncle, Alfred Watson, got a job working for "Mr. Bell," as Mr. Bellingrath was known.

"My uncle," Carl explains, "was Mr. Bell's valet and chauffeur."

Carl began to work at Bellingrath Gardens, too. His first task at the gar-

Edward Carl, who was Walter Bellingrath's valet and chauffer, and later
Bellingrath's personal aide, reminisces in the courtyard of the Bellingrath
home. Photo by Kate Mercer, courtesy of the *Mobile Press-Register.*

dens was to help show flowers. "Miss Bessie" as he calls Bessie Bellingrath,
taught him the names of the camellias and had him stand amid them as tourists roamed through.

"I'd stand in the camellias and tell the visitors the names. Pink perfection,"
he says, recalling one of the camellias. "Oh, they were pretty."

The Bellingraths had built a fifteen-room mansion at the gardens in 1935, furnishing it with grand, rococo revival furniture and English antiques, and using it to hold formal dinners.

"Miss Bessie had me start working at the door of the house," Carl says, "to make sure guests' shoes were not dirty."

"Then," he recalls, "Miss Bessie asked me to come into the house and that she would teach me how to serve."

First, he needed the proper attire—a white shirt, tie, blue serge pants, and white shoes. Bessie Bellingrath sent him to Hammel's Department Store to buy the wardrobe, he remembers, on her account.

He entered, he recalls, a world different than any he had known.

Inside the house was a "modern" 1930s kitchen, where a full-time staff prepared many-coursed meals for the visitors to the Bellingrath table. Carl's role was to assist at the table—removing the centerpiece before a banquet, adding leaves to the table, carrying out the big trays for "left side serving."

He grew adept at setting the table—"knives and spoons on the right, forks on the left," he recites. At home he is still the one who sets the family dinner table.

And he became schooled in the fancier practices of formal dining—some not even known to the very guests at the table.

"We set out finger bowls at each place setting," he says, referring to the artfully blown glass containers where guests were to rinse off their fingertips between the main course and dessert. But all the guests, he says, were not familiar with the practice.

"In the kitchen," he says, smiling, "we'd watch to see who drank the water from the finger bowls."

The story of Bellingrath Gardens has been told many times—from the announcement of its opening to the public in spring 1932 to the fine biography, *Mister Bell: A Life Story of Walter D. Bellingrath,* by Howard Barney (1979, Bellingrath-Morse Foundation) and countless travel magazine stories about the gardens located on Fowl River near the western shore of Mobile Bay.

Edward Carl's version of the story begins at the front door of the mansion and ends up behind the wheel of Walter Bellingrath's car.

But first there were some detours.

In 1943, Carl entered the U.S. Army Air Force and was sent to India as a technical sergeant. Before entering the service he married Mary Evelyn Jackson, whose father had worked on the original construction of Bellingrath Gardens. After the war, the couple decided to set up a general store in the Fowl River community. They started their family—the Carls have three children—and settled into a hard-working life close to the patches of soil where they had come of age.

Carl's uncle Albert Watson, the Bellingrath valet and chauffeur, had decided to move on to work at Brookley Field.

One Sunday, recalls Carl, Albert Watson found Carl at church and whispered that Walter Bellingrath wanted to talk with him. Bellingrath, it turned out, wanted Carl to follow in his uncle's footsteps. Carl accepted the position.

Part of that job included working as Bellingrath's valet.

"I'd shave him in the mornings," Carl says matter of factly, "lay out his clothes, help him get dressed, line him up for breakfast."

Although he had no experience behind the wheel of a limousine, he did have driving under his belt. "I drove a Model-T Ford when I was eight or nine years old," Carl says. "Mr. Bell" offered more than a Model-T.

Describing the Packard, Carl speaks of it dreamily—its sleek black color, its leather seats and hand-straps, its straight-eight engine purring along with subtle power. He also talks of its ability to impress the authorities. He would sometimes surpass the speed limit on Government Street.

"But nobody stopped me. They knew it was Mr. Bell's car."

He drove Bellingrath's Buick limousine, too.

There was a radio, but the men rarely listened when they drove.

Bellingrath had made his fortune as a bottler and distributor of Coca-Cola in the Mobile area, from 1903 to his death in 1955. During his tenure as driver, Carl ferried the beverage executive back and forth to the Coca-Cola offices in downtown Mobile, originally located on Water Street, then at the corner of Royal and St. Anthony streets. When he picked up Bellingrath and there were other businessmen with him, Carl sat alone in the front, driving. "They'd talk business," he says.

He acknowledges that he overheard many business conversations but would not divulge what the talks were about.

The code of the chauffeur only changed when it was just the two men.

"If it was just Mr. Bell, he'd ride in the front seat with me. And we'd talk. Mostly tell jokes."

Often the men traveled together to New Orleans, where Bellingrath had a doctor at Ochsner Clinic. Once they arrived in the Crescent City, they would go separate directions—Bellingrath to the Roosevelt Hotel, Carl to a small hotel for black guests that was owned by a friend of his.

On the way home, they would ride along together, separated only by a few feet of upholstery, two men in the front seat of a shiny car, watching the Gulf Coast beaches slide by.

Bellingrath Gardens was the result of one of the most unusual medical prescriptions in the history of this area.

As Mobile advertising executive Howard Barney wrote in his biography of Bellingrath: "The effects of influenza, business anxiety over the shortage of sugar and Coca-Cola syrup and the inroads of age considerably weakened Walter toward the end of the World War I. Instead of relying again on the magical powers of mineral waters at a distant resort, Walter consulted his Mobile physician, Dr. P. D. McGehee. He was advised to create his own spa, get out in the country more often, reduce business activities, learn how to play with greater regularity and beyond the pressures of urban life."

As a result of jaunts on Fowl River with his fishing guide, Frank Woodard, Bellingrath discovered a plot of available property. According to Barney's book, in February 1919 Bellingrath wrote a letter to his beloved mother: "Ma, I have bought me a beautiful site on Fowl River, 21 miles from Mobile."

McGehee would provide more than medical advice to Bellingrath. Two generations later, the doctor's grandson, Tom McGehee, became director of the House Museum at Bellingrath.

To walk through the Bellingrath home with McGehee is to step back in time. He tells of the pleasures Walter took in a little drink of whiskey but how Bessie disdained liquor. When Bessie came up the driveway, McGehee says, Walter would put away his flask, telling Bessie the smell on his breath "was Listerine."

Prohibition outlawed alcohol between 1919 and 1932. But there was moonshine to be had. McGehee says there were moonshine stills near the property. "Not on the Bellingrath property," he emphasizes.

But the headiest drink of all for the Bellingraths was not alcohol but Coca-Cola.

McGehee tells of an era in early-20th-century American life, where families like the Bellingraths rose to wealth on the fizz of that sweet beverage. Walter was one of several Bellingrath siblings who came to prominence through securing Coca-Cola distributorships—in Montgomery, Andalusia, and Selma, and in Little Rock and Pine Bluff, Arkansas, in addition to Mobile.

The country home at Bellingrath Gardens, McGehee says, is an expression of a family that achieved great social and financial status. In one of those rooms is a portrait looking down from the wall—Asa Candler, who built up Coca-Cola in its early years.

McGehee shares a letter by Walter Bellingrath that suggests the couple's fascination with a more glamorous realm. In 1912, the Bellingraths had vacationed among millionaires, including the Vanderbilts, at a resort in French Lick, Indiana, where the Coke distributor exclaimed in the letter to his mother: "I tell you, it is some sight to see all these rich people come down in the evening with their glad rags and numberless diamonds and other jewelry on."

At the Bellingrath Gardens home, McGehee says, the lengthy, formal meals, the bone china and crystal and finger bowls on the table, were the vision of Bessie Bellingrath aspiring to the utmost sophistication.

After all, McGehee explains, Bessie was Walter Bellingrath's secretary before she became his wife. And both husband and wife had humble beginnings. "Bessie probably read in the society pages about parties on Fifth Avenue in New York and at Newport."

She created, in the wilds of a former fishing camp near Mobile Bay, with garden paths and silver goblets and diamond-cut glassware and valets, her version of elegance.

The Bellingraths had no children, and Bessie passed away in 1943. Walter Bellingrath seemed to lean, ever more heavily, on Edward Carl as someone he trusted, someone he could talk to about personal matters.

The trips to Ochsner Clinic grew more frequent, and when Bellingrath developed cirrhosis of the liver, it was Carl who assisted the doctor, who flew to

Mobile. When the doctor made an incision in Bellingrath's stomach to drain off the fluid from his condition, Carl held the hose, he says.

In the early 1950s, as Bellingrath's health declined even more seriously, the Ochsner doctor told him, Carl recalls, that his boss did not have long to live, that he should "get his affairs in order."

"The doctor pulled me aside and said, 'Edward, I told Mr. Bellingrath this, but I don't think he was listening. You tell him, too.'"

The old-time chauffeur and valet spoke to Bellingrath. Soon after, "Mr. Bell" started getting his affairs in order, Carl says.

In the hospital during his last days in 1955, Carl says, Bellingrath allowed few people into the room. "I was the only one he'd let turn him," he says quietly.

Carl was home, though, when the telephone rang with the news that Walter Bellingrath had died.

"He was a friend to me," Carl says, his voice getting soft. "Like a brother."

Then, tears filling his eyes, Carl leans back in his chair and stops talking, wipes his silver mustache, and looks away.

William Bolton and Herbert Henson

VISITING OLD PALS

Cherokee

With 154 years of rural living between them—and most of those in the company of their beloved dogs—cousins William O. Bolton and Herbert Henson wander through the Key Underwood Memorial Coon Dog Cemetery, saying hello to old friends. "You love your dogs just like you do your kids," says Bolton. "You get took up with them."

As secretary and treasurer of the Tennessee Valley Coon Hunters Association, Bolton, 80, knows whereof he speaks. "Coon hunting used to be a famous thing," he muses. "Everybody had dogs. They didn't sit and watch television as they do now."

Love of dogs, to some, means a desire for their proper resting place, and the Coon Dog Cemetery—the only one in the world, contends Bolton, who acts as its caretaker—is both unusual and bucolic. It's situated in the northwest sector of the state, about an hour west of Muscle Shoals and just outside Cherokee.

A traditional "pet cemetery," says Bolton, it is not.

"We got stipulations on this thing. A dog can't run no deer, possum, nothing like that. He's got to be straight coon dog, and he's got to be full hound. Couldn't be a mixed-up-breed dog, a house dog. We wouldn't have nothing if we had every kind of dog out here."

Key Underwood, the graveyard's founder, started it after his own coon dog, Troop, died in 1937, Bolton says.

William O. Bolton, secretary and treasurer of the Tennessee Valley Coon Hunters Association, recalls a fine old coon dog named Bear at the Coon Dog Cemetery near Cherokee, Alabama, in the northwest corner of the state. Photo by Roy Hoffman, courtesy of the *Mobile Press-Register*.

The Coon Dog Cemetery has rows of headstones that vary from those scrawled or crudely chiseled to fancier ones from monument companies. Photo by Roy Hoffman, courtesy of the *Mobile Press-Register*.

"They dug a hole three-foot deep and put him in a cotton pick sack. Mr. Key Underwood took this rock out of an old chimney and took a hammer and screwdriver and put his name in it."

He points to a screwdriver-cut stone.

"Troop was half redbone and half birdsong," Bolton says, referring to two strains of coon dog. Black-and-tan and blue-tick are other kinds. "And he had an awful cold nose on him. That means he could trail a trail a long ways."

Bolton walks to another plot. "I got one here I call Red—a fine coon dog. He wasn't a real fast dog, but he was real gritty. No doubt knew how to kill a coon."

Henson, 74, nods. He's buried several of his own dogs here, too. One is named Fanney, another Trael, and "Trael's daddy, Old Blue. Trael was a better dog than his daddy because he trailed a colder trail. Both of them"—he pats the hand-lettered stones—"just dogs."

Henson says he could not afford a fancier headstone; now, the cemetery asks hunters to provide granite monuments. If the dogs all enjoyed similar existences on earth—howling in the night, running after raccoons, salivating and whimpering—they are remembered differently, even with invented spellings.

"Moma," reads a piece of wood lying flat on the ground, "Good Bye Good Freind."

"Black Ranger," states another, "He Was Good As The Best And Better Than The Rest."

Another deceased dog, recalls Bolton, was brought all the way from Kentucky with family mourners and a clergyman, of sorts, presiding. "He wasn't no preacher," Bolton says, "but a lawyer playing a preacher."

One grave proclaims its inhabitant a "Night Champion," which Bolton says refers to a nocturnal hunting competition.

"That's not like a regular coon hunt," says Bolton. "I just go over to his house"—he gestures to Henson—"and we turn a-loose. We get the dogs in the truck, and we hunt the natural way."

What about the prey?

"I bet some old coons at night come through here, and some of these dogs might want to rise up," says Bolton.

He grins. Apparently he's told this joke before. One of his duties is to welcome tourists. Although the site is seemingly lost among the pines—down two-lane highways and endless, snaking, dusty Coon Dog Cemetery Road—it is highlighted in Colbert County tourist brochures.

The men defend the tradition of coon hunting, saying that the new method of catching the animals—luring them into traps—is unfair.

"It takes the coons away from us," says Henson. "Part of the sport was to give the coon a chance. You'd jump him, and he could get away. We'd sometimes hold the old dogs back—they had the experience to catch him—and use the young ones."

Henson says he's caught raccoons by hand, "when they're young. You catch them about the neck, they'll scratch you all over the arms. Me and my kids raised them on bottles."

Henson can communicate with them, too.

"I can squall them down," he says.

By "squalling," he means the making of a noise that sounds like a coon being attacked on the ground by dogs. A raccoon high in the branches, he says, will come to the aid of his fellow raccoon facing off with slavering dogs.

"I've made a lot of them jump out of the tree."

He demonstrates, putting his chin down, flaring his lips, and making a reedy, mouth-clearing noise.

As much as the men have relished catching the coon, though—the animals used to sell, they say, for $10 to $12 a hide, and the meat's good barbecued—what they seemed to love most of all was the boyish adventure of it all.

Henson spent his working years driving a forklift for Wrangler; Bolton toiled as an aluminum worker for Reynolds. Questing for coons provided roughly sweet therapy.

Henson tells of coming home, downing supper, and heading out with his dogs. Sometimes the hunt would last all night. He'd head on back to work, bleary-eyed.

"A lot of times, the boss man would come by and say, 'I know what you done last night.' I said, 'What?' He said, 'You been-a coon huntin'.'"

Bolton thrilled to the baying of the dogs—"one's got a coarse mouth, the other one's got a soprano, the other's got a fine mouth. That's music. And when they're running the coon, and they get him up the tree, they change voices. It makes your hair rise on your head."

Both men lament that the rambling days of coon hunting are largely gone by. "You might have a lot of troubles today," says Bolton, "but you could call your buddy up you been coon hunting with, and y'all could get out here in the open, and you'd get away from your troubles, and hear them dogs run, and the next day it'd be a lot better for you."

Scoop, Red, Moon, and Shorty

THE OAK TREE SOCIAL CLUB

Mobile

In the cool shade next to a sweltering parking lot, the members of the Oak Tree Social Club lean over a small table as Sylvester "Scoop" Brown shuffles the domino tiles and parcels them out to the others.

"Dominoes' more fun than cards," says Scoop, 68, who picks up seven tiles for himself, cups them in his hands to study them and figures out his strategy.

"We play cutthroat," he says. "Every man for himself."

Scoop, who has a gray walrus mustache and wears several gold finger rings, is president of the club, a group of men, mostly retired, who started playing dominoes twenty years ago.

After meeting up originally at a barbershop, they moved to their beloved tree on Montgomery Street near South Broad, on the south edge of Mobile's Oakleigh neighborhood, about a block from the Magnolia Cemetery.

"This is the headquarters," says Scoop, who collects the $2 monthly fee, which is put toward snacks, cold drinks, and cookouts.

"If somebody's sick, we buy them a card," says Willie "Red" Washington, 83, who, along with Scoop, is one of the original members. The men also take up collections, Red says, for friends in the hospital.

There's plenty of conversation—one man is nicknamed CNN, "because he likes to tell the news," says Scoop, and another is called WGOK, the call letters of a Mobile radio station, "because he likes to talk."

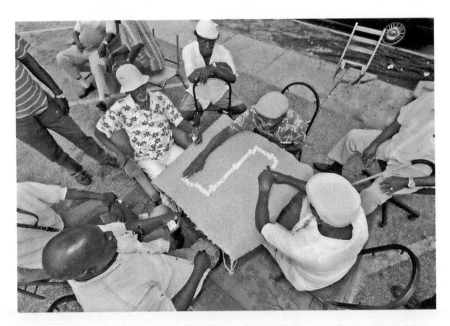

A group of men play dominoes under the shade of an oak tree in the parking lot of the Greer's Food Tiger on South Broad Street in Mobile, Alabama. Photo by Bill Starling, courtesy of the *Mobile Press-Register*.

But the four men who are at the table at any given time are expected to refrain from chit-chat, and play.

After Scoop lays down the double-six tile in the middle of the table, the others build on, matching the numbers of their tiles—they call them bones—going clockwise around the table. While Scoop and Red move quickly, holding their bones in the air with great flourish before thumping them down, Harold G. "Good Looking" Beck, 84, is gentler with his touch.

Good Looking studies his tiles hard. The challenge, he explains, is mathematical—determining which bone to play based on the calculation of what's on the table and what's being held.

"But you ain't going to have no strategy unless you got the right bone," he says.

"We got the best domino players in the world right here," says Scoop.

There are some younger men among the old lions, including Donald "Duck" Seltzer, 47, who works at the Mobile Water Board and visits the game on his off-time. He is concentrating on the table hard, looking at his tiles, making his moves.

But Red "dominoes," putting down his last tile. The others count up the tiles they're holding. The high man will be out.

Duck is the high man. "I can't believe I let these old guys beat me," he says, shaking his head.

"Give me another child, another child," calls out Red, using the expression for a newcomer to the table.

Duck stands up to let Leonard "Moon" Johnson take his place, and Red shuffles the bones.

All year long, every day of the week but Sunday, the dominos game goes on. There is a rhythm to the day—at eight every morning, Moon sets up the chairs and table—and soon afterward, the men arrive from all over town.

As the day unfolds, and the tree's shade moves like a sundial, as many as forty men may be sitting on the chairs or on the overturned cabinets. About half of those are dues-paying, domino-playing members.

The wooden sign nailed to the tree reads: "Oak Tree Social Club. Spirits. Sports. Fun. News."

"People get stressed and don't know they got stressed," says Scoop. "Things get balled up in your mind. This will let go of your mind."

Scoop worked as a laborer for the city of Mobile, and used to play dominoes during his dinner break. As president of the club, he has a calm but forceful manner, keeping a watchful eye out over the parking lot of Greer's Food Tiger and the Family Dollar Store, making sure all is quiet.

When two men start drinking wine near the table, he tells them, "Take that outside of the tree!" As president of the club, he says, he tolerates "no foolishness, no actin' up."

At the table there is no smoking, he says, and no alcohol. Scoop has put members "on probation" for misconduct at the table, keeping them from sitting at the table until he deems the probation time is up.

Good Looking, whose wife died two years ago, says he found out about the club at church, when he was talking with Scoop.

"It gave me somewhere to go," Good Looking says.

He admits to having been intimidated at first by the intensity of the play. He watched for several months before taking a turn at the table.

Richard Barnes, 66, who has no vocal cords—he had throat cancer—says, in his halting way, that his game of choice in earlier years was shooting pool. But, like Good Looking, he loves the camaraderie of the Oak Tree Club.

"It gets boring sitting up in the house watching TV," Barnes says.

Moon, as one of the younger members of the club, finds in the men a model of good conduct. "I used to stay in trouble," Moon says of his life before joining the club.

"He's still a fool," says Scoop, teasing him at the table.

"He's a little bit better," says Red, who used to be a coal miner in north Alabama.

"I learned a lot from these old men," says Moon, who got disabled, he says, after being hurt working on a ship.

Another man arrives. "Brown, Brown, what's going down?" he says, slapping Scoop's hand.

Others look on: Pizza Man, Low-Down, Cigar.

Then a red pickup truck rolls in and comes to a halt.

Good Looking gets up from his chair and heads over to the back of the truck, opens up the tailgate and takes down a wheelchair. He rolls the chair to the door of the truck. A man with a big smile and a prosthetic leg climbs down, huffing, and gets in the chair. Good Looking rolls him toward the table.

Samuel "Shorty" Dubose, 67, had his left leg amputated, he says, from diabetes. He lives in a neighborhood on the other side of town. "I'd be riding by and see them." He had stopped once and introduced himself. Now he's part of the club.

"I enjoy being with the fellows," he says, "and shooting the bull."

As Scoop wins the domino game, Moon gets up as the loser.

"Give me another child, another child," cries Red.

Good Looking rolls Shorty up to the table, and the next game begins.

The losers and winners revolve—soon Red gives up his chair, then Scoop— and others sit down. Before long, Scoop is seated again. Then Red.

When the sun drops lower in the sky, and the shade moves again, the club members stop their game and move the table and chairs over a few feet to follow it.

A young man in his 20s in a sport-utility vehicle, hip-hop music thundering from his sound system, drives right up next to the table, looks down over the men, and says, "I've been wanting to play some professionals."

The men do not answer him. Scoop glances up, then back to the table.

"Hey," the youth says, "I want to play."

"This is a club," says Scoop. "You got to be a certain age."

The youth sits watching, his music pounding.

The men continue to ignore him. Finally, he drives away.

"He was looking for trouble," says Scoop.

The game ends, another begins. "They got the devil in them," Scoop says of the younger generation. "All colors, white, black, yellow. An older person can't tell them what to do."

"When I was coming along," says Red, "anybody old tell you what to do, you did it. Now they want to go get a gun."

"If they got a gun, they're bad," says Scoop. "If they don't got a gun, you can run them in the river with a switch."

Dusk comes, and it's time to box up the dominoes, fold up the tables and chairs, and stash them beneath the tree.

Overhead, battered by hurricanes and drought, hot weather and sleet, enduring all, the headquarters awaits the next round of games.

PART VI DIFFERENT WINDOWS ON DIXIE

*W*hatever sets one apart from the mainstream can make for an un-usual angle of vision on home. In a way, many of the people I've profiled in Alabama Afternoons *look through different windows on the Dixie they inhabit. Their views are distinctive, idiosyncratic, passion-ate, and creative.*

Three widely varying stories in this section offer distinctive windows on Ala-bama and the South.

The first is the tale of Yolande "Bebe" Betbeze, Miss America 1951, whose rav-ishing beauty as a young woman impacted her point of view. The two days I spent with Betbeze at her Georgetown townhouse in Washington, D.C., were fascinat-ing to me on many levels. The Miss Alabama of a half century ago who had won the national crown was still lovely, and still tied, in her stories and vivid rec-ollections, to her native state. Betbeze had been controversial, too, in her early stances on women's liberation and racial equality, and the national press she received for her opinions had not gone unnoticed back home by admirers—or critics.

The second is the story of a young man of Native American heritage, Alex Alvarez, on the Poarch Creek reservation in Atmore. For all the times I had driven on Interstate 65 past the Poarch Creek community, I had never explored its streets, certainly never sat in a class where the Muskogee language was being taught.

Abby Fisher, who may have composed the first African American cookbook in the nation, offers another kind of window on the culture. We see her through the shadows of history. The quest to find out more about her is expressive of another kind of journey I enjoy, a sleuthing back through time. The culinary tradition of Alabama, and the larger South, is central to regional culture. Abby Fisher is a representative of that tradition, one that holds appeal for all the senses.

Yolande "Bebe" Betbeze

CINDERELLA IN CHARGE

Nearly a half-century after she was crowned Miss America in 1951, Bebe Betbeze welcomed me into her home far to the north of her native south Alabama.

Washington, D.C.

In a grand old townhouse in the elegant Georgetown neighborhood of Washington, there lives a woman from Mobile once known as "America's Own Cinderella." Ravishing during her youth—with compelling brown eyes, lustrous dark hair, and a smile that ignited the room—Yolande Betbeze Fox, now 71, is lovely still, the gracious elder of the bewitching girl that she was long ago.

Over the course of the last fifty years, "Bebe," as she's nicknamed, has enjoyed an especially glamorous time for a teen who once pored over school books within the nurturing confines of Mobile's Visitation Convent. Her life has traced a dramatic arc, from an early marriage to the boss of Universal Pictures, to friendship with actors like Cary Grant and Elizabeth Taylor, to her activism in politics, reflected, in 1960, in her picture in the *New York Times*, carrying a civil rights placard.

Widowed in her 30s, Bebe became a darling of the gossip columnists, who linked her romantically—and imaginatively, she emphasizes—to Joe DiMaggio and other celebrated men.

Some Mobile women still whisper of a friendship with President Kennedy. ("I knew him," Bebe says crisply, settling into a chair in the living room.

Yolande Betbeze, Miss America 1951. Photo courtesy of the *Mobile Press-Register.*

"Enough said.") George Wallace, she suspects, may have even had his eye on her as a potential first lady of Alabama. Wallace friend Jimmy Hatcher, as Bebe tells it, had tried to pair them up.

This Cinderella's fairy tale began in 1950 when Bebe, who'd not yet shed her dental braces, was an opera student in Mobile. One night, the arts critic of the *Birmingham News,* who heard her in a Mobile Opera Guild production, gave her a glowing review, then proposed to Bebe that she enter the Miss Alabama pageant.

Bebe, by then, had already captured a local crown—judged Spring Hill College's Miss Torch of 1949. She insists that she nursed no further ambition to be a beauty queen, preferring to lose herself in Proust and Mozart.

But the invitation flattered her, and the city of Birmingham—the pageant's home—seemed enamored of her. At the time, she recalls, Mobile gave her no backing, "not even a handkerchief," as she once complained to an interviewer.

After performing Schubert songs in the pageant preliminaries, and reaching the finals, she resolved to win, she says. "It was off with the braces and on with the show!"

In August of that year, at a theater in Birmingham, she sang "Summertime" from *Porgy and Bess* and clinched the crown.

Photos astonished her friends back in Mobile. She laughs. "'That's Bebe?' they asked? 'Where are her books? Her braces? Her braids?'"

Atlantic City was next.

In the Thursday night swimsuit competition, dressed in Catalina swimwear, Bebe won first place. For the Saturday night finals, in a white taffeta gown, she performed the "Caro Nome" aria from *Rigoletto* that she'd studied with Madame Rose Palmai-Tenser, founder of the Mobile Opera Guild.

As her friends back in Mobile gathered at the Cawthon Hotel to hear the pageant on the radio, Bebe awaited the judges' decision. . . .

Our new Miss America: Miss Alabama! Yolande Betbeze!

With a crown atop her head and a cluster of roses in her arms, she started down the famous walk.

It was the next morning that her duties as Miss America 1951 were outlined at a breakfast hosted by Catalina. The company, she says, had planned for her to tour the country modeling Catalina swimwear, as had previous Miss Americas.

She refused, telling them she was a singer, not a pin-up.

Catalina threatened to sue, but she held her ground.

When the pageant backed Bebe's decision, Catalina pulled out as a sponsor, founding Miss America's chief competing contest—Miss Universe.

"I wasn't born yesterday," she says of her decision to defy the sponsors. "They were funny old men, and I always knew how to make them march."

As a result of her savvy, her fees as Miss America—for everything from cutting ribbons to promoting products—went up four-fold, reaping her $50,000 that year. Indeed, according to Frank Deford's 1971 book about the pageant, *There She Is,* Bebe once declared of yesteryear's competitions, "'The pageant uses its Miss Americas, and most of them don't even know they're being taken.'"

From the outset of her reign, America's Cinderella had made it clear. If her life was to unfold like a fairy tale, she would take control of the script.

To spend a few days with Bebe Betbeze is to enter a realm where stories about hometown folks blend with those of figures on the world stage.

Welcoming few interviewers into her home—and even then, not allowing a visitor to tape their conversation—she is down-to-earth, dressed in slacks and cotton T-shirt with over-blouse, and at the same time regal, recounting the stories of her life with the presence of a woman used to speaking to reporters, cameras, and crowds. She wears little make-up, no nail polish, and still keeps her dark hair shoulder-length. She has an Audrey Hepburn–like bearing, relaxed, warm, clear-voiced, yet controlled.

The photographs in her study suggest the range of her acquaintances—Henry Kissinger, Eudora Welty, Luciano Pavarotti, Muhammad Ali—and those in her living room, among them Al Gore and Hillary Clinton, show her political loyalties. On the top of her grand piano are photos of her mother, who passed away in 1986, and Bebe's daughter and granddaughter, Dolly and Paris Campbell. There also is a portrait of Clark Clifford, her daughter's godfather. Clifford, who passed away in 1998 at age 91, had served as an adviser to presidents Truman, Kennedy, and Johnson.

As Bebe tells the story of her life, the lore of her house serves as backdrop. Built in the late 1700s, and having been the residence of Newton Baker, secretary of war during World War I, the mansion is a place where tour buses idle and tourists gawk. Across the street live Ben Bradlee, the former executive editor of the *Washington Post,* and his wife, writer Sally Quinn. On the same block is the former home of Bebe's late friend, Pamela Harriman, the grand dame of the Democratic Party.

But the presiding spirit of the house will always be Jackie Kennedy, who lived here with little John-John and Caroline in the year following President Kennedy's assassination.

"It's again like Jackie would have liked," says Bebe, "chintz and pillows and children running around."

It is Bebe's fair-haired, snaggle-toothed, 7-year-old granddaughter, Paris, who has brought back the happy noise of kids.

Bebe shows her visitor the back patio of the house, pointing out a gate deep in the shrubs where Jackie would make her escape to elude the pesky crowd out front. Some tourists, Bebe says, still have the nerve to come banging on her door, demanding to see Jackie's former domain.

"I've known five presidents," she says, adding sweetly, "I had a crush on Adlai," referring to the man who was a Democratic candidate for president twice—in 1952, the first year after her Miss America reign, and 1956. Bebe sang "The Star-Spangled Banner" at his 1952 rallies. Stevenson lost both elections to Republican Dwight Eisenhower.

In recent years she befriended Virginia Blythe Kelley, President Clinton's mother, and threw a party for her at her Georgetown home. She describes a festive soiree, with Mickey Rooney at the piano. Bebe took a trip to the horse races with Mrs. Kelley just weeks before she passed away in 1994.

Bebe has even gone out on the stump. During Bill Clinton's first run for president in 1992, she sometimes filled in for Mrs. Clinton on speaking engagements in the New York primaries. One of these speeches, she says, was to a group of Mississippians living in New York, a group best known for its annual Mississippi-in-Central-Park picnic.

"I love a southern accent," Bebe says, likening it to a "slowed-down British accent." Although her own voice, clear and resonant, bears little trace of an Alabama drawl, she acknowledges that, sometimes, "I put one on."

Among the objects of cultural value that surround her—an original painting by the French impressionist Corot, a signed Andy Warhol silkscreen of Jimmy Carter—there is an object of deep sentimental value. She shows her Mobile visitor a black banner with the white lettering, "A L A B A M A." It is the sash she wore in Atlantic City on that victorious night half a century ago.

"I would probably be in Mobile still," she replies, when asked how her life might have turned out if not for the Miss America crown, "active in historic preservation and pouring a lot of tea."

Born on Thanksgiving Day 1928, Yolande—a name her mother took from a book of medieval history—was the sole child of William and Ethel Betbeze.

She was reared during her early years on Montauk Avenue, a block in Midtown Mobile of mostly stately homes.

She describes her father—remembered by many in town as a good-looking man who took pride in his pit barbecue—as often absent during her childhood, a "good ol' boy" who preferred bunking at his hunting camp, and who sold off pieces of family property for income. He passed away when she was a teenager, and she speaks of him as though he were a shadow drifting across the back porch of her years, lingering, then gone. Her aunt, Lelia Sauer, active in civic circles, seemed more interested in Bebe, taking her on cultural trips north.

Her mother, though, is the sustaining force who occupies center stage when Bebe remembers Mobile.

It was not spacious Montauk Avenue that was home to Bebe, Ethel, and Ethel's mother, Elizabeth Green—a household of women on their own. They relocated to a humbler block on Spring Hill Avenue, across from Father Ryan Park. Although Bebe is vague as to when they moved there, she recalls the feeling of letdown she had to wake up in a home that was far more cramped than the one they'd left.

But Bebe had found an outlet for escape, the world of the arts.

Her passion for music was fired early on by two Mobile teachers, she says, the first being her accompanist, Alma Fisher, a concert pianist who'd arrived in Mobile from Germany in the aftermath of World War II. The other was her voice teacher, Madame Rose Palmai-Tenser, who'd fled Czechoslovakia during that same war, and arrived in Mobile to become, in Bebe's opinion, one of the great cultural influences on the city during the 20th century.

She was more conscientious about following the guidance of her music teachers than of the nuns at her Visitation Convent school, she says.

Bebe's preferred academy was one of her own making, composed of time spent by herself in the public library, or walking through Ashland Place, near the convent, practicing her recitative. She remembers a day that she wandered through the Church Street Graveyard in downtown Mobile, reciting aloud the "Rubaiyat of Omar Khayam."

"Because I was a loner," she says, "some people thought I was a snob."

Whatever they thought, no one could dispute that she was captivating.

Bebe's visitor tells her that many a man in Mobile crows he went out with Yolande Betbeze, Miss-America-to-be. "If I had a hundred dollars for every man in Mobile who claims he went out with me, I'd be a billionaire," she huffs.

"We had lots of dances and you had lots of formal gowns," remembers Joan Young Tonelli, a year behind Betbeze at Visitation Convent. "With her olive skin and long glorious hair, she would catch people's eye. Her hair was dark and kind of floated when she moved."

Tonelli also remembers an amusing habit of Betbeze. "She would step into this ballroom in the Admiral Semmes hotel, this beautiful person. If you caught her eye, she'd make a monkey face."

"Do you want to see the monkey face?" Bebe asks her visitor today. She scrunches up her mouth and nose. Her granddaughter, Paris, giggles at the result.

Relaxed, her face is beautiful again, a softened, aged image of the woman who was photographed in the *New York Mirror* magazine, for a 1957 article, "What Is Beauty?" Grace Kelly and Kim Novak were pictured on the same page.

It was one thing to be acclaimed Miss America at 21—the city of Mobile held a fireworks celebration for her one Friday night at Ladd Stadium; The University of Alabama Million Dollar Band spelled out "B E B E" in a football half-time show there the next day—but another to venture out on one's own as a 22-year-old former Miss America.

"It's not easy being young and pretty," she says. "It's hard work."

The movies came calling. Among the offers was the role of Jane in the Tarzan series, following in the jungle steps of Maureen O'Sullivan (mother of Mia Farrow) who'd played Jane in the 1930s to Johnny Weismuller's loin-clad king of the apes. Ever independent-minded, Bebe declined. "In those days, the studio owned you for a year," she says. "They told you what to wear, what to say, who to go out with."

She was squired by the golden boys of her generation. She broke the hearts of strangers. In a piece for *Look* magazine just after her year as Miss America, she wrote: "I have received and rejected 163 proposals of marriage sent through the mails."

At a New York party thrown for an actor in the early television cop-show *Dragnet*, Bebe met and fell in love with a "brilliant and gentle and wonderful man" nearly twice her age. Matthew "Matty" Fox had been president of Universal Pictures during the era of W. C. Fields and Mae West, and had just launched a television venture. They got married in Beverly Hills, California, on July 4, 1954.

"He was the father I never had," Bebe reflects today, "the father I was looking for."

For ten years, until he succumbed in his sleep to a heart attack, Miss America and the movie mogul led a star-struck existence. They globe-trotted, they threw parties for the rich and famous, they had homes on two coasts.

"Gloria Swanson was our next-door neighbor in Hollywood. She used to come over and throw out all my pots and pans," Bebe says. Swanson, Bebe explains, fretted eccentrically about hygiene.

The Visitation Convent student, though, who'd loved Proust and Faulkner, continued to flourish as a thinker. Her Miss America reign had coincided, she points out, with a searingly divisive era in American politics—the McCarthy hearings in Washington—and her dislike of McCarthy's communist-hunting tactics crystallized her political convictions. In 1953, she recalls, she even stood vigil "at the front gate" at Sing-Sing Prison in upstate New York to protest the executions of Julius and Ethel Rosenberg, the U.S. couple accused of spying for the Soviets.

She began to attend a circle of intellectuals at the home of Deems Taylor, a New York music critic. One of the other regulars at Taylor's salon was Ayn Rand, the conservative ideologue and author of the best-selling novels *Atlas Shrugged* and *The Fountainhead*.

"Ayn Rand hated me," Bebe remembers. "She said to Deems Taylor, 'I'm not coming here if Yolande Fox comes here.'

"He told Ayn Rand, 'Well, then, don't come back.'"

She took up the cause of the early civil rights movement. On June 15, 1960, she was shown in the *New York Times* carrying a protest sign that read, "Theatre Supports Southern Students." The *Times* reported:

F. W. Woolworth was picketed on Forty-fourth and Broadway at noon yesterday by Southern Negro students, Broadway actors and Alabama's 1951 winner of the Miss America contest, Yolande Betbeze Fox.

"I'm a Southern girl, but I'm a thinking girl," the brunette from Mobile said yesterday, holding a sign supporting the sit-ins of Southern Negro students at Woolworth lunch counters throughout the South. "Every Southerner I know in New York, without exception, is in favor of the Congress of Racial Equality (CORE)."

"Yes, I received a lot of hate mail for my position, saying, 'How could a flower of the South say something like that?'" Bebe recalls. "But I don't like hate of any kind. I tore it up."

She says she also received letters of encouragement from all over the country. Joe Langan, Mobile's mayor from 1953 to 1969, doubts anyone in her hometown could have thought too badly of Bebe. For all that she'd accomplished, "Everybody was pretty proud of her," says Langan, who knew her family.

Ironically, it was not living in the North that had fired Bebe's convictions but her upbringing in the South, she says.

She describes a painful but revelatory moment of her childhood. After she'd addressed a black man as "mister," one of the elders in her family tore into her, criticizing, "Don't you know better than that? I thought we raised you better!"

She tells this story as though she is still amazed.

The Bebe of the 1960s did not shy away from turning her ire on the very organization that had launched her into fame.

A lily-white pageant, she proclaimed to cameras and microphones, was hardly in keeping with the diversity of the nation. She disassociated herself from the Miss America pageant until it changed its profile.

"'How could we say it's Miss America,' I asked, 'if it's not open to all Americans?'"

She levied other criticisms at the pageant for what she perceived as a decline in its standards, especially in its depiction of women. "In the seventies it was sexist," she says unstintingly. "It was like parading meat out there. It needed to straighten up."

Her thinking at the time was reflected in a profile story, "Miss America Was a Rebel (and still is)," by Barbara Raskin in the Sunday magazine of the *Washington Post*. In photos with the story, Bebe struck a bookish, Gloria Steinem pose—long, straight hair, oversized eyeglasses, dark turtleneck, knee-length skirt, knee-high boots.

When Raskin asked Bebe if she continued to go to the Miss America pageant, Bebe retorted:

"Good Lord, no. I love to watch it on TV, though. It's great to see the essence of mediocrity chalked up on a point system . . . You get to watch some blonde twirling a baton through a hoop of fire . . . Usually they don't have a talent at all and they have two weeks in which to learn how to do something, a cultural thing, you know." But the pageant, Bebe underscores, has transformed itself since those days, and she takes some of the credit.

During the 1980s, she says, the pageant began regularly to have black and Asian-American contestants, and the general focus became less about looks than about what the women thought and had to say. "It's a serious, scholarship foundation," she explains. "We gave away $36 million in scholarships last year."

In recent times, she has opposed certain proposed changes at the pageant that, in her opinion, would undermine its traditions. Last year, for example, there was rancor within the Miss America organization about whether the ban should be lifted against participants who were divorced or had ever been pregnant. Ultimately, the ban remained.

Bebe believes this degree of "openness" would have been going too far.

"Miss America," she explains, "should represent an ideal, the All-American wholesome girl, well-rounded. Somebody you'd be proud to bring home to your mother. 'Miss America' is a wholesome word, like 'apple pie.'"

A generation after she was frequently at odds with the pageant, its contestants have come to look up to her. "People tell me I've become the 'darling,' of the pageant," she says with obvious pride.

"Yolande definitely is a spokesperson and a role model," says Nan Teninbaum, president of the Miss Alabama pageant. Teninbaum says she agrees with stands on difficult issues that Bebe took in the past.

"Back in Yolande's day, it was a beauty pageant," Teninbaum says. "Today, they have a platform. Something to stand for."

If there was a time when Bebe's relationship with Mobile seemed on uneven footing—she first visited Birmingham after her Miss America victory, a fact lost on no one a half century ago—perceived insults have long faded.

Deford wrote in *There She Is* that civic Mobile's failure to promote Bebe in her Miss America quest "was to prove expensive to mercantile Mobile some months ahead" when Birmingham took her under its wing. Bebe's attentions to Birmingham seemed to annoy the *Mobile Register*'s society columnist, Cornelia McDuffie Turner. As late as 1962, Turner wrote: "Bebe Betbeze Fox had a daughter a few days ago. Her wire to the *Birmingham News* (not Mobile, mind you) stated, 'Future Miss Alabama born today.' Figure that one out."

But Bebe expresses nothing but deep affection for her hometown, remembering the adulation she received after winning the pageant, not to mention a diamond bracelet financed by public donations.

If there were slights, "Mobile," she says, "has more than made up for it."

"I've thought about going back there to live for a year," she tells her visitor. Trips home, in recent times, she says with melancholy, have too often been to the final rites of a family member or dear friend. She lists some of the Mobile friends now deceased—Tommy McCown, Jane Rogers Guthrie. As she says of Guthrie: "I can't think of going there and not seeing her."

So in Georgetown Bebe remains.

She has never remarried, but enjoys a longtime friendship with Cherif Guellal, the former ambassador from Algeria to the United States. The couple, when she was a young widow and he a dashing Arab diplomat, were often the subject of Washington gossip columns.

Joining Bebe and her visitor for lunch, Guellal recounts a story of how his political rivals back in Algeria tried to disgrace him by showing their president a photograph in the U.S. press of the ambassador dancing with the former Miss America. Guellal, laughing, recalls that the president, upon gazing at the photograph, raised his hands and declared, "Let God give him more of this!"

After lunch, Bebe sees her visitor to the front door and lingers a moment beneath the magnolia trees profuse in her urban yard. Like long-dormant ghosts stirred to brilliance again, the images of yesteryear—Bebe as opera singer, as beauty queen, as new bride—have been brought to life these last few days as she recounted her fairy tale. But, she acknowledges, those are pages long turned.

Through the front window, Bebe's granddaughter peeks out mischievously. A delivery man climbs the walk. Her maid, Maria, summons her to the telephone. Bebe heads back inside, Atlantic City receding to once upon a time long ago.

Alex Alvarez

Poarch Creek Reservation, Atmore

Growing up in Fort Walton Beach, Florida, Alex Alvarez knew little at first of his family's American Indian heritage. Creek on his mother's side, Alvarez went to a powwow when he was 8 years old and was captivated by the stories of the elders.

"An old Indian sat beside me and started talking to me like he'd known me for a long time," recalls Alvarez, 24, at his office at the Poarch Creek Band of Indians reservation near Atmore. "I just sat and nodded my head."

That powwow began Alvarez's interest in Creek music, drumming, religion, and the Creek language, known as Muskogee.

Now serving as cultural education coordinator at the Poarch Creek reservation, Alvarez is teaching a new generation of kids—and their parents—to speak the language of their forefathers.

"This is the heart of what I call cultural revitalization and retention," he says of the Muskogee tongue.

He began his work only a few weeks ago.

Daniel McGhee, chairman of the Poarch Creek education committee, says the language instruction is the first at the reservation in at least ten years, and the most ambitious yet.

"I think it's a way to get in touch with your past, with your identity," McGhee explains. "You have something very specific to Native Americans—a different language altogether."

It's a challenge to learn Muskogee. Even the alphabet is tricky.

Alex Alvarez, of Creek ancestry, teaches culture, history, and the Creek language, Muskogee, as he writes Creek vocabulary words on the marker board in the front of the class at the Poarch Creek Tribal Complex education center. Photo by John David Mercer, courtesy of the *Mobile Press-Register.*

On Alex Alvarez's desk is a copy of the textbook he uses for his twice-weekly classes: *Beginning Creek,* published by the University of Oklahoma Press. Beneath the English letters are the words in the native language: "Mvskoke Emponvkv."

The "v," he explains, is pronounced "uh," the "p" as "buh," and the "k" usually as "ghee." The "k" is sometimes pronounced as a traditional "k."

He sounds out the words: "Muh-sko-ghee Em-bu-nah-ga."

"I've been learning Creek since I was sixteen," he says. "Ever since then, I've been trying to pick up words. Now, I'm trying to pick it up on a more professional level. On my trips to Oklahoma, I try to ask elders as much as I can. I try to listen to everything they tell me."

Alvarez has a dark, cherubic face and straight black hair that he keeps in a braid down his back. He explains that in addition to his mother's Creek heritage, he has Cuban lineage on his father's side and some white ancestors, too.

But it is the American Indian side of his background that spellbinds him, in part because of his closeness to his mother.

"I might go to a Hispanic dinner or an Irish gathering, but I am Indian. I go to sleep an Indian and wake up an Indian.

"Ever since age eight, I've been performing, dancing, and singing in pow-wows."

As a teen, he traveled often from Florida to the Poarch Creek reservation and made friends among other young tribal members.

He now travels, for example, to drum and dance in Ahoskie, North Carolina, with the Meherrin tribe; to Niceville, Florida, for an intertribal gathering; and to a powwow of the Mississippi Band of Choctaw Indians.

He composes some of his own music, too.

When asked to offer a number in Muskogee, he stands straight and chants a song he wrote. He translates the lyrics: "When we sing, we can shake the earth."

The Poarch Creek reservation, on the western edge of Escambia County, covers 386 acres about a mile from Interstate 65, eight miles south of Atmore. The tribe, says Arthur Mothershed, tribal council treasurer, owns about 6,200 acres altogether.

Mothershed explains that the Poarch Band of Creek Indians was historically part of a Creek nation that covered parts of Alabama and Georgia.

Shortly before it's time for class, Alvarez drives a van through the reservation, pointing out the flat landscape of one-story brick homes, the ball field, and rodeo ring. "The reservation is like its own city," he says. "We even have our own police."

The tribe is one of several federally recognized ones in the Southeast, Alvarez explains, the remnant of Indians who stayed behind—"hiding, escaping, surviving in godforsaken places"—after the Indian Removal Act of 1830. He lists others: the Eastern band of Cherokee in Cherokee, North Carolina, the Mississippi Choctaws near Philadelphia, Mississippi, the Seminole and Miccousuke in Florida, and the Catawba in South Carolina.

Alvarez's Indian ancestors were from the tribal town of Eufaula—the site that inspired the Alabama city of the same name—and "were removed to Oklahoma. But some escaped and came to Florida, where they ran moonshine in the backwoods."

Members of the Poarch Creek community affiliate with an array of Christian churches. But there are ancient Creek rituals, too. Alvarez says the older spiritual practices appeal to him greatly.

He points down one road where the ceremonial grounds are tucked into the woods. He has spent many nights there, he says, doing all-night stomp-dancing as a form of ritual prayer.

While the grounds are not officially off-limits to visitors, on this particular afternoon, it is inhabited by elders mourning a tribal leader who has just died. Alvarez drives on.

Beyond the reservation, Alvarez finds that American Indians are stereotyped by people outside of his culture. "People ask me," he says, "'Do you live in a teepee? Are you a real Indian?'"

He says that for decades in Hollywood films, Indians were depicted in certain ways. One of them, he complains, was as "a drunk Indian going 'woo-woo,' chasing a white woman around the cabin."

And the Indian roles, he says, were often played "by white people with brown shoe polish on their skin. The real Indians were used for extras."

He sees the opposite movement, though, in popular culture today.

"Now, Indians are glamorized, glorified. People want to claim native blood."

As Alvarez tours the reservation, he sees a young teen ambling down the road. He rolls down his window and calls out to him, "Coming to class tonight?"

"I don't think I can make it."

"Hope to see you next time," Alvarez says.

Teenagers are of particular interest to Alvarez, who has helped in efforts to prevent substance abuse by Indian teens in Louisiana and Kansas. He says that his focus on language and culture helped save him from traveling perilous paths of his own.

Young people "are less inclined to mess up their lives with drugs and juvenile crime when they are involved with culture, when they have that as an outlet."

"Creek is in the process of dying," he says about the language, estimating that only 5 percent of the Creek population of Oklahoma is fluent. The Muskogee speakers, he says, are mostly of the older generation.

Too often in the past, he says, Indians had to choose between "giving up their culture and surviving."

His goal is to encourage other Indians "to have one foot in the past and one in the present. To speak Muskogee and suit up in a three-piece suit."

The students who show up for Alvarez's evening classes are of all ages.

There's Johnny McGhee, 56, whose great-uncle, Calvin McGhee, was a famous chief. "My parents and grandparents could say a few words," McGhee says of Muskogee. "The language died out."

There's Rosalind Smith, who has long, curly black hair and attends the class with her son, Tyler, 10. Smith emphasizes how important cultural education is to the sense of "being proud." Language, she says, "is a part of it."

Daniel McGhee, the tribal council member, also a descendant of Calvin McGhee, comes to the class with his sons Brice, 10, and Xan, 8.

McGhee manages the Poarch Creek gaming hall with its twenty-four-hour bingo, which helps generate the revenue for education funding, including Alvarez's salary.

McGhee says he's delighted to be able to take the class with his sons. "This is our home," he says, speaking of his Creek ancestors. "This is where it originated."

Looking at dark-haired Brice and blonde Xan, McGhee explains that, as Indians, "we run a spectrum of how we look."

Part of that spectrum comes from other racial and ethnic groups that may be mixed into a Creek heritage.

Mazie Gartman, 78, says she is three-quarters Creek and that her father, who was full-blooded Creek, had few educational opportunities open to him and his generation. "He was illiterate," she says.

"That's why I've enrolled in this class," she says, expressing her commitment to lifelong education.

Young and old, the classmates turn their attention to Alvarez as he stands before the blackboard. The evening's lesson is animals.

With chalk he writes: "este-papv," pronouncing, "este-bah-buh. Lion." He says the words literally mean "person eater."

"Este bah-buh," the class repeats.

"Kono," he says. "Skunk."

"Kono," they chorus back.

"Kowike," pronouncing it, "ko-we-ghee. Whale."

"Ko-we-ghee."

Pony. Horse. Dove. Buffalo. He goes through the list in Muskogee, with call and response on each one.

Then they play a game, each person offering clues to an animal, having the rest of the class guess the animal's name in Muskogee.

Council treasurer Arthur Mothershed is at the second class of the evening with his three daughters, Katie, 15, Shelley, 11, and Kamryn, 7.

Alvarez has the class play a game, in which students think up an animal, then tell a few clues as to its identity. The others have to guess the animal, calling out its name in Muskogee.

Little Kamryn Mothershed is having trouble coming up with clues. She summons Alvarez to help her, but quickly dismisses his advice.

She reads her clue aloud: "It likes cat food."

The class, in a spirit of camaraderie, laugh and in unison chime the answer: "Pose," pronouncing it, "boh-zay."

"Yes, boh-zay," Alvarez says. "Cat."

Abby Fisher

"WHAT MISS FISHER KNOWS ABOUT OLD HOME COOKING"

I learned about Abby Fisher and her cookbook from Phil Hyman, a Mobile native who lives in Paris and is a food historian and scholar. The story of Abby Fisher led me to Karen Hess. I visited with Hess in 2000; she passed away in 2007, at age 88.

New York City

On a brisk, Manhattan afternoon, surrounded by thousands of books about food, Karen Hess, 80, is talking about the woman she believes composed the first African American cookbook in the nation—Abby Fisher, of Mobile.

Abby Fisher was an ex-slave, Hess believes, born in South Carolina to a white, French father and a black mother. "She had to be a slave," Hess says. "Any other explanation would be tortured."

Hess bases her sketch of Fisher on scant information available, mostly garnered in San Francisco, where Fisher set down her recipes. The esteemed culinary historian is the first to acknowledge—indeed, hope—that the mysteries of Fisher's shadowed life will be unraveled in Mobile, perhaps by the reporter visiting her this day.

According to Hess, Abby married Alabama-born Alexander C. Fisher. Both were designated by census records as "mu," for "mulatto." Together, in Mobile, they had ten children, and after the Civil War, carrying the young ones, headed west. "She cooked on a wagon train," Hess speculates.

WHAT MRS. FISHER KNOWS

ABOUT

Old Southern Cooking,

SOUPS, PICKLES, PRESERVES, ETC.

Awarded Two Medals at the San Francisco Mechanics' Institute Fair, 1880, for best Pickles and Sauces and best assortment of Jellies and Preserves.

DIPLOMA AWARDED AT SACRAMENTO STATE FAIR, 1879.

San Francisco:
Women's Co-operative Printing Office, 420, 421 & 430 Montgomery Street,
1881.

The title page of Abby Fisher's *What Mrs. Fisher Knows About Old Southern Cooking* from 1881.

While in Missouri, along the way, Abby gave birth to their eleventh child.

As if it were not enough to arrive in California with a passel of children, Abby Fisher carried something else, too—166 recipes, fashioned in the plantation kitchens of the Deep South.

As Hess said in a speech on Abby Fisher to the Culinary Historians of New York: "It was the African American cook in the slave owner's kitchen who was responsible for the legendary quality of southern cookery."

San Francisco society, in Hess' view, went wild for Abby Fisher's calf's head soup, chicken gumbo, watermelon rind pickles, and coconut pie. Fisher was "awarded several prizes and diplomas at various fairs in California," she says, and her fans insisted she record her dishes.

But Abby Fisher was illiterate, as she admitted in her cookbook's preface, and Alexander Fisher, who took down her words, had not received a formal education: "Not being able to read or write myself, and my husband also having been without the advantages of an education—upon whom would devolve the writing of the book at my dictation—caused me to doubt whether I would be able to present a work that would give perfect satisfaction."

Nevertheless, she "concluded to bring forward a book of my knowledge—based on upwards of thirty-five years—in the art of cooking Soups, Gumbos, Terrapin Stews, Meat Stews, Baked and Roast Meats, Pastries, Pies and Biscuits, making Jellies, Pickles, Sauces, Ice-Creams and Jams, preserving Fruits., etc. The book will be found a complete instructor, so that a child can understand it and learn the art of cooking."

She signed it: "Respectfully, Mrs. Abby Fisher, Late of Mobile, Ala."

If it were not for Karen Hess, the story of Abby Fisher might be forever lost. "Cookery," Hess explains, "especially women's cookery, is looked down upon as a menial occupation, so that historians have never stooped to examine this facet of the history of the human race." She adds, "African American culinary contributions are even more denigrated by historians."

After discovering Fisher's cookbook at a public auction of culinary artifacts, Hess saw it through to republication in 1995. Its publisher is Applewood Books in Massachusetts.

Hess' research on Abby Fisher is in keeping with her look into the kitchens of the past. She developed an interest in the origins of cuisine—and an early love of French cooking—when she lived in Paris with her husband, John, an award-winning correspondent for the *New York Times*.

After returning to the states, the Hesses coauthored, *The Taste of America*, and John did a stint as the *Times'* restaurant critic. Karen turned her interest to an 18th-century recipe book, *Martha Washington's Booke of Cookery*.

She became intrigued by the South when she worked on *The Virginia House-*

Wife, written in 1824 by Mary Randolph, a white Virginian. Mary Randolph's dishes, Hess realized, had an African flavor, particularly in their use of garlic and okra. "It was the presence of the black cook in the big house," she says. "Once I got that, everything else fell into place."

In her book, *The Carolina Rice Kitchen: The African Connection,* Hess explored these connections further, writing in its first chapter: "The ancient way of cooking rice developed in the primeval rice lands of India and Africa became the Carolina way . . . The early history of the rice kitchen in South Carolina is inextricably bound up with slavery; it was the black hands of African slaves who cultivated the rice and cooked it."

Mobile native Philip Hyman, a culinary historian who lives in Paris, says that Karen Hess has done "outstanding work as a food historian, editing previously neglected culinary texts and annotating them with scholarly comments . . . Insofar as Mrs. Fisher's book goes, I can only applaud its publication. It is the first American cookbook written by an African-American and gives us a glimpse of cooking in Mobile in the mid-nineteenth century."

Hyman, who has coauthored with his wife, Mary, an encyclopedia of the foods of France, points out that Fisher's cookbook has a white Mobile parallel: *The Gulf City Cook Book,* compiled in 1878 by the ladies of the St. Francis Street Methodist Episcopal Church.

"It is very interesting to compare the two recipe books," Hyman says. "Are they giving us two visions of Mobile cooking of the late nineteenth century, black and white? Or simply individual variants on popular recipes of the day?"

Consider, Hyman says, the different recipes for succotash. For the ladies of the St. Francis Street church, "the corn and beans are cooked separately, mixed together, simmered with milk, seasoned with salt and pepper before serving."

In Mrs. Fisher's version of the same dish, he says, she adds a dozen tomatoes to the butter beans and corn plus "'fat pork cut in fine pieces.'"

There was another difference, too: Mrs. Fisher called the dish "circuit hash."

"I have close ties to the women of the nineteenth century," says Karen Hess, moving through her Upper West Side apartment, barefoot in a blue house dress, her silver hair in a bun. "As a child, I chopped wood, wrang chicken's necks."

In Nebraska, as the daughter of a Danish Lutheran minister, she learned to cook by standing on a chair at her grandmother's knee.

Next to the apartment's kitchen window, looming like a black box, is what Hess calls "the iron monster"—her cooking range. "Until the iron monster came along," she says, speaking of culinary history, "things hadn't changed."

Prior to the range, Hess says, cooks did their work at the hearth—the fireplace. As she said in her speech to the Culinary Historians of New York: "While the iron monster may have replaced the hearth in city mansions here and there, it was not in general use in the South, even among rich people, until well after the close of the Civil War, particularly in the plantations. But by the time Abby Fisher wrote her book, she had long truly mastered the art of cooking on the range. Particularly striking is her mastery of roasting methods, showing how to achieve properly roasted meats in the iron box."

Fisher included eight recipes for croquettes in her book, among them lamb, liver, and crab croquettes. As Hess wrote in historical notes: "While croquettes were not absent from northern cookery—indeed, they are all but universal—it has generally been accepted that black women were particularly adept at their confection and frying. They were fried in lard or, rarely, butter. Nasty, artificial shortenings had not yet been invented."

Other recipes suggest that the flavor of the antebellum South was succulent, indeed—plantation hoe cake, turnip soup, roast venison, crab apple jelly, spiced cherries. In Fisher's recipes, one catches glimpses of the woman behind the food. In her prescription for "Blackberry Syrup for dysentery in children," she notes, "This recipe is an old Southern plantation remedy among colored people."

When telling of how to mix "Pap for Infant Diet," she says, "I have given birth to eleven children and raised them all, and nursed them with this diet. It is a Southern plantation preparation."

Outside of a few facts that Fisher reveals about herself, little is still known about her. Through a researcher in California, Karen Hess found reference to Abby Fisher and her family in the 1880 census in San Francisco. Later records indicated that Fisher survived the San Francisco earthquake of 1906.

Through the California census, Hess also came across the name of Abby's husband, Alexander C. Fisher, and learned that the family was in the business of making pickles and preserves.

Hess believes that the publishers of the original cookbook in 1881—the Women's Co-operative Printing Office in San Francisco—were suffragettes, and may have had their origins in the abolitionist movement.

"As fascinating as it would be to know about Abby Fisher's life in detail," Hess says in her historical notes to the recipe book, "we shall have to content ourselves with what we can deduce from such facts as we have."

Karen Hess never got the chance to travel to Mobile while researching Fisher's life behind the recipes.

More information about Abby Fisher is available, though, in the Mobile Public Library's Local History and Genealogy division.

In the 1870 census for Mobile County, the Fishers were living in Mobile. While Abby Fisher's profession was listed as "keeps house," Alexander C. Fisher's was stated as "minister."

Abby Fisher was shown as neither being able to read nor write; but Alexander was literate, though perhaps not formally schooled, as Abby's cookbook preface would later bear out.

In their household of 1870 were four of their children, the youngest, a newborn, named Jennie.

Also in the household was 60-year-old Jennie Anderson. The census noted that the older woman, and Abby, had been born in South Carolina. Might Jennie Anderson have been Abby's mother and baby Jennie's grandmother?

Mobile city directories from 1870 to 1876 show that the Reverend Fisher, identified as "colored," had a pulpit at the "State Street Methodist Church" in downtown Mobile. Could that have been what is now the State Street AME Zion Church, one of the oldest black congregations in the city, at its location in downtown Mobile since 1852?

The Reverend James French, minister of the church, says that he has never come across references to the Reverend Fisher in researching his church's history. But an early history of the AME Zion movement, kept in the church's

State Street office, does refer to a "Rev. A.C. Fisher," who, in 1869, was helping to organize churches in Key West, Florida.

One of the church leaders at Key West during that time was the Reverend Wilbur Strong, who became one of the first ministers of the State Street AME Zion Church, according to French.

Assuming that Fisher was not the full-time minister at State Street AME Zion, might he have been what French calls "a missionary spirit moving around?"

But there was another black church only two blocks away, on the corner of Hamilton, the "African M. E. Church" that appeared briefly in directories of the 1870s. Might this have been the Reverend Alexander C. Fisher's church?

In an interview from Nashville, Tennessee, Dennis C. Dickerson, a historian for the AME church body, says that it was not unusual to have several black churches close to one another, given patterns of segregation.

State Street AME Zion, with its denominational roots in New York, and State Street AME, with its origins in Philadelphia, would have "drawn from the same constituency," but been different congregations.

Dickerson, a history professor at Vanderbilt University, whose great-grandfather, Dave Jordan, was an AME minister in Dothan, Alabama, says that there were early AME ministers who had preached while being slaves, circumstances that could have applied to Alexander C. Fisher.

There was a westward expansion of the AME movement during the 1870s, says Dickerson. If Fisher were an AME minister, he might have taken his family to California, sent by an AME bishop as part of that expansion. In this scenario, Abby Fisher, the minister's wife, would have departed with her husband and children as they made their way toward the Pacific, pausing in Missouri only long enough for her to give birth to their eleventh child.

But Vanderbilt's Dickerson is not convinced that Fisher was with the AME Church, since he shows up nowhere in the history of the AME church in Alabama after a cursory review.

Again, the Fishers grow elusive.

Another piece of the puzzle is in the archives of the Mobile County Probate Court. In 1866, the Fishers bought a house at the corner of Gaston and Lyons streets—a block behind what is now Bishop State Community College—from John H. Woodcock, for the sum of $250. In 1876, as another deed shows,

"Alexander C. Fisher and Abby Fisher (his wife)" sold it to Frederick Walker—for $500.

"As to how the Fishers made the terrible trek from Alabama to California, we can only speculate," Karen Hess wrote in historical notes to the cookbook. "The Union Pacific Transcontinental Railroad was completed in 1869, but such a journey by newfangled rail would have been costly."

Would the Fishers' $250 profit, in 1876, have been used to buy tickets to travel to the West on that train?

Yet another question, of course, is this: How had they managed to accumulate $250—money they had "in hand," records show—to buy a house in 1866, within a year after the end of the Civil War? With Mobile's sizable population of free people of color, had Abby and Alexander Fisher, in fact, even been slaves?

Perhaps, we will never know the final answer—the 1850 and 1860 "slave schedules" for Mobile County list only first names and ages for thousands of humans kept as "property." Last names are given only for the owners. "If you don't know the name of the owner," explains Charlotte Chamberlain, historian with the Mobile Public Library, "it would be difficult to locate someone."

And prior to 1866, no record has yet turned up pertaining to the Fisher family.

"Researching African American history in that time period is rough," admits Judy Busby, records supervisor for Mobile County Probate Court. The records are scant, she says. Little was recorded; much was lost.

What we do have, of course, thanks to Karen Hess' investigation and republishing of the first African American cookbook—born in the kitchens of Mobile—is a record of the roast pig, and jelly cake, and snow pudding, and circuit hash, that Abby Fisher and her sisters at the hearth prepared so very long ago.

PART VII PERSONAL SOJOURNS

I am an Alabamian too, my self-portrait a work in progress, as is everyone's, no matter where we hail from, what language we speak, or which cultures shape us.

In a way, ironically, all of the pieces in Alabama Afternoons have involved personal sojourns. Although I appear in these profiles and conversations rarely as "I," I, of course, am there. As the great nature photographer Ansel Adams said even of images with no human, presumably, present: "There are always two people in every picture: the photographer and the viewer."

So like you, the reader, I am in the picture, too, though most often behind the literary lens.

I have included at least one profile in this collection in first-person voice, my role that of narrator. But in this section I have included pieces in which my role is key: as explorer, as involved portraitist, as memoirist.

In a visit to Brooklyn, Alabama, I look in the mirror as well as at the colorful, tiny village. In a reminiscence about one summer I drove an ice cream truck during high school, I offer a story of my friendship with an old family friend, Joe Bear, whose immigrant tale was bound up in the ice cream enterprise.

No one figures into this collection more than my dad, here represented by a personal essay of mine centered in his former law office shortly after his passing in 2006. During his last years one of his greatest pleasures was to read my stories, commenting on each and every one. One of my deepest pleasures was to have him do so.

He helped give me my appreciation of living history, of story telling, of language, of humor. He read deeply. He understood.

Greetings from Brooklyn, Alabama

Brooklyn

You might think it's in the middle of nowhere—down a two-lane Alabama highway lined with pine trees, farmhouses, and mobile homes—but to Janice Matthews and a hundred or so other residents of this crossroads with one general store and a gas pump, it's Brooklyn. "Our Brooklyn," says Janice, petite, fair haired, and chatty, who runs Janice's Fill-A-Sack store with her husband, Dale, lean and philosophical in a black cowboy hat.

Ice cream, pickled eggs, stuffed olives, garden hoses, cap pistols, cat food: as I go down the rows, I'm put in mind of a back roads bodega, a southern version of a general store in the Brooklyn, New York, neighborhood where I used to live. But here you can buy chicken feed or catfish-skinning pliers.

"Brooklyn's the meeting point," I'm told by Charlie Philyaw, who's driven five miles from Johnsonville to buy supplies for a party. He chats with me while he pumps gas in front of the store, the "gallons" and "amount" columns slowly spinning. He tells me his buddy Anthony Williams has a special barbecue sauce that he'll be preparing and invites me to the party. I decline but inquire about the recipe. "It's a secret," Charlie says.

I reach for my cell phone to call my daughter, who spent her first years in Cobble Hill before we moved to the South. I'm eager to announce, "Hey, I'm in Brooklyn!" But the phone is useless.

"We're in a dead-cell area," Janice says.

Television reception's not much better, which is why a radio plays in Janice's store. "Fifty percent of the people around here have a satellite," she tells me.

The U.S. Post Office in Brooklyn, Alabama, 2002. Photograph © Michael E. Palmer.

"Satellite's a must. It goes up there with a pack of cigarettes, a gallon of gas, and a six-pack of beer."

Dale, who left his hometown to work in shipbuilding but returned, seems like a worldly man. The Brooklyn up north seems daunting, though. "I'd like to go visit so I can see the town and meet the people," he says, "but I think it would be confusing."

But Janice knows what she would do upon arriving. "I'd say: 'I'm Janice. I run a convenience store in Brooklyn, Alabama.'"

There is Rome, Georgia; Carthage, Tennessee; Toronto, Ohio; Manhattan, Kansas. America is full of place names that merge the great and the small. The director Wim Wenders made a movie, "Paris, Texas," whose bleak lyricism seemed to play off the name of that locale.

Brooklyns are plentiful. One only need punch a weather request for Brooklyn into an Internet search engine to be met with these choices: Alabama, Connecticut, Iowa, Indiana, Kentucky, Maryland, Michigan, Mississippi, New York, and West Brooklyn, Illinois. But I find in the name Brooklyn, Alabama, the charm of opposites. Stickball versus pond fishing. Mean streets, red clay roads. Klezmer music, banjo. Coney Island hot dogs, pit barbecue. Youse guys, y'all. These legends of place may not be wholly real—I have listened to banjo music on the Brighton Beach boardwalk, and eaten Nathan's Famous at a fast-food franchise in Alabama—but the mythologies endure.

My interest in this particular Brooklyn—in south-central Alabama some twenty miles north of the Florida line—may also spring from that I grew up in Mobile, about an hour and a half southwest of tiny Brooklyn, and lived for twenty years in New York City, eight in big Brooklyn, before returning to my hometown. When I watch the movie *My Cousin Vinny*, whose comedy turns on Joe Pesci's deeply Brooklyn Vincent Gambino finding himself deep in Alabama, I wonder how the story would have played out had Vinny left one Brooklyn to arrive in yet another.

My grandparents Morris and Mary, Romanian Jews, met as new Americans in Flatbush at the outset of the 20th century, and Morris proposed to Mary in Prospect Park, repeating the pun for generations to come that "she thought I was a good prospect." In 1907, when they made their way to Alabama's Gulf Coast, they might have noticed Alabama's Brooklyn on the map. In those days, the town hummed with activity.

I learn that I'm not the first person to set foot in the two Brooklyns.

In the summer of 2001, a couple from Brooklyn, New York, rolled into town and announced they were visiting Brooklyns around the country. Janice spent an afternoon talking with them. Then there was the throng of long-distance bicyclists who took a rest stop at the store. "One of the cycle riders said he was from Brooklyn, New York," Dale recalls. "He sat out there on the bench and told me of his Brooklyn."

Dale thinks about making up a postcard for visitors. In the meantime, since the store also houses the post office—a stray letter addressed Brooklyn, New York, has been known to find its way here—Janice concedes that a postmark will have to do.

Although much of Brooklyn has vanished, its history is close at hand. Betty Jo Alexander, a store customer hearing of my interest, offers to drive home and pick up her copy of a short history of Brooklyn. It is a two-page essay written by Ed Leigh McMillan for the Brooklyn Year Book, 1949–1950, a publication of a long-gone school.

Brooklyn, Alabama, McMillan wrote, was named by Edwin Robinson, who came south in 1821 from Brooklyn, Connecticut. The town had a landing on the Sepulga River, where keelboats in the 1800s stopped to load cotton, then headed south to the port of Pensacola, Florida. When cotton fell into decline, Brooklyn did, too, until timber brought the village back to life.

When river traffic was replaced by freight trains, Brooklyn was eclipsed yet again, until a company from nearby Brewton extended its logging railroad into the area. This prosperity, Mr. McMillan stated, "lasted until 1926, when the logging operation by railroad through the territory was abandoned."

I realize that the somnolent crossroads has been a capsule of much rural southern history: cotton and riverboats, timber and trains, boom followed by a slow dwindling. Had Brooklyn been closer to the central artery of the state— Interstate 65, half an hour to the west—it might have continued to thrive.

What sustains the locals at all? Most people have to drive a long way to make a dollar. Janice nods. "If they want education, they have to leave Brooklyn. If they want jobs, they have to leave Brooklyn. If you're not a logger or a farmer and don't want to work from can to cain't fifteen hours a day, you have to leave Brooklyn."

"Can to cain't" suggests from when you can see to when you can't; or, for Janice, dawn to dark. "Nights I walk out of here," Janice says, "I'm almost squalling. But if somebody offered me a million dollars, I wouldn't trade."

Outside Janice's Fill-A-Sack, I meet a friend of Dale's, Jack Feagin, who's watched changes come and go. Talking to me while idling in his truck, he gestures down the empty road and tells me of a blacksmith shop, a cotton gin, a flowing well long dried up, even a hotel.

Dale adds there was also a casino. A casino?

"It was back of an old barbershop," he says, "where the men used to play cards."

I leave the men and amble down the road, in one direction finding an abandoned tin-roofed building with the words "Brooklyn Volunteer Fire Department" scrolling across a wall webbed with brittle vines. A new volunteer fire department is nearby.

In the other direction I come to the Brooklyn Baptist Church, as picturesque as a calendar picture with its white plank walls, deep green shutters, and wreath on the door. I step into the cemetery alongside the church, by weathered tombstones from as early as the 1840s.

I head back to the store. When I arrive, Janice and Dale are outside, closing up for the day.

I tell them their tiny town is lovely, and that I wonder what folks in the real Brooklyn would think about this one.

Dale looks askance at me. "You cut your tongue out now. This is the real Brooklyn."

Joe Bear

ICE CREAM MAN

Mobile

I will never hear the clang-clang of an ice cream truck bell come our first hot weather without remembering the truck I drove for Bear Ice Cream the summer I turned 17, and the owner of the enterprise, a Polish Jewish immigrant to Mobile.

With the truck windows cranked open and the sultry air blowing in the cab, I'd hold fast to the bell cord, yanking it to keep the clapper going.

Clang-clang. I carried nutty buddies, fudgesicles, and blueberry Popsicles.

Clang-clang. Dreamsicles and push-ups. Ice cream sandwiches and vanilla cups.

The noise was a summons through the neighborhood: Ice Cream Man was on his way.

While many folks thought Bear Ice Cream got its name from the animal pictured on the trucks—a polar bear, sitting down about to lick a chocolate-covered vanilla stick held between its paws—I knew the name was for the owner, my boss, Joe Bear. The man I knew as Mr. Bear, 70 years old that summer, was a kindly man with thick eyeglasses, a silver mustache, and a Polish accent.

Surely he knew ice cream, as he showed on my tour of the plant on my first day on the job, explaining pasteurization and homogenization. I was fascinated by the big vats with churning cream, the conveyor belts chopping the desserts into different shapes. I liked best watching the vanilla ice cream dipping into chocolate, being readied for boxing.

"Don't eat up your profits," Mr. Bear cautioned that first day while I peeled

Ice cream trucks lined up in front of the Bear Ice Cream Company, circa 1953. Photo courtesy of Jay C. Bear.

off the wrapping of a grape Popsicle and polished it off before climbing up into my truck.

He handed me the keys. I turned the ignition. The truck bolted forward. I stepped on the brake; no, it was the clutch. I had never driven a stick-shift before. Finally, with some instruction from the kindly old gent, I went bucking out of the parking lot, Mr. Bear waving good-bye to me in my rearview mirror.

Clang-clang. Up Springhill Avenue. Clang-clang. Over to Old Shell Road.

How well I remember the heat of the asphalt that summer of 1970, the rattle of the bell, the children in bright shorts and T-shirts scurrying toward me over the lawns.

How vividly I see Joe Bear, there, too, come back to me after these many years.

❋

Like most teenagers, I was too worried about the confines of my own world, and too dismissive of my elders, to think that Joe Bear might have a fascinating story to tell.

I'd met him through my dad, who'd gotten to know him not long after Bear arrived in Mobile in the 1920s. I knew that he'd come from far away to make a life for his family in coastal Alabama. He and his wife, Adele, had raised three children—Albert, Bootsie, and Jay C.—who were friendly with my older sisters, so there was an ongoing connection. Mostly, though, to me, he was another of my parents' silver-haired friends.

While in college, I had other part-time summer jobs. Whenever I bumped into Joe Bear, he asked about my studies, and seemed especially interested that I nursed ambitions to become a writer. One day, after I'd graduated and was home visiting, my father told me Joe Bear had a favor to ask.

He wanted me to tape his life story. I figured it could not take long.

The date was January 10, 1977. Mr. Bear was widowed and living alone in an apartment complex off Airport Boulevard. Bear Ice Cream, by then, had sold its Springhill Avenue plant to Barber's Ice Cream, though its polar bear trucks continued to roll through town until the mid-1970s.

As I drove up, he was standing at the window, waiting for me. On the table were two bowls. Two spoons. "My good friend," he said, reaching out to grasp my hand. He seemed excited, that he had something he was eager to tell.

First, he opened the freezer and brought out a bucket of ice cream and scooped out enough of a rich vanilla to fill our bowls. "We are ready?" he said.

I turned on my tape recorder.

Eighteen ninety-nine. Ostrow, Poland. It's where Joe Bear's story began.

The grandson of a candle maker, and the son of a wine merchant, young Joe grew up in a "shtetl," a rural village where the Jewish families—the Bears among them—lived in communities surrounded by land owned by their gentile countrymen. The Jews, clustered together, were nurtured by their houses of worship, their schools and shops. The ethnic Poles, working as farmers, were like "plantation owners" in the old South, Joe explained.

The relationship between the two communities was not always benign. On Sundays, some Poles would go to church, then go to bars, drink too much, and "the first thing they did was beat up some Jews. I was beat up many times," Joe said, "and sometimes got stranded just one or two of us in the outskirts of the city, attacked by the Christian boys either with bats or with stones and many times we came home bloody."

The life within the Jewish quarter was sustaining, though. He told me of beginning school—or "cheder"—each morning at seven and not arriving back home until it was dark. At school there was little distinction between secular and religious studies. Rabbis taught the boys how to read Hebrew and to understand and discuss the sacred texts: the Torah, the prophets and writings, and the Talmud, involving the many books of interpretation and discussion.

Winter snows were no obstacles. Joe remembered that "going to cheder in the snowstorm and coming back at night with a lantern or candle was a pretty tough job but we found our way."

When students misbehaved, the teacher sometimes hit them with a book. "It was not permissible," Joe explained, for a student to return home at the end of the school day and "complain to the father or the mother about the treatment of the rabbi." Further infractions at school often meant "we had to do some housework for them like clean the snow and wash the dishes." By not complaining of being disciplined, the student fulfilled what Joe called the "code of honor."

The worlds of men and women were distinctive in the shtetl. After the age of 13, when the boys had their bar mitzvahs and were adult members of the religious community, they would continue their studies. When they married—match-makers were still used in Joe's time—the men were allowed to spend long hours at the synagogue in prayer, while the women tended to the children and the family shops.

The steam bath was the place where the men, in the evening, sweated and talked. "For steam," he told me, "they got a big stove, a big open fireplace, and they pour water on it and the water evaporates into steam and it comes in and falls down on the people. And it's made with benches, like a football stadium.

The higher you go, the hotter the steam is. A lot of business was conducted in the steam bath."

Friday at dusk, the start of Sabbath, was the holy time, lasting until Saturday dusk.

As Joe told me his story, it seemed as though the world he'd left had a strong appeal. The families were large—Joe was the youngest of seven brothers and sisters—and religion defined the daily comings and goings. Grouped together, the Jewish villagers had protection against the violence of the outsiders.

But they could not protect themselves, living in northern Poland, subjects of the Russian government, against military conscription. The Russian army came into the villages periodically, looking for the boys who had turned 19. "They drafted you for a period not less than four years and sometimes eight and you could be sent to God-knows-where, even to serve in Siberia. My father and mother decided there was no future for [their] sons to remain in Poland or Russia."

Joe's older brothers, and one sister, soon left the shtetl, made their way to Western European cities, and on to America.

But Joe, still at home with his parents when he was 15, found himself unable to leave. The world was falling apart by then. The year was 1914—the start of World War I.

Near the outbreak of the war, Joe started his first business enterprise.

As a boy, he'd come to own half a bicycle with a friend. The friend's family had fled Poland, so the bicycle was now all his. Joe managed to acquire a few other abandoned bicycles and opened a shop. "I was renting out the bicycles and supporting the family," he said. With the war under way, his father, a wine importer, no longer had open access to his markets in other countries.

While I had been a teenager driving a Bear Ice Cream truck, I never paid much attention to what it meant that Joe Bear was speaking English as a foreign language. It turned out that, in addition to his native Polish, he spoke Russian, French, German, and Yiddish—that international language of European Jews, a variation of German. Those languages helped sustain him as his corner of Poland was chewed up by different nations.

In 1914, the Russians came into his village, called all the Jews into the town square, and told them they would take fathers and grandfathers to the front line to build trenches. Were there any youths who would be brave enough to take their elders' places?

Joe, at 15, was one of the young men who volunteered, enabling his father to stay home. "My mother fixed me up a little pack on my shoulder with something and they marched us out," he said.

After they dug trenches, they waited while the Russians went into combat. To their astonishment, the Russians scattered and the Germans "took up our trenches and they put us in the back to dig up more trenches."

One day, a German officer announced to the Jewish conscripts that he needed someone who spoke Russian. Joe held up his hand. He could also, of course, speak Polish. Germany was looking for men under its control who spoke the native languages essential for organizing logging crews and shipping fresh-cut Polish timber.

A few German officers saw a future in young Joe, and he in them. Working together, they smuggled goods from Warsaw to the front line. Joe would take a wagon to the capital city, buy silks and cognac for the officers, then return. He sent the money he pocketed to his parents in the village.

In 1920, World War I was over, but the fighting hardly stopped in Joe's native land. That year, Joe, 21, was drafted into the Polish army to help defend the new nation against the Russians.

"By 1920," he recounted, "Russia attacked Poland and they got as far as Warsaw." Before long, "we broke the Russian front and started chasing them. We chased them a thousand miles. As we chased them, if a man were lying dead, the first thing we looked for was boots. Many times, I had two left boots or two right boots. Our rifles gave out of ammunition. The dead or the wounded soldier laying over there, we picked up his rifle and his bullets. With no food we had to find our own food. In the cold of the winter we used to raid farms and get potatoes and boil them and then put them in our pockets, wrapped them around in newspaper to keep our bodies warm. When we didn't have potatoes we used to warm up rocks."

But back home, Jews in Poland were being violently persecuted by the very nation in whose army Joe fought. In a half-dozen years, he'd been with three different armies—Russian, German, and Polish—and had even been wounded.

He'd had enough! On a thirty-day furlough, leaving his remaining family behind, he took off his uniform and went to the office of the American consul and obtained a visa, then crossed the border to Danzig, a free city.

Making his way to Antwerp, he sailed on the ocean liner *Rotterdam*. In steerage, he traveled in "the bottom of the boat for thirteen days, sick as a dog. It was nasty, filthy, we didn't have water to bathe or to wash with."

But finally, on August 21, 1920, he looked up to see the New York Harbor and the Statue of Liberty.

As we talked, we ate one bowl of ice cream, then another. I realized I had already used up three cassette tapes—each an hour long—when I put in the fourth. I had arrived at seven in the evening and it was now well past ten.

He told me how his older brother, Benny, had traveled to Pensacola from New York as an umbrella salesman, but had been cheated by a partner and left stranded in Florida. Benny had found work in a delicatessen, so Joe headed south, too, to Mobile.

In time, Joe studied the dairy industry, taking college classes at Auburn.

For many years, as he and Adele started their family, he ran an ice cream shop on Dauphin Street downtown, but in 1950 he opened his plant on Springhill Avenue and marshaled his fleet of trucks.

Shortly after eleven o'clock, Joe's story wound down. Concluding, he told me he would not want to live his life over again, that he would not wish it on his children—his own childhood, in war-ravaged Poland, had been too hard. He had seen too much hatred, too much fighting.

In Mobile, he was proud of all he had accomplished and of his contributions to his town and country. He had been, he said, "a good citizen."

I will never forget the way Joe Bear looked that night after I gathered my things and my tapes—I would make copies for myself and his family—and went outside, back to my car. He was standing there, in his picture window, waving and smiling broadly. He looked both tired and happy. The Ice Cream Man had told his story for all time.

I never saw him again after that.

❋

Clang-clang.

Ice cream trucks today do not often make that sound, many blaring pre-recorded jingles. Even so, the hammering of that truck bell is what I hear this week, and next, as summer begins to unfold.

I don't recall if I made much money that summer. Probably not. As Mr. Bear had amiably warned, I ate up some of my profit—we worked on commission—gave away too many nutty buddies to friends, and was a soft touch for the kid with only five cents in his hand when the cost for a Popsicle was fifteen cents. "OK," I'd agree. "A nickel will do."

Of course, as I came to understand, the ice cream trucks were far more than vehicles carrying frozen confections to street-corner consumers. They were symbols, to Joe Bear, of a new life he had made, a good life. They were like little ships of freedom and prosperity rolling through the Deep South heat.

Clang-clang. They sounded their own little liberty bells.

Windows

A SON REMEMBERS

Mobile

S itting at my dad's old walnut desk, my elbows on the leather desk pad cracked dry with time, I gaze out his twenty-fourth-floor law office window. Past his now-silent Dictaphone, over the two dozen black bindings of the Code of Alabama lined up on his windowsill, over the snapshots of my mom, who passed away three years ago, I see the view that, like the possessions in this office, will forever belong to him.

There's the red terra-cotta dome of the Gulf Mobile & Ohio railroad station, now restored for offices and a bus terminal, where he took the train to Atlanta during the late 1920s to go to Emory Law School; the grain elevator and loading berths of the Alabama state docks, which he represented as legal counsel for four years after World War II; the port of Mobile with its lazy brown river opening out to Mobile Bay, and all the sites where we launched a boat to go fishing when I was a boy.

For forty years, he looked out this window, having moved into this building once it opened in the mid-1960s, a thirty-four-floor, white, cast-concrete structure—until this year the tallest, by far, in town—across the street from the 19th-century iron fountain and ancient oaks of Bienville Square, the historic heart of town. The office, with its sheetrock walls, is three rooms and a connecting hallway: the entrance area, with its secretary's desk and a typewriter giving way over the years to a computer; a small library with 1930s oak and glass-paneled bookcases; and the spacious room near the windows with his desk.

Charles and Evelyn Hoffman. Courtesy of Roy Hoffman.

In the former AmSouth Building in downtown Mobile, Room 2401, a doorway welcomes clients—and a son—to the offices of Charles Hoffman. Courtesy of Roy Hoffman.

For thirty-five years prior to that, his office had been housed in the 1905 First National Bank Building, a solid structure with arched windows and elegant brickwork that was torn down once the modern bank building was ready. He overlooked an airshaft there, but no matter. He was a young attorney on the way up. I've got a news clipping from the *Mobile Register,* July 24, 1931, headlined, "New Law Office Opens. Charles Hoffman, Native Mobilian, Is Graduate of Emory University." The article, in part, reads, "Returning to Mobile, his native city, Charles Hoffman, son of Mr. and Mrs. M. Hoffman, has opened a law office on the seventh floor of the First National Bank Building. Mr. Hoffman was licensed to practice law in Alabama in the fall of 1930, having passed the state examination in summer of that year."

Dad recalled with satisfaction that he had passed the bar exam even before finishing law school, and on the wall behind where I sit hang his 1931 Emory law diploma and 1930 Alabama law license. In 2004, I accompanied him to bar association events where he was honored for being the oldest practicing attorney in Mobile and the entire state of Alabama. I heard him speak, with a catch in his voice, of his pride in what had always been, for him, a "noble profession," and, on a lighter note, regale audiences with tales of that long-ago bar exam. It had been administered in the Montgomery courthouse, then under construction. "They were working in the courthouse," he recounted, "and the desks were made of sawhorses with pine wood across them. Air-conditioning was a nonexistent word, and fans were limited in their scope. Beads of sweat would occasionally drop from your forehead while you were writing and smear the ink."

I can read many histories from the pictures on these walls, the memorabilia on these shelves. Atop a brick on his desk is the framed picture of the YMCA building where he boxed as a youth, the start of a lifelong willingness to "put up your fists," even into his 90s, when an insolent young lawyer insulted him in court and Dad challenged him to "step outside."

Both the brick and the photo were gifts from his trusted secretary, Debby. The photograph is from the local archives, and the brick from the recent demolition of the building, which stood two blocks from the square and five from where he grew up over his parents' general mercantile store on Dauphin Street. On a hallway wall are copies of the instruments of surrender of Germany and Japan in World War II. Already a seasoned lawyer in 1944 when he was drafted by the Army, after basic training in Michigan he ended up in

Washington, D.C., with the military police, then worked in the Pentagon with the Secretariat of the Joint Chiefs of Staff, handling paperwork and orders. Few visitors have come to my dad's office without his pausing to show them the facsimiles he made, for souvenirs, of those surrender documents.

In addition to the sunny photos of my mother, Evelyn—he put up ever more of them when, after sixty-seven years of marriage, he lost her to a long illness—there are pictures of us four children and spouses, the six grandchildren, the three great-grandchildren. One photo, a favorite of mine, is of Dad with four of his nephews and great-nephews. In a rogues' gallery they bow, heads down, to the camera—five bald men showing off their shiny pates. I got my thick head of hair from my mom's side of the family.

And there is the empty chair.

How often I sat there, facing this desk, while he sat here, in the swivel chair I now occupy on this hazy, Gulf Coast afternoon. As a child, I visited him rarely at his office—he was out the door with hat and briefcase after breakfast, returning from the far-off world of work for dinner—but as a teenager I began to see his work world more often. In the office or when I tagged along to court, he tried to entreat me, persuade me, and downright insist that I set my sights on law school, too. Our hometown was steeped in father-son law practices. I was fascinated, I must admit, by the struggles and triumphs of his storied career, from his rite of passage as a fledgling criminal attorney taking court-appointed cases to his later involvement in business law.

His had always been a one-man practice, and when a lawyer friend of mine from a huge firm in New York asked him his specialty, Dad answered, "People law." Estates, real estate deals, criminal defense—he did it all, and sometimes for generations of the same family. "There is no end," he told me philosophically, "of human complication." He handled divorces but felt a matchmaker's delight when he got couples, about to split, back together again. He incorporated one small Protestant church for the African American community, then another and another. One church even asked him to help write its creed. "But I'm Jewish," he said. No problem.

Didn't I wish to join him in helping people deal with their complications, and make a good living at it, too? When I graduated from college in 1975, to appease him I took the Law School Admission Test. But I sat in his office, in the chair across from his desk, and told him, really and truly, I wanted to try wandering a different path.

He became my most attentive reader, of works both published and unpublished, and I remember calling him from various offices in Manhattan and Brooklyn, including home offices, where I looked out other windows. Often, if only in my mind, I sat in that chair across from him as we talked.

On August 1, 2006, a Tuesday, I sat in that chair while he sat in this one. Having moved back to Mobile a decade ago with my family, and working several blocks away at the newspaper, I walked over to this office almost daily for lunch. We even had an unconscious comedy routine, playing into my father's love of old-timey puns. "I'm running a little behind," I'd sometimes say, calling him from my cell phone. "A little behind," he'd ask, "or a big behind?"

As usual that Tuesday, we made our way to the elevator, Dad ambling slowly with his cane, dressed in pinstripe blue suit with suspenders and two-tone shoes. In recent years, finding a necktie uncomfortable, he'd taken to wearing bolo ties brought to him by my sister who often travels out west. That afternoon he sported a bolo with two Indian head nickels on a circle of silver as the clasp.

"Hey, Charley," said a colleague when we stepped onto the elevator, "nice to see you."

"At my age," he quipped, "it's nice to be seen."

Downstairs in the basement lunchroom, Zitsos, a homey cafeteria with green flowered wallpaper and old brick, Claire Zitsos, the owner, said, "Happy Birthday, Mr. Hoffman."

"You know who wants to be ninety-seven years old?" he asked her.

"No sir, Mr. Hoffman."

"A man," he said, "who's ninety-six. And who wants to be ninety-eight? A man who's ninety-seven."

He was that exuberant 97-year-old man.

She brought him a piece of baklava, light desserts being one of his rare gustatory pleasures amid a no-salt, low-fat diet prescribed by his cardiologist a year before. Three years earlier he had learned he had heavy calcification in his arteries and opening them up with stents would be too complicated. He had the option of a heart bypass operation but waved it off.

"I never wanted to be Methuselah," he'd told the doctor, "but I would like a few more years. And I'll go to meet my maker just as I am."

With medication, he'd returned to work and scrapping in court, continuing to drive his 1999 gold Lincoln Town Car, meeting up with me to catch a weekend movie or baseball game, and returning to the seniors dance club he'd joined with my mom. With his legs too weak to dance as he used to, he liked to have a little Scotch with water, then stand in place rocking side to side, stretching his arm out while a lady friend turned about holding his hand.

After lunch, we went back to our respective offices, and I called him at the end of day to make sure he was soon heading home. We had a family birthday dinner scheduled for early evening. "I'm just winding things up here," he said.

Our dinner was celebratory. The next day, his heart nagging him badly, he checked into the hospital, summoning his legal secretary once and calling the office several times to take care of paperwork for clients. A week later, we brought him home with round-the-clock hospice care. Our family, from all over the country, hurried to be at his bedside, keeping vigil until the night of August 10.

He never sat in his office chair again.

My father, a practical man, was organized at the time of his passing. Although he fully expected, I have no doubt, to be back at work the day after his 97th birthday, he had planned for what he knew would come, sooner than later, with time. Like the artful attorney he was, he had consolidated his assets, streamlined his will, and made sure we wouldn't have to spend a lot of money, well, consulting a lawyer. With a colleague's simple signature and Debby's expertise, we handled matters all on our own.

Dad had asked, in notes he had given us weeks before, that we keep the office door open for several months, with Debby on the payroll. There was the matter of settling the estate, getting files back to longtime clients, selling the law books, and distributing the furniture. There were some fees still coming in, enough to meet the overhead in the short term.

And there was his desk.

For all the times I had sat on the other side of it, and now in its commanding chair, I had never taken it upon myself to open its drawers. After all, if the office was his domain away from home, the desk was its sacred center.

Inside it I find objects and paperwork that tell even more stories of his life. History reveals itself here in unexpected ways. There's a travel itinerary from a trip he and my mom took to Europe in 1962—they departed from Idlewild

Airport in New York and, as part of their continental tour, visited the Berlin Wall. There's an envelope marked "Birth Announcements," with newspaper clippings and copies of birth certificates for me and my three older sisters. There's a color slide of me receiving my college diploma, and copies of letters from relatives in Israel. There are jokes he jotted down that he liked to tell, and a plastic bag with a snack of peanut brittle. There are condolence letters addressed to him in 1956, when his dad died, and in 1960, when he lost his mom. Those letters have an immediacy to me now.

In the lower left drawer, behind a long file of financial papers, he kept a pair of 10x50 binoculars he liked to use to survey the scene below. I take them out and, as he often did, scan the horizon. I can see the newspaper office where I have sat many afternoons, gazing out at his building. My desk is near the window, too.

I imagine him peering out at my building, fiddling with the focus, seeing if he can spot me. He's not looking out at me, so much as looking out for me.

He still does.

Acknowledgments

I owe thanks to many people who have helped in my creating the works and bringing them to life that make up *Alabama Afternoons,* from direct editorial input, to the dialogue among friends, colleagues, and family:

At the *Press-Register* in Mobile, where most of the pieces originally appeared: editors Mike Marshall, Dewey English, Paul Cloos, K. A. Turner, Jackie Byrd, Debbie Lord, Steve Joynt, Jim Van Anglen, and Dave Helms; photographers Bill Starling, Mike Kittrell, Glenn Andrews, Mary Hattler, John David Mercer, Kate Mercer, and Victor Calhoun; colleagues Doug Dimitry, Chris Hall, Debby Stearns, Frances Coleman, J. D. Crowe, Tom Harrison, Judi Rojeski, Sherry Lee, George Talbot, Rena Havner, and Ben Raines; and a special thanks to Howard and Dorsey Bronson, and to Ricky Mathews.

For the pieces that originally appeared in other publications: Connie Rosenblum and Dana Jennings of the *New York Times;* Arnold Berke, of *Preservation;* and the editorial staff of *Garden & Gun.*

At The University of Alabama Press: Dan Waterman, who has been key to envisioning the individual profiles and essays as a collective whole, and shepherding the book into publication.

In the Alabama writing community: Don Noble, Rick Bragg, the Clarence Cason Award selection committee, and the late Bailey Thomson at The University of Alabama; Jeannie Thompson at the Alabama Writers Forum; Jake Reiss of Alabama Booksmith in Birmingham and Karin and Kiefer Wilson of Page & Palette in Fairhope; Sue Walker at the University of South Alabama.

My writing and reading friends around the country: John Sledge, Karl Hein, Charles Salzberg, Al Kassan, David Alsobrook, Walter Edgar, John Hafner, Eli Evans, Bill Pangburn and Renee Magnanti, William and Nancy Oppenheimer, the Mosteller family, David Weiner, Lynn and Cori Yonge, Russell and Billie Goodloe, Gordon and Geri Moulton, Judy Culbreth, Karen Zacharias, Alida Becker, Joelle Delbourgo; Spalding Brief-Residency MFA in Writing Program colleagues, among others, Karen Mann, Kathleen Driskell, Katy Yocom, Luke Wallin, Dianne Aprile, Rich Goodman, Ellie Bryant, Mary Waters, Bob Finch, Molly Peacock, Julie Brickman, Charles Gaines, Elaine Orr, and Phil Deaver; and folks I've profiled here who have become friends, Sena Jeter Naslund, Diane McWhorter, Winston Groom, Howell Raines, and Frye Gaillard.

My family, for their love and support for all my writing: my mom and dad, my sister Sherrell and her husband, Charlie, all of them gone now, but who read with depth and care so many of these pieces early on; my sisters Becky and Robbie and brother-in-law John Nadas; my nieces and nephews Lezlee Peterzell-Bellanich, and Rob Bellanich, Marisa Nadas, Scott and Amy Peterzell, Sandro Nadas, Aaron Grean.

My wife, Nancy, for patiently hearing about everything I write—or sometimes don't—from first inception to my feelings about it once it's on the page, and always being there for the sojourn.

And our daughter Meredith, a keen-eyed reader and critic, and a writer whose own voice is beginning to flourish beautifully on the page.

Permissions

PART I: THE MAKERS

"William Christenberry: Pilgrimage of the Heart" was originally published in the *Mobile Press-Register,* August 13, 2000.

"Charles Moore: Witness to Change" was originally published in the *Mobile Press-Register,* January 2, 2001.

"Bernice Sims: A Folk Artist's Stamp on History" was originally published as "Bernice Sims: Brewton Artist Puts Her Stamp on History" in the *Mobile Press-Register,* October 16, 2005.

"Kathryn Tucker Windham and Charlie Lucas: Kathryn and the 'Tin Man'" was originally published as "Kathryn and the Tin Man: Two Alabama Treasures" in the *Mobile Press-Register,* November 16, 2003.

PART II: THE TELLERS

"Mary Ward Brown: Black Belt Storyteller" was originally published in the *Mobile Press-Register,* March 6, 2005.

"Sena Jeter Naslund: A Story Deep Inside Her" was originally published in the *Mobile Press-Register,* August 15, 2003.

"Diane McWhorter: Taking Pictures from the Inside" was originally published as "Not Just Who, But Why" in the *Mobile Press-Register,* March 18, 2001; and as "Living the Pulitzer" in the *Mobile Press-Register,* May 19, 2002.

"Frye Gaillard: Writing His Way Home" was originally published in the *Mobile Press-Register* on March 29, 2004.

"Artelia Bendolph: The Girl in the Window" was originally published as "The Artelia Bendolph Story: The Girl in the Window" in the *Mobile Press-Register* on June 16, 2002.

"Eugene Sledge: 'With the Old Breed'" was originally published as "WWII Veteran Eugene B. Sledge, 'With the Old Breed'" in the *Mobile Press-Register* on February 5, 2001.

PART III: THE JOURNEYERS

"Mel Allen: 'Voice of the Yankees'" was originally published as "The Late Mel Allen: Alabama's Voice of the Yankees" in the *Mobile Press-Register,* July 6, 2003.

"Gay Talese: Made in Alabama" was originally published as "Made in Alabama: The Gay Talese Story" in the *Mobile Press-Register,* April 23, 2006.

"Howell Raines: Coming Full Circle" was originally published as "Howell Raines: 'I've Come Full Circle'" in the *Mobile Press-Register,* May 19, 2006.

"Winston Groom: The House That Gump Built" was originally published as "The Bard of Point Clear: The Inimitable Winston Groom" in *Garden & Gun* magazine, Summer 2007. Copyright Roy Hoffman.

"Tommy Tarrants and Stan Chassin: Deliver Us from Evil" was originally published in a three-part series, "Deliver Us From Evil" in the *Mobile Press-Register:* "Encounter With Hate," January 6, 2008; "I Deserved to Die," January 7, 2008; "Forgive Our Trespasses," January 8, 2008.

PART IV: WITNESSES TO THE MOVEMENT

"Neil Davis: Tough, Sweet Voice of Reason" was originally published in the *Mobile Press-Register,* April 1, 1997.

"Vivian Malone and James Hood: The Stand in the Schoolhouse Door" was originally published as "'I Wasn't Afraid': UA's First Black Students Take a Look Back 40 Years Later" in the *Mobile Press-Register,* June 9, 2003.

"George Wallace Jr.: The Loyal Son" was originally published in the *Mobile Press-Register,* September 12, 1999.

"Johnnie Carr: Sustaining the Dream" was originally published as "Sustaining the Dream: The Story of Johnnie Carr" in the *Mobile Press-Register,* January 21, 2001.

"Theresa Burroughs: In Beauty's Care" was originally published as "In Beauty's Care: Theresa Burroughs' Safe House" in the *Mobile Press-Register,* April 25, 2004.

PART V: DOWN BACK ROADS

"Sara Hamm: Keeping the Faith" was originally published in the *Mobile Press-Register,* January 18, 2004.

"Restoring Rosenwald: The Oak Grove School" was originally published as "Restoring Rosenwald" in the *Mobile Press-Register,* July 21, 2002.

"Bessie Papas: A Malbis Life" was originally published in the *Mobile Press-Register,* July 31, 2005.

"Edward Carl and Walter Bellingrath: Driving Mr. Bellingrath" was originally published as "Driving Mr. Bellingrath: Edward Carl's Story" in the *Mobile Press-Register,* May 12, 2002.

"William Bolton and Herbert Henson: Visiting Old Pals" was originally published as "Coon Dog Cemetery: Visiting Old Pals" in the *Mobile Press-Register,* August 22, 2004.

"Scoop, Red, Moon, and Shorty: The Oak Tree Social Club" was originally published as "The Oak Tree Social Club" in the *Mobile Press-Register,* July 30, 2006.

PART VI: DIFFERENT WINDOWS ON DIXIE

"Yolande 'Bebe' Betbeze: Cinderella in Charge" was originally published as "Cinderella In Charge, Yolande Betbeze: Mobile's Miss America," in the *Mobile Press-Register,* June 11, 2000.

"Alex Alvarez: Voices from the Past" was originally published in the *Mobile Press-Register,* October 22, 2006.

"Abby Fisher: 'What Miss Fisher Knows about Old Home Cooking'" was originally published as "In Search of Abby Fisher" in the *Mobile Press-Register,* February 6, 2000.

PART VII: PERSONAL SOJOURNS

"Greetings from Brooklyn, Alabama" was originally published in the column, New York Observed, City section, *New York Times,* September 15, 2002.

"Joe Bear: Ice Cream Man" was originally published as "The Ice Cream Man" in the *Mobile Press-Register,* April 29, 2001.

"Windows: A Son Remembers" was originally published as "Windows: A Son Finds Memories and Solace in His Late Father's Mobile, Ala., Law Office," in the column, Place, in *Preservation: The Magazine of the National Trust of Historic Preservation,* March/April 2007. Reprinted in *Emory* magazine, Summer 2007. Copyright Roy Hoffman.